The Big Rig

The Big Rig

TRUCKING AND THE DECLINE
OF THE AMERICAN DREAM

Steve Viscelli

UNIVERSITY OF CALIFORNIA PRESS

University of California Press, one of the most distinguished university presses in the United States, enriches lives around the world by advancing scholarship in the humanities, social sciences, and natural sciences. Its activities are supported by the UC Press Foundation and by philanthropic contributions from individuals and institutions. For more information, visit www.ucpress.edu.

University of California Press
Oakland, California

Library of Congress Cataloging-in-Publication Data

Names: Viscelli, Steve, 1974- author.
Title: The big rig : trucking and the decline of the American dream / Steve Viscelli.
Description: Oakland, California : University of California Press, [2016] | "2016 | Includes bibliographical references and index.
Identifiers: LCCN 2015035773 | ISBN 9780520278110 (cloth : alk. paper) | ISBN 0520278119 (cloth : alk. paper) | ISBN 9780520278127 (pbk. : alk. paper) | ISBN 0520278127 (pbk. : alk. paper) | ISBN 9780520962712 (e-edition) | ISBN 0520962710 (e-edition)
Subjects: LCSH: Independent truck drivers—United States. | Trucking—United States.
Classification: LCC HD8039.M7952 U573 2016 | DDC 388.3/240973—dc23
LC record available at http://lccn.loc.gov/2015035773

[Manufactured in the United States of America / Printed in China]

25 24 23 22 21 20 19 18 17 16
10 9 8 7 6 5 4 3 2 1

In keeping with a commitment to support environmentally responsible and sustainable printing practices, UC Press has printed this book on Natures Natural, a fiber that contains 30% post-consumer waste and meets the minimum requirements of ANSI/NISO Z39.48–1992 (R 1997) (*Permanence of Paper*).

Contents

Preface

The sociologist C. Wright Mills (1959) argued that sociology is valuable because it helps us to understand the relationships between the individual and society and between biography and history. The *sociological imagination,* Mills claimed, allows us to see how the beliefs, decisions, and actions of individuals are shaped by—and then in turn reproduce or change—our social world. The sociological imagination explains how society changes by examining the changing nature of these relationships over time. And, when needed, it is the sociological imagination that allows us to understand personal troubles in a way that can reveal underlying social problems. This book applies the sociological imagination to the trucking industry, one of the largest and most vital industries in the United States. It thus moves back and forth from examining the details of the actual work of truckers and how they think about it to looking at the larger historical transformation of class power in the trucking industry, and then attempting to explain the relationships that connect these two realms. The book covers both the micro and the macro, from individual ambitions, fears, economic opportunities, constraints, and decisions that truckers told me about, to the rise and fall of worker power, the onset, retreat, and reformulation of state regulation, and the transformation of employment relations and the work of moving freight itself.

This book is the outcome of ten years of research. I began by reading a few books on the trucking industry. I then took a job as a long-haul driver, immersing myself in the daily routines, goals, and difficulties of the work for almost six months. Though I ended my career as little more than a rookie, I came to understand personally the sense of pride truckers feel in their skills and the care they take to ensure safety despite the enormous demands of their work. I also came to understand the kinds of sacrifices they make and the indignities they suffer. I then looked at the bigger picture of labor markets. I interviewed drivers with experiences both similar to and different from my own. Many were new to the industry and figuring it out just like me. Others, with a little more experience, were wrestling with the question of whether to buy or lease a truck and become an owner-operator (i.e., an independent contractor). However critical this book may be of independent contracting across much of the trucking industry, I came to deeply respect the ambitions and efforts of many of the drivers who choose to become independent contractors. Unfortunately, I also came to agree with the most experienced truckers I interviewed, that the dreams of these less-experienced drivers were played upon by employers and others who have rigged independent contracting to their advantage.

Are there any opportunities for drivers to be independent contractors that aren't bad? I'll let the voices of the most experienced drivers, including the most experienced contractors, answer that question in the pages that follow. In fact, drivers with the most experience often pointed me in the direction of the bigger structural and historical issues at play. Much of what value may be contained in this book resulted from me trying to understand in sociological terms the insights shared by these truckers. On many points I have been a research assistant to them.

I have benefited from conversations with hundreds of truckers and others working in or studying the industry. At every step in the process of writing this book, I have had those people mind. The most basic goal that has guided me throughout is the desire that all those individuals, especially the drivers, would agree that I have accurately represented their experience. At my most hopeful I have imagined my most experienced interviewees reading this book and concluding that not only did I get it right as they see it, but that by putting their experiences together with those of other drivers, the perspectives of carrier managers and owners, and in the context of statistics and historical facts, they can now understand their own experiences in a new way. Even more importantly, I hope that this book may allow the knowledge and advice of those veteran insiders (for better and worse organized and narrated by a sociologist) to be passed on to those new to the industry.

Relative to the academic literature, my goal is to draw the reader's attention to the critical links between ideology, discourse, state policy, and individual workplaces, as well as the decisions of workers as they invest in their work lives. It's there, in that interaction, that we find the labor market, a woefully understudied arena of class power and class action. It is at the level of the labor market that key parts of the disturbing story of rising inequality and bad jobs in the United States need to be investigated.

For readers interested in public policy my goal is to show why the transformation of employment relations in trucking that produced the troubles of the drivers described in this book should be understood as a pressing issue to be addressed, regardless of whether their ultimate concern is workers and their families, highway safety, traffic congestion, economic efficiency, the social safety net, or environmental sustainability. Indeed, the story told in this book is important to all of us as consumers, workers, the motoring public, taxpayers, and citizens. The workplace of truckers is a public space that we share with them as they follow the laws of the road, comply with the direction of employers, and meet the demands of customers. While the public may see truckers primarily as a problem or a danger, the importance of the work they do and how it is regulated by government cannot be overstated. It is their work that moves our economy, bringing us the goods that sustain and entertain us, whether those goods come from a hundred miles away or halfway around the world. How truckers are trained, how they work, how they are treated by their employers, and what social safety net programs they have access to—these issues affect all of us.

In the end I cannot escape the conclusion that we would all be better off if truckers had greater control over how they work and what they earn. We would be better off if truckers had greater power in the labor market, both individually and collectively. The reader might suspect that these conclusions were preordained, that regardless of what I was told or experienced,

I must be a liberal, left-leaning academic who wants independent contracting, and the freedom of workers to choose it, to be restricted. Or that I was just interested in finding evidence to support arguments suggesting that unions are the answer. Unions, or collective action of some other sort, may indeed be a key part of the answer to truckers' problems. Ultimately that's a question truckers would have to decide and act on themselves—though the rest of us may have a role to play in ensuring that they, and millions of workers like them, are free to make those kinds of decisions.

In fact I began this project with little knowledge, and even less of an opinion, on the role of independent contracting in trucking. It was truckers themselves who initially pointed me to its importance. And it was truckers who first suggested some of the most disturbing aspects of the industry's labor markets. They argued that truckers were underpaid, overworked, disrespected, and lied to. The most experienced all saw these problems as systemic and tied to labor turnover, cutthroat competition, and ultimately deregulation of the industry. They argued that the system was causing truckers to work themselves to death—sometimes literally. They saw independent contracting as a scam meant to pay truckers less while getting them to work harder. They argued that the government subsidized the whole thing by paying part of the cost to train hordes of new workers who had no idea what they were getting into and who wouldn't last a year behind the wheel.

It did not take me long to find strong evidence supporting some of the most critical opinions I had encountered. But as a sociologist I knew that I had to understand these perspectives in the context of larger industry structures, through the experiences, goals, and constraints of managers and owners, and historically. I did that by gathering every kind of data I thought might be relevant (see the methodological appendix to learn more about this process). In the end, not only did I come to agree with some of the most strident critics, I learned that few in the industry would disagree. Truckers are overworked and underpaid. Just about everyone in the industry knows that's true.

Many also wouldn't be surprised by my conclusion that the industry systematically mistreats and misleads drivers, transferring to them much of the cost and risk of the industry's inefficiencies. What was for me one of the most shocking findings of my research—that employers keep wages low and encourage workers to take on the risk of owning trucks by supporting third-party companies that are allied with them—probably would not surprise the most experienced truckers either. But I suspect that even those drivers would be surprised by how sophisticated this coordination is.

Throughout this project I consistently played the role of detached analyst. I formulated, tested, and retested my hypotheses and conclusions as open-mindedly and thoroughly as I could. But ultimately this book is about the experiences of hundreds of thousands of workers. As I write this, many of them are out on the road in the middle of a fourteen-hour (or longer) workday, hundreds of miles from loved ones they may not see weeks or months at a time. Many are working under a form of debt peonage to pay for their training. Many others are on the edge of destroying their credit and working for far less than they are worth to buy a truck, become an independent contractor, and get their piece of the American Dream. This book is my attempt to tell their story to the best of my ability.

Acknowledgments

This book would not have been possible without the contributions and support of many. Most obviously it would not exist without the hours given by hundreds of truckers and others involved in the trucking industry who gave their time and knowledge freely to me. My heartfelt thanks go out to all of them.

I would like to thank my dissertation committee at Indiana University: Pam Walters, (chair), Art Alderson, Bill Corsaro, and Ethan Michelson. My dissertation advisers provided a wonderful mix of tough criticism, constructive insight, and generous support as I pursued what was for me an intimidating research agenda. During that time I also benefited from a departmental fellowship from IU's Department of Sociology. My fellow graduate students at IU provided willing ears and were a frequent source of vital feedback. As the dissertation evolved, and then developed into additional research, and eventually into this book, I was the beneficiary of conversations and comments from many, including Elizabeth Armstrong, David Bensman, Michael Belzer, Issac Martin, Monica Prasad, Ann Swidler, Mike Hout, Howie Becker, and Andrew Abbott.

In 2010 I was awarded a two-year American Sociological Association/ National Science Foundation postdoctoral fellowship in economic sociology at the University of Wisconsin. That fellowship provided me with great opportunities, allowing me to continue my research on the effects of the Great Recession and to write the first draft of this book. The W. E. Upjohn Institute for Employment Research and the Center on Wisconsin Strategy provided research funds to cover the cost of this additional research. More importantly, during this time it was my good fortune to have the mentorship of Joel Rogers and Erik Wright. Joel challenged me to see trucking within the bigger picture of economic change, showed me the potential of my research to address public policy, and then generously supported its development in that direction. Erik spurred me to think more deeply about the historical and structural explanations of the inequalities involved and the potential of alternative ways of organizing the trucking industry. Having Joel and Erik as guides as the book emerged, and as my research expanded in directions I never foresaw, was the intellectual opportunity of a lifetime. While at Wisconsin, the staff of the Center on Wisconsin Strategy welcomed me and provided essential support. Daniel Cox wrestled my files into order. Matthew Wyndham and the incomparable Michelle Bright provided all manner of support and good humor, making my time in Madison both more productive and more enjoyable than it otherwise would have been.

The book as it actually exists really began with the involvement of Naomi Schneider at University of California Press. In her very first email, responding to my book proposal and sample chapters, she contributed the vision that turned a dense and sprawling dissertation into this book. Her contributions have been critical. At key decision points in the writing of the manuscript, I have been lucky and grateful to have Naomi's patient and sage guidance. I also received excellent suggestions from an anonymous reviewer of the manuscript. Thanks go to the staff at UC Press for guiding this first-time author through the production process. Thanks also to Meg Wallace for helping to reorganize the structure of chapters and to Thomas Frick for copyediting.

There are several individuals who have contributed so much to the development of this book that it is hard for me to imagine what it would look like without them. Christine Williams provided many useful contributions over the years, beginning with her comments during an ASA presentation before the manuscript even existed. Her assistance has been invaluable and continued right up to the last draft. Annette Lareau has read multiple drafts and provided some of the toughest and most valuable feedback. Beyond her comments, her faith in and support of this book have been humbling to me. It is my hope that at some point in my career I will be able to contribute to the work of another as generously as Annette has to mine. Finally, my wife, Melissa Wilde, has helped and supported me throughout the entirety of this project, from the initial idea for the dissertation to the lengthy absences during fieldwork to the final editing. She has spent more hours reading drafts and discussing the project than can be counted. To her I owe more than I can ever express in words.

Introduction

WHERE DID ALL THESE BAD JOBS COME FROM?

Several months into my work as a trucker, I recorded the following notes in my audio journal:

5/18, 8:30 p.m.: I am stuck at a railroad yard in New Jersey just across the Hudson River from Manhattan. I got here around 6:30 after fighting rush hour traffic all the way from Long Island through New York City. When I arrived, the clerk said my company needed to fax my name, driver's license number, and company codes for the load I am picking up before he could process it. It took more than an hour and half for the evening shift dispatcher to fax the information. Why can't they have that stuff ready? Now I'm really screwed. According to government regulations I can only work one more hour today before I have to take a ten-hour break. The load is headed to Rhode Island and I was planning to make it to Connecticut tonight, and I still don't have the load. I don't think I will be able to find parking north of the city now, which means I've got to find a place near here tonight. And I'll have to fight traffic on the Cross Bronx Expressway tomorrow morning. That will cost me a lot of time, not to mention stress. *I hate that damn road.* Once again, the only one who isn't getting paid is me. My company's dispatchers are getting paid. The guy in the guard shack is getting paid.

5/18, 10:00 p.m.: My load is still not ready. I just backed my tractor between a couple of trailers in the yard. I am not allowed to stay here once I get the load, but I'm hoping the security guards won't give me any trouble for spending the night. Maybe they won't notice the truck or will lose track of how long I am here after the next shift change. I can't legally drive, and the only place I'll find to park now is on a nearby street. But that would be like putting out a "please hijack this truck" sign.[1]

These notes are from one of the many bad days I spent working as a long-haul trucker in the early stages of research for this book. That night I slept in a railroad yard without food or access to a bathroom. By the time I recorded the second note, I was dead tired and frustrated. Having started my workday at 6:00 a.m., I had spent sixteen hours driving through traffic, delivering and picking up freight, and waiting, but I would only be paid for the 215 miles I drove. At twenty-six cents per mile, I had earned a grand total of fifty-six dollars, or three-fifty per hour.

Hundreds of thousands of truckers experience days like this regularly, because they absorb the inefficiencies of the system that moves virtually all of the goods you and I consume. They crisscross the country for weeks at a time, living out of their trucks and working extremely long hours, often for little more than minimum wage. Why would truckers want that kind of job? The answer is that they don't. They want better working conditions and better pay.

This book explains why trucking jobs are so bad, why workers take them anyway, and why, when workers become dissatisfied, there is little they can do to solve the problem except find another line of work. It explains how companies can continue to get workers to do jobs—at least temporarily—on terms that they don't really want to accept. Of course, trucking is not the only industry in which American workers are finding it increasingly difficult to get a decent job or improve the one they have. What has happened to the trucking industry over the last few decades can tell us a lot about the dramatic rise in inequality in the US.

Truckers' working conditions and problems today have a precedent. In the early days of trucking, truckers often toiled long hours for low pay. But by the 1950s they had organized across much of the nation. Those collective efforts, along with government regulation of the industry, which began during the New Deal, made trucking good, well-compensated work. From the 1950s to the late 1970s, when the industry was deregulated, truckers were the best-paid and most powerful segment of the US working class.

In light of this history, and how bad things have become for so many truckers, I wondered: Why do today's truckers accept such conditions and pay? Why can't they achieve through collective action the situation truckers had in the past? So, in the winter of 2005, I left my low-paid but relatively comfortable life as a graduate student in sociology and became a long-haul trucker to begin answering those questions. I wanted to know how trucking went from being one of the best blue-collar jobs in the US to one of the worst, and what that transformation could tell us about the way labor markets work in the contemporary economy. I spent about two months training to learn how to drive a tractor-trailer and then almost four months working for a leading long-haul trucking company. I drove tens of thousands of miles across the eastern half of the United States hauling what is known as "general freight"—almost anything that could be put into a cardboard box or on a pallet and loaded into a fifty-three-foot-long "box" or "dry van" trailer. I worked, lived, and slept in my truck for weeks at a time, rarely leaving it for more than the time required to uncouple a trailer, take a shower, or grab the occasional hot meal. I typically worked either twelve or nineteen days at a time and averaged almost fourteen hours of work per day, for which I earned on average about nine-fifty per hour. On the worst days I worked as many as eighteen hours and made far less than minimum wage.

The harsh reality of working as a trucker taught me a lot. I learned how the work was done and began to understand a little about how the workers I encountered in my training, on the job, and at truck stops thought about it. I quickly learned that my fellow truckers pretty much agreed with my own take on things: the work was bad and the pay was worse. They wanted something better. Knowing in broad strokes the industry's history, I assumed that workers would consider unions a possible answer to their problems. But when workers commiserated—as we often did during the brief moments of human contact at loading docks and truck stops that randomly punctuate the long, lonely hours on the road—the topic of unions almost never came up. No, unions were not the solution on these

JS. union

workers' minds. Instead, many talked about the possibility of becoming an owner-operator, a self-employed trucker who owns their own truck.

At the outset of the project, I was aware that owner-operators existed, but I didn't immediately realize that many were working right alongside me. Other truckers hauling "dry vans" for large, long-haul companies like mine were doing exactly the same work I was, and I assumed that they were all employees. Owner-operators, I thought, wouldn't look like employees. I sometimes imagined them as popularly portrayed in movies: modern-day cowboys, complete with boots, oversized belt buckle, and hat, and driving trucks gleaming with chrome. As a sociologist, I suspected owner-operators would be mostly older, white men from rural areas where they were "born into trucking." I knew the cultural stereotypes were likely a caricature, but the academic literature on trucking gave little reason to doubt my demographic hunches. Furthermore, while I had some uncertainty about who owner-operators were, I had none about what they would *do*. On this the literature seemed to universally agree. Owner-operators had greater control over what work they did and how they did it, they were small business owners independent from companies, and they valued that independence. So I expected to see owner-operators on the phone dealing with freight brokers, cold-calling customers to find the best loads, haggling over prices and negotiating delivery times, and focused on hauling good-paying niche freight that rewarded the specialized skills, experience, and equipment that they supposedly possessed.

After just a few weeks of driving and meeting fellow truckers, however, I realized that owner-operators surrounded me, but could not be distinguished by how they looked, who they were, or what they did. Unlike independent owner-operators, who deal directly with customers or brokers to find loads, the owner-operators I was working alongside were contractors. These owner-operators owned or leased their own truck but then leased their services for a year or more at a time to a larger firm that provided them with freight to haul.

Though I could not initially find any significant differences between what contractors and employees *did*, as I talked with them at loading docks and truck stops I began to notice differences in *how they thought about what they did*. Some contractors seemed convinced that contracting was far better than being an employee, and it didn't take much to get them to say so. Experienced employees and contractors voiced the opposite view, but only when pressed on the issue. While I had no intention of studying contractors when I began this project, by the time I finished working as a driver I knew that I had stumbled upon a remarkable puzzle: here were workers with similar labor-market opportunities doing the same kind of work, often for the same company, but some wanted to be employees while others wanted to be self-employed. Why? Did contracting return more pay and control over work, as some claimed? If so, why weren't all truckers contractors, particularly the most experienced? Were different values and/or personal backgrounds the answer? Was it simply a matter of who had the financial means to buy a truck?

Immediately after my experience working as a trucker, I began visiting trucking firms and interviewing company owners and managers that used contractors. I started gathering statistical data on contractor and employee compensation and productivity, seeking to first determine why firms wanted to hire contractors. Then, to find out what workers wanted and got out of contracting, I began regularly visiting a large truck stop near the junction of two major interstate highways in the Midwest. There, from 2005 to 2007, I conducted in-depth interviews with an initial sample of seventy-five truckers. Of these, twenty-eight were working as contractors and another nine had done so in the past. In 2008, in the midst of fuel price spikes and labor unrest among trucking contractors, I conducted another twenty-five in-depth interviews with contractors and had informal conversations with several dozen more. (The reader interested in learning more about how I conducted my fieldwork, and who I interviewed and how, can find more information in the methodological appendix at the end of the book.) After the fieldwork and interviews I collected a wide range of other data from trucking Web sites, magazines, industry publications, and academic studies.

Altogether these data tell an important story about the rise of inequality in the US, and how deregulated labor markets disadvantage workers and benefit employers by allowing employers to shape the way that workers understand the costs and benefits of different employment relationships. In order to understand that story, we need to start with a bit of background about the trucking industry and its labor and regulatory history.

THE LONG-HAUL TRUCKING INDUSTRY

On any given day the US economy depends on the movement of more than *54 million tons* of freight worth more than $48 billion. That's about 350 pounds of freight for *every American every day*.[2] Though rail, barge, and pipeline play key roles, at some point nearly all of the goods you and I consume are moved by truck. As you can imagine, given the variety of goods being moved, the types of truck transportation vary widely. Some manufacturers and retailers own their own trucks and haul the goods they make or sell. These are known as private carriers. But for-hire carriers move the vast majority of freight.

For-hire carriers can be defined by the types of goods they haul, the quantities they typically carry, and how far and fast they move the freight, all of which determine the kind of equipment they use and how they organize the services they provide. Typically trucking companies specialize in freight that requires just one or a few of the dozens of kinds of trailers out there—regular box trailers, refrigerated trailers, flatbeds, tank trailers, and so on.

The distance the goods are moving is also important. Carriers that typically haul loads less than 150 miles are considered local, and those that travel greater distances are considered long-haul or over-the-road (OTR). The vast majority of long-haul carriers are truckload (TL) carriers, moving shipments that fill their trailers to capacity or approach the maximum weight of trucks allowed on most highways without a special permit (eighty thousand pounds).

This book focuses on the largest and most important kind of trucking in today's economy, long-haul TL trucking—particularly its general freight segment. General freight is anything that can be put in a box or on a pallet and loaded into an unrefrigerated trailer. For the most part, general freight truckload companies do little more than move a trailer full of freight from one loading dock to another; they rarely handle or process freight that requires special care or attention.[3] But the range and volume of goods— from steel coils to consumer electronics to beverages—that can be moved in this way is enormous. General freight carriers play a critical role, moving the majority of goods to and from nearly all of the ports, railroad yards, factories, warehouses, distribution centers, and large retail stores in the US.

Of the some 1.7 million tractor-trailer drivers in the US, roughly eight hundred thousand work for long-haul truckload carriers and six hundred thousand of those are employed by general freight carriers.[4] There are more than one thousand long-haul general freight TL firms that make more than $3 million dollars in revenue annually, and tens of thousands of additional carriers with one or just a few trucks that might compete in the for-hire segment. The high level of competition means low profits for most of these companies. In some years even medium and large general freight carriers have had average profits of less than 1 percent.[5] Very large companies, however, benefit from economies of scale in purchasing equipment and fuel, and in the ability to handle high-volume customers, and some of these do significantly better in terms of profit. Several dozen of these large companies, each of which employs thousands of the lowest-paid drivers, set rates that are the competitive standard for the entire general freight segment, while earning substantial profit.

Low carrier rates are the fruit of low wages and bad working conditions for drivers. The typical general freight driver lives out of a truck and is away from home for almost two weeks at a time. Though many of them put in hours equivalent to two full-time jobs or more, a new driver might earn $35,000 annually, while the average driver might earn around $45,000. If we count the total time they are required to be on the road, many of these drivers are earning less than minimum wage.

The combination of low wages and bad working conditions results in extraordinarily high turnover, typically averaging over 100 percent a year at large companies.[6] The best recent studies of turnover have focused on a unique set of data collected at a large firm similar to the one I worked for. I will call this firm "Federal." Steven Burks and his colleagues looked at the retention rates for more than five thousand drivers hired by Federal from September 2001 to the end of March 2005. Ninety-two percent of the drivers hired by Federal were inexperienced—that is, new to the industry. Within about ten weeks of being hired, 25 percent of the drivers had left the company. Half of those hired were gone by twenty-nine weeks. The authors suggest that these turnover rates are consistent with other industry data, a fact which indicates that "several hundred thousand people train for and try out this job each year, only to leave it within a few months, probably having incurred debt for training that most have little hope of repaying."[7] It appears that having enough inexperienced drivers available to fill TL carriers' eight hundred thousand or so seats requires training somewhere in the neighborhood of 150,000 to two hundred thousand drivers per year.[8]

Turnover is expensive. The cost of replacing a single driver varies by segment and carrier, but industry figures and academic studies suggest that turnover costs the industry as a whole several billion dollars annually.[9] In fact, carriers and their industry associations are almost constantly claiming that the industry is facing an imminent labor shortage. So why don't they fix the turnover problem by improving wages and working conditions? Because it is more profitable to manage the problem than to fix it.

Carriers know that being a long-haul trucker is so tough that wages would have to be much higher to retain drivers. In a 2011 survey, an industry consultancy asked trucking executives what drivers' wages would need to be to retain them more effectively. Almost 95 percent said that wages needed to rise above $50,000 a year. Sixty-five percent said that they would need to top $60,000. And almost a third said that they needed to be over $70,000.[10] In other words, these executives believe that they would need to nearly double the pay of drivers in order to solve their turnover problem.[11]

Instead of paying such high wages, companies employ a number of strategies to reduce problems related to turnover or shift the problems and costs to others. First, rather than operating training programs at their own expense, most carriers bring in a steady stream of drivers through public and private truck driving schools that charge workers for their training. A few of the largest carriers operate their own trucking schools and charge students around $4,000 to learn to drive a truck. If then hired, most of these workers sign a contract with a carrier stating that this debt will be forgiven if they work for the company for a year or so. If they quit before that time, they usually must repay the cost of training to the carrier, which most likely charges high interest on the debt. In other words, these workers work under a form debt peonage.

Once workers can leave without penalty, carriers prevent them from bidding up wages by using benchmarking companies to track wages and avoid paying above the market rate that others in the sector are paying.

As workers gain more experience—even just one or two years can make a huge difference—options at local, niche, or private carriers with better work routines and pay begin to open up. To retain these more experienced drivers, TL carriers and trucking media convince workers to become independent contractors, promising that contracting will be financially rewarding and give workers additional control over working conditions. But contracting ends up being even worse for most truckers than being an employee. Simply put, it allows carriers to pay the most productive drivers far less than they are worth for their labor and to shift much of the cost and risk of owning and operating a truck to them.

Without a doubt, these practices hurt the workers who are unfortunate enough to pass through the industry's revolving door. But we all pay the costs of trucking's dysfunctional labor market. Our tax dollars subsidize the costs of training the constantly needed stream of new drivers through worker training grants. And inexperienced drivers operate less safely and efficiently than experienced drivers, so the public pays the price by way of more highway accidents, higher insurance costs, and increased oil consumption and air pollution.

The industry and its advocates claim there is little they can do about their labor troubles. If they raise pay and improve working conditions, they say, they will be priced out of the market. They insist that their pay rates are simply the outcome of natural market processes of supply and demand, particularly as they compete for the business of increasingly large and powerful customers, like Wal-Mart.

But it's not that simple. Trucking companies have collectively developed a number of widespread and sophisticated labor supply and management strategies to ensure profit. These strategies keep wages artificially low, coerce workers to stay in the job longer than they want to, and shift risks and costs onto workers and the public. To begin to understand why, we need to look at the history of these jobs and how the current system of labor relations in the industry developed.

WHAT WENT WRONG FOR TRUCKERS?

Trucking jobs weren't always so bad. Hauling general freight, in particular, used to be one of the best blue-collar jobs in the US—until the late 1970s. That's when trucking's highly unionized labor force began losing control of trucking's labor markets, and the federal government began deregulating the industry. Deregulation led to complete deunionization of much of the industry, as employers responded to hypercompetitive conditions. Many companies went belly-up, and wages plummeted and working conditions deteriorated among those that remained, as new, low-cost firms emerged.

The history of trucking can be divided into three periods according to the way the state regulated the industry over time. The first, the preregulatory period, extended from the advent of motorized trucks in the early 1900s to 1935. The second, the regulatory period, began with the Motor Carrier Act of 1935, which authorized federal economic regulation of the industry under the auspices of the Interstate Commerce Commission (ICC). The third period began after a series of executive and legislative efforts, most notably the Motor Carrier Act of 1980, removed federal economic regulation.

These three periods represent fundamentally different state approaches to the industry's central tendency toward destructive competition—competition so severe that it undermines profitability to the point that it causes underinvestment by firms, industry-wide inefficiency, market instability, and poor service quality. According to economists, two factors cause this tendency. First, trucking lacks asset specificity: the capital investments required for trucking are not generally tailored to narrow or specific product markets, and trucks are, for the most part, cheap and interchangeable. This means that the barriers to entry into the industry are low, so when trucking is profitable new firms are able to enter the market and existing firms can increase capacity quickly.

Second, trucking is a derived-demand industry. That is, what trucking produces is entirely dependent on the immediate demand for its services from customers. Trucking firms cannot store what they produce for later sale. When demand slackens, some portion of their equipment, facilities, and labor will be immediately underutilized. When that happens firms may have strong incentives to keep the wheels rolling by cutting the rates they charge customers, even taking a loss on individual loads to maintain market share or generate revenue to cover fixed expenses and survive slack periods.

These two characteristics of the industry have always presented significant challenges. In the preregulatory period, collusive arrangements between trucking firms to limit entry and prevent rate-cutting, often enforced by strong worker organizations, occasionally allowed firms to overcome these problems. In the regulatory period, government regulation through the ICC restricted entry into markets by issuing a limited number of hauling authorities that gave certain firms the right to haul specific kinds of freight to and from particular geographic locations. Regulation also exempted firms from antitrust regulation and encouraged firms with the same hauling authority to collectively set rates by freight type and route to ensure a profitable environment for investment. However, just as in the preregulatory period, strong worker organizations were critical for firms to maximize profit during regulation, as I'll explain below.

Regulation had other important effects for labor as well. The terminal systems that existed during the regulatory period strengthened the position of labor relative to carriers. Because retailers were smaller and hauling authorities limited the types of freight and geographic reach of specific carriers, much regulated freight was shipped in less-than-truckload (LTL) size shipments, and the biggest carriers found it advantageous to develop terminals where small shipments could be combined and broken down. These facilities and the relationships between carriers they created provided an expanding set of interconnected leverage points for union organizing.[12] Quite simply, terminal systems gave unions the opportunity to disrupt shipments throughout whole companies and the firms they partnered with, once the union had control of one or more important terminals. At the same time, regulation gave carriers the means to pass additional costs of unionized labor on to customers through higher rates. But they could only do that if carriers with similar authorities were also unionized.

Throughout the preregulatory period, truckers struggled collectively to improve their pay and working conditions, and often enjoyed significant success in major cities. Under regulation, unionized truckers gained control throughout the US in every sector but the hauling of agricultural goods, which was always exempt from regulation. In the process they built the largest and most powerful union in American history, the International

Brotherhood of Teamsters (IBT). By the 1950s, the IBT had achieved better working conditions and pay for most truckers across much of the US. And by the 1970s IBT members were among the best paid blue-collar workers in the country, earning as much as 20 percent more than even unionized auto and steel workers.[13]

Much of the IBT's progress came between 1957 and 1967, when Jimmy Hoffa was the union's president. Without doubt Hoffa deserves much of the credit, but what he did was bring to fruition a set of strategies Teamsters had been using for more than half a century. What successful IBT leaders had almost always done was try to improve wages by increasing the profitability of the firms they worked for. They did this by reducing competition. As one academic study published the year Hoffa became IBT president concluded, "The IBT is unusually alert to the needs of the industry and has striven to strengthen the competitive position of trucking vis-à-vis other forms of transportation."[14]

Hoffa was important and innovative not so much in terms of strategy, but in terms of the magnitude of his goals. He wanted to gain national control over trucking's labor market, and in 1964 he did, when he successfully negotiated the first National Master Freight Agreement (NMFA). The NMFA set the wages and working conditions for 450,000 long-haul and local drivers working for hundreds of companies, including all of the most important companies in general freight trucking, the industry's most profitable and important sector at the time.[15] The agreement raised wages substantially for most truckers, particularly those in South and in low-paying areas of the Midwest. The 1964 NMFA was the outcome of years of careful planning and organizing by Hoffa to tame both labor and employers and create a centralized bargaining process that would set the standard for truckers' wages and working conditions across the nation until the 1980s.

Once Hoffa had organized the industry's employers within a national centralized bargaining system, he used his power to benefit both employers and workers. By reducing competition among trucking firms and disciplining labor, he was able to ensure both profitability and high wages, while protecting the industry from outside competition.

In the first major attempt at nationwide bargaining negotiation, in 1960–1961, the employers and union had started far apart. The employers put up resistance, but eventually the two groups agreed to a contract they believed was in their mutual interests. Arthur Sloane, an economist who interviewed trucking executives about the negotiations, concluded, "Their opinion is that the settlement stemmed basically from a competent presentation of the industry's problems to Hoffa by the employer negotiating team and (in the words of one manager) 'Hoffa's willingness to develop a program for solving these problems.'"[16]

Similarly, a husband and wife team of Harvard economists that Hoffa allowed to study his negotiations wrote:

> Without Hoffa's centralized power, the trucking operators would have to deal separately with each local over its limited geographical jurisdiction. . . . Trucking carriers are keenly aware of the plight of the closely-related railroad industry, where unions have historically impeded improved efficiency and technology. Consequently, many of them applaud Hoffa's progressive domination of the Teamsters, and are willing to pay the price.[17]

Larger carriers in particular came to favor multiemployer contracts with the union as enforcement vehicles. Sloane surveyed dozens of managers and owners of medium-sized to large firms and found that they respected Hoffa greatly; he even suggested that some of their opinions "bordered on hero-worship." Smaller carriers feared a one-size-fits-all approach, but saw a great advantage in the central control of a competent leader rather than potentially overreaching local leadership.[18]

Though Hoffa wanted the most comprehensive contract uniformly applied on the widest basis, he often tailored the nationwide agreement to meet the needs of specific employers. According to Sloane, Hoffa carefully considered appeals for conditions based on economic necessity. Over time he made more and more exceptions, and as the scale of bargaining grew, employers would have best of both worlds, "stability for their industry and individual dispensation from contractually imposed uniformity for themselves where this was genuinely warranted."[19] Once contracts were signed, Hoffa made sure they were strictly enforced. An employer told Sloane that Hoffa "honors his contract immaculately, even to the point of placing himself in political jeopardy."[20]

Hoffa's efforts not only raised wages, they also took wages out of competition by standardizing them. Uniform wages provided a hedge against companies seeking to lower pay rates and thus minimized legal and illegal rate competition. Major firms appreciated the IBT's ability to enforce rates and help to eliminate marginal carriers who could compete only by paying lower wages.[21] But Hoffa's influence over the industry and the benefits to the strongest carriers extended beyond this. To some extent he determined the number and size of firms in the industry. Hoffa could influence the investments companies made to expand or change their operations, and companies consulted him on plans, because if he wanted to, he could prevent mergers and acquisitions by putting political pressure on the ICC or by threatening to disrupt the supply of labor to companies.[22] In general, however, Hoffa preferred to work constructively with large trucking companies. If the number of companies was few, this would enhance profitability and create a more cohesive leadership among employers to address the industry's long-term problems. Hoffa used contract terms and union boycotts of nonunion carriers to eliminate less efficient firms.

Under regulation, higher wages also helped to raise profits and return on investment. The ICC would approve shipping rates that resulted in a 94 percent operating ratio (operating expenses as a percentage of revenue). So if labor costs increased, firms could receive a far better return on invested capital. Convincing regulators to approve an increase in shipping rates was an important part of Hoffa's strategy. When asked if he thought a strike was likely during a negotiation in 1962, Hoffa replied, "Only if we need one to convince the ICC to grant a rate increase."[23] Sloane concluded:

> By the readily acknowledged, if sometimes embarrassed admission of the trucking companies, Hoffa represented all of their labor cost interests better than these historically close-to-the-margin, mistrustful, highly individualistic, and zealously competitive operators could ever have done themselves. . . . He infused a once-chaotic industry with a great deal of stability and allowed it to prosper. Trucking was undoubtedly better off for there having been a Hoffa.[24]

Hoffa helped the industry to become more profitable than ever,[25] and it appears that most employers were not unhappy with their dependence on him. As Slone summarized: "If they viewed him as an autocrat (as most did), they also saw him as a benevolent autocrat, an enlightened unionist who had generally attempted to act in the best interests of trucking."[26] On the other hand, they were concerned about how such power might be used by others. Hoffa had gained employers' trust, but his sometimes ruthless approach to dealing with companies, fellow unionists, and the government had resulted in repeated scandals and numerous criminal charges. It was clear that Hoffa was at risk. Employers worried that Hoffa's potential successors did not possess the knowledge and relationships to control both employers and the internal politics of the union. As James and James put it at the time:

> While the formal bargaining structure in freight may well outlast Hoffa, his potential successors would play the leverage game differently—without the intricate strategies and subtle sophistication which characterize Hoffa's maneuvers—and therefore, not nearly so well. This is what made the struggle to get Hoffa so fascinating and extremely significant: for if Hoffa goes, the power balance will change, both between the union and its employers, as well as within the Teamster organization itself.[27]

Employers were right to be concerned. By 1962, legal troubles were mounting for Hoffa. He negotiated the first NMFA in 1964 under the cloud of a jury-tampering trial in which he was accused of bribing a grand jury. He set up Frank Fitzsimmons, the IBT vice president, as his replacement and hoped to control the union from prison if need be.[28] Despite the ongoing trial, which would ultimately lead to his conviction, the IBT's 1966 international convention was completely under Hoffa's control, and support for him among the membership was strong. As a demonstration of that support, the convention delegates quadrupled Hoffa's pay, which was already the highest of any union official in the US.[29]

But when Hoffa went to jail in 1967, after eventually being convicted of both jury tampering and misuse of the IBT's pension funds, things began to fall apart. In a bid to build support and head off challenges to his leadership, Fitzsimmons negotiated a big pay increase for truckers in the NMFA. He almost immediately began to give up the centralized control Hoffa had painstakingly achieved, restoring responsibilities to regional and local officials and hoping to build loyalty within the union in return.[30]

Instead Fitzsimmons lost control of powerful locals. The 1967 and 1970 NMFAs prompted major wildcat strikes, the first such rebellions within the IBT in its history. By the time Hoffa was pardoned in 1971 the union was imploding, as rebel rank-and-file groups appeared in almost every major city and power struggles consumed the leadership.[31] Leaders jockeyed to fill the power vacuum left by Hoffa by promising better contracts. From 1967 to 1973 this competition produced a 20 percent real wage increase for IBT members.[32]

But the IBT's success at the bargaining table was reducing the competitiveness of the unionized segments of the industry. This would have been unlikely under Hoffa, who "always cast a wary eye on the market and avoided pushing trucking wages too far in any segment."[33] The increased aggressiveness of the IBT drove up costs and prices and caused carriers and their customers to seek alternatives, such as building their own in-house trucking fleets.

By 1979 the biggest problem for union members and their employers was a rapidly declining share of freight and a corresponding drop in the number of truck drivers in the Teamsters—a 20 to 25 percent drop from 1967 to 1977.[34] Still, despite declining market share, profits and Teamster wages at regulated unionized companies were stronger than ever, with hourly wages 50 percent higher than for manufacturing workers.[35] These developments alienated supporters of regulation and hardened the resolve of the IBT's enemies.

Amid the sluggish economy and double-digit inflation of the 1970s, the IBT may have flexed its muscle too much and too frequently. The dramatic rise in IBT wages, the increased cost of trucking services, and the inefficiencies caused by regulation created significant political pressure to deregulate the industry. At the same time, the economic woes of stagflation were prompting policy makers to question government regulation in general. Advocates for economic deregulation were gaining ground rapidly, and they wanted to deregulate trucking as much as, if not more than, any other industry.

Conservative think tanks, economists, and politicians had been criticizing trucking regulation since passage of the Motor Carrier Act of 1935. New Dealers had argued that regulation was needed to ensure stability in the industry, but conservative economists suggested that regulating trucking the way that railroads were regulated made no sense, because unlike railroads, trucking did not tend toward monopoly. Trucking's low investment cost and flexibility would naturally lead to a more atomized structure that would not allow for high levels of concentration or inadequate capacity or service. From this perspective, collective rate setting and limitations on new entrants into the industry would create monopolies, resulting in inefficiency and artificially high freight rates.[36] Although these arguments had failed to sway the Roosevelt administration, every administration from Eisenhower to Carter revisited the issue of deregulating trucking with increased interest.

Proponents of deregulation persistently gathered academic backing for their position, with private foundations, think tanks, and university academics collaborating to build a broad case.[37] Over time, leading academic economists arrived at a nearly universal consensus that economic regulation in key industries, most notably utilities, transportation, and communications, resulted in inefficiency and should be eliminated. In the 1970s, think tanks politicized this consensus through a series of intellectual and lobbying efforts that promoted an agenda of deregulation.[38]

A revolving door between universities, think tanks, and government—for example, membership on the Council of Economic Advisers—gave deregulation advocates access to the highest levels of decision making. In tandem, the American Enterprise Institute, the Brookings Institution, and other think tanks published papers and ran conferences on concrete proposals to deregulate various industries. Trucking was at the top of their wish list.[39]

Their argument centered on the assertion that regulation was creating economic rents in trucking—or excessive benefits at the expense of consumers—and that 66 to 75 percent of these rents went to labor as higher wages.[40] The remainder of the benefits went to the carriers as profit. On the eve of deregulation, eighteen thousand carriers were authorized to haul regulated freight. These were known at the time as common carriers. About seventeen thousand common carriers typically hauled a single type of specialized freight in truckload-size shipments, and the other thousand or so owned the authority to haul general freight. By the late 1970s the general freight carriers were generating up to two-thirds of all regulated trucking revenue and a substantial profit.[41] Between 1964 and 1973 large general freight carriers averaged a 19.4 percent return on equity, pretax. All manufacturing firms had a 15.8 percent return over that period.

In 1976, these carriers had a 23.7 percent rate of return, while for manufacturers it was about 14 percent.[42] In 1977, the eight largest general freight carriers "earned a rate of return on equity that was twice that of the average Fortune 500 company."[43]

In the late 1970s, with the scholarly case against regulation unopposed, think tanks and lobbying groups went on the political offensive and developed a powerful coalition of consumer advocates and shippers to pressure for deregulation of the industry. The public face of the effort highlighted efficiency gains and cost savings to consumers, but it was well understood by key supporters that deregulation was also aimed at "breaking the back of the Teamsters."[44] But first the deregulators would need to overcome the formidable lobbying power of both regulated trucking firms and the IBT.

President Carter, meanwhile, was seeking a way to address stagflation and increase fuel efficiency. His chief economic adviser, Charles Schultze, pointed out one reason Carter was inclined to favor deregulation: "If you polled 500 economists you'd get 499 to say you ought to do it."[45] Backed by presidential support, the proderegulation coalition developed into a remarkably broad and novel mix of conservative groups like the American Conservative Union and more liberal groups like Common Cause and Ralph Nader's Consumers Union, along with agricultural groups such as the American Farm Bureau.[46] Also eventually included were two dissident conferences of the American Trucking Associations (ATA), representing private and contract carriers. This diversity lent great legitimacy to the claim that the deregulatory agenda was in the public interest.[47] As one writer in *Barron's* summed it up:

> Any movement that lines up such diverse organizations as the Consumer Federation of America, National Association of Manufacturers, National Federation of Independent Businesses, American Farm Bureau Federation and Common Cause on one side [with] the American Trucking Associations and the Teamsters Union on the other, must be in hot pursuit of sound public policy.[48]

Although the public face of the coalition was often its nonbusiness members, its earliest participants were shippers, some of them with large private fleets of their own. Many of the largest manufacturers in the US were involved: DuPont, General Mills, Georgia Pacific, Lever Brothers, Procter and Gamble, Kraft, Kimberly-Clark, Union Carbide, International Paper, and Whirlpool, among others. Also involved were more than two dozen associations representing manufacturers and retailers of many kinds. These companies stood to benefit substantially from deregulation, and because some of them, like Sears, Roebuck & Company, had sophisticated distribution systems that included private fleets, they understood the economics of trucking—particularly that the biggest gain would come from reducing the size and power of the IBT.[49]

Regardless of coalition members' ultimate motives relative to the IBT, the consequences of deregulation for the union and labor were well understood and had already been embraced by the Carter administration, which remained officially silent in anticipation of the expiration of the NMFA in 1979. Observers suggested that the next NMFA would test the price and wage guidelines Carter had issued to counter inflation.

When the IBT opened negotiations for a new NMFA with wage demands far in excess of Carter's guidelines, the administration broke its silence. A spokesperson announced that the administration would quickly press for thorough deregulation of the industry if the labor union won wage increases "substantially" beyond the guidelines. Ignoring the threat, the IBT went on strike and won large wage increases. Powerless to stop the contract, the administration declared it in compliance with the guidelines. But *U.S. News and World Report* called the contract a "body-blow" for Carter's use of the guidelines to fight inflation.[50]

The ensuing congressional battle to pass trucking deregulation was hard fought. The ATA and IBT mounted what has been characterized as one of the most intense lobbying campaigns in the history of Congress.[51] They repeated the same basic arguments that were used to create regulation in the first place: that without regulation there would be chaos, service quality would deteriorate, small shippers and communities would be hurt, and safety would suffer as drivers pushed themselves to gain a margin and had less to invest in their equipment.

However, their arguments about the public good were overshadowed by their focus on the economic interests of IBT members and the firms that employed them. The IBT president told one member of Congress that even watered-down deregulation would "result in complete destruction of qualified motor carriers who now employ 500,000 of our members."[52] Many considered the IBT's lobbying tactics crude and ineffective compared with those of their opponents. The union was even caught trying to bribe a key senator; five Teamsters, including the IBT's president, were eventually convicted on conspiracy to commit bribery.[53]

In the end, the ATA and IBT were easily defeated. Accounts suggest that many votes the truckers thought they could count on were lost on the perceived merits of the case. After decades of academic and think-tank promotion, the economic case for the benefits of deregulation was taken for granted by lawmakers in the late 1970s.[54] There were few concerns about the negative consequences of deregulation, which, it seemed, would be borne by labor and industry special interests. In a series of legislative and administrative decisions, restrictions on new entrants, product-specific hauling authorities, and virtually all other important components of regulation were eliminated. The complete deregulation of interstate trucking, including elimination of the ICC, would not occur until 1985 under President Reagan, but the 1980 legislation clearly spelled the end of regulated trucking.

After signing the 1980 Motor Carrier Act, Carter stated:

> This is historic legislation. It will remove 45 years of excessive and inflationary Government restrictions and redtape. It will have a powerful anti-inflationary effect, reducing consumer costs by as much as $8 billion each year. And by ending wasteful practices, it will conserve annually hundreds of millions of gallons of precious fuel. All the citizens of our Nation will benefit from this legislation. Consumers will benefit, because almost every product we purchase has been shipped by truck, and outmoded regulations have inflated the prices that each one of us must pay. The shippers who use trucking will benefit as new service and price options appear. Labor will benefit from increased job opportunities. And the trucking industry itself will benefit from greater flexibility and new opportunities for innovation.[55]

The rapid deregulation of the industry gave existing carriers little time to prepare, and conditions in the industry were chaotic for several years as carriers tried to adapt. During the decades of regulation, the industry had developed far more capacity than was needed after deregulation. Large manufacturers and retailers had developed private fleets to avoid the inflexible and expensive services of common carriers. As deregulation took effect, this private fleet capacity and less-than-truckload overcapacity drove down freight rates dramatically. In addition, a remarkable number of firms entered the market. At the start of deregulation, 18,045 carriers had ICC hauling authority. In 1981, carriers filed 28,700 applications for new or expanded authority with the ICC.[56]

The first year of deregulation coincided with the recession of 1981, when freight volumes dropped. In the competitive environment that had developed, companies slashed freight rates. Discounts of up to 70 percent from regulation freight rates were commonplace.[57] Nonunionized companies that had focused on TL freight were well positioned for this competition and flourished. Owner-operators, previously unable to easily access regulated freight markets, entered new segments and further weakened the influence of the IBT, which was making wage concessions in an unsuccessful attempt to prevent carriers from going bankrupt or developing low-cost nonunion operations. Within a few years the general freight market was split into a low-cost, almost entirely nonunionized TL segment and a much diminished, unionized, terminal-based less-than-truckload segment handling smaller, more profitable loads.

This transformation forced existing trucking firms to fight simply to survive, and profits plummeted. By 1982 operating ratios of general freight carriers averaged nearly 99 percent, and close to 40 percent of all regulated carriers had net losses.[58] A handful of well-capitalized, previously regulated less-than-truckload carriers gambled on long-term returns and continued to undercut rates, drove competitors out of business, and gobbled up market share. Many regulated carriers, saddled with expensive and now underutilized terminal systems and expensive and inflexible Teamster labor, failed.

In the first five years of deregulation 6,740 carriers went out of business and 57 percent of general freight carriers with more than $1 million in revenue exited the industry.[59] When the full shakeout of the industry was completed by the end of the recession of 1991, only five of the largest fifty carriers operating in 1965 remained.[60]

Deregulation resulted in productivity gains that continued steadily until the mid-1990s.[61] But even after the shakeout of less competitive firms, the general freight TL segment remained intensely competitive two decades after deregulation. Having enjoyed above-average profit margins under regulation, trucking was now barely profitable. General freight, still the dominant freight type, became the least profitable to haul. Despite productivity gains, cost cutting, and tremendous growth in demand, general freight carriers had a profit margin of just .6 percent in 2001.[62]

Outcomes for the IBT, its members, and nonunion drivers were equally dramatic, as remaining carriers shifted to using nonunion labor and drove down wages across the industry. The IBT lost about 25 percent of its membership, almost five hundred thousand members, in the first decade of deregulation.[63] Union membership dropped from 56.6 of all truckers in 1978 to 24.1 percent in 1990.[64] By 1997 this had declined to 19.7 percent, with just 10 percent of over-the-road drivers unionized.[65] There have not been any representative surveys conducted of over-the-road drivers in recent times, but I can say that in my six months of training and driving over-the-road, and then months spent at truckstops conducting interviews, I talked with hundreds of truckers. Only one of those was working for a unionized company. There are essentially no long-haul truckload union drivers today.

In terms of the explicit goals of deregulators, trucking is arguably the most successful and important case of deregulation in US history. Large companies now pay much less to move goods. But deregulation also brought lower wages, greater amounts of unpaid work, and less-desirable working conditions for truckers. Estimates suggest that more than 60 percent of the cost reductions achieved in the years immediately after deregulation came from lower compensation. Total employee compensation per mile, including benefits, fell by 44 percent in over-the-road trucking from 1977 to 1987.[66] These wage declines affected drivers in every category.[67] Although the remaining union drivers maintain about a 20 percent wage premium, their wages have also fallen sharply.[68]

Within two decades of deregulation conditions had deteriorated so much that Michael Belzer, a leading scholar of the industry, characterized over-the-road trucks as "sweatshops on wheels."[69] If we take into account the very long hours they work today, long-haul truckers are producing twice the amount of measurable output, compared with the late 1970s, for wages that are 40 percent lower.[70]

MAKING SENSE OF THE TRANSFORMATION OF
TRUCKING'S LABOR MARKETS

The strength of labor to build formal labor market institutions such as the Teamsters rested on high levels of what sociologist Erik Olin Wright calls worker associational power; the ability of workers to collectively articulate and act on a common set of economic interests. Economic theories, whether Marxist or neoclassical, suggest that the development of worker associational power, and the formal institutions it fosters, inherently disadvantages firms in realizing their goal of maximizing profit.[71] These theories assume that there is an inverse relationship between worker power and capitalist interests: as workers grow more powerful they can both capture a larger share of profit and interfere with capitalists' ability to determine capital investment and control the production process to maximize profit.

Wright suggests, however, that the relationship between worker power and capitalists' interests is more complicated. Although the initial growth of worker power may disadvantage employers, at a certain point it can begin to provide benefits. This is because when worker power is substantial and no longer regularly contested by employers, it can result in higher productivity and be used to solve collective action problems that capitalists cannot solve for themselves, thus increasing the financial benefits for both.[72]

The trucking industry exemplifies how this can work. As workers gained control of the industry's labor markets, their collective action enhanced the profitability of unionized firms in ways firms themselves could not. The IBT disciplined labor to the requirements of capital accumulation, moderating power at the point of production—for example, by nearly eliminating strikes, by streamlining union grievance procedures, and by facilitating labor consent to labor-saving technology. It also standardized wages across the industry, helped to limit the entrance of new firms, and prevented firms from undercutting each other. Finally, the IBT supported beneficial state regulation and helped to protect the industry from outside competitors. A strong IBT was not only better for workers, it resulted in greater profits for their employers.

Deregulation of the trucking industry ended this arrangement, and chaos ensued as competition intensified. Most importantly, the labor market began to churn, as workers moved from company to company in response to deteriorating pay and working conditions. Firms began competing against each other to attract labor at the same time that cutting labor costs became the critical source of competitive advantage. As trucking jobs continued to worsen, many workers began leaving the industry altogether, and soon employers lacked a sufficient supply of trained and experienced drivers. By disrupting trucking's formal labor market institutions, deregulation dis-embedded the industry's workers.

There was no quick way to reembed workers in trucking's labor markets, but the basic requirements of a labor strategy that would lead to profits were clear. After deregulation, trucking firms increasingly needed cheap, compliant truckers who were willing to work more hours for less money and to travel large swaths of the country without returning home often. A sufficient number of those workers simply didn't exist. The industry needed to create them.

For an individual employer this would have been an impossible project to carry out, even without labor opposition. The cost of recruiting and training new workers would be impossible to justify and sustain if competitors could draw them away with slightly higher wages once training was completed. Similarly, radically transforming the way drivers work, and requiring more work for less pay, required an industry-wide process. No individual company could require more work for less pay and more time away from home if workers perceived better options elsewhere. In other words, employers faced a problem that could be solved only through collective action.

STRUCTURE AND CONTRIBUTION OF THE BOOK

Today, trucking companies coordinate their relationship to labor through a range of efforts that reembed workers while increasing their exploitation. These efforts begin with the ceaseless and extensive recruiting efforts trucking companies employ to attract new workers, whom they then funnel to various (often state-supported) training programs. Chapter 1 tells the story of how labor is, and historically was, recruited and trained by the industry.

Once workers are recruited, companies work hard to get them and keep them working cheaply. Chapter 2 describes what it is like to work as a long-haul trucker, explains how that affects the way workers understand their opportunities in the labor market, and shows why truckers are thus open to "buying their own jobs" by becoming contractors.

Chapter 3 describes how workers buy their own jobs, by describing how contracting is promoted and made attractive to workers, and how employers and allied third parties have developed the institutions that support contracting. By promoting contracting, employers have gained back some of the advantages that worker associational power provided during regulation, but without losing control in either the workplace or the labor market.

In Chapter 4 the reader will learn what the harsh reality of contracting is like for most workers, and why it is so attractive to employers. While keeping wages low, contracting shifts much of the risk and cost of equipment to workers. It also creates more productive workers with better retention who, for a time, *believe* in contracting. In other words, employers now achieve consent without compromise.

The final empirical chapter of the book, Chapter 5, demonstrates that this new labor arrangement is the result of a coordinated set of actions on the part of companies. Companies keep wages low by avoiding competition with each other as they buy labor, and by collectively shaping the work that is performed for them and the terms under which it is done. They do so primarily through third-party firms that provide labor research, recruiting, training, and management services. Although these firms are typically considered simply private businesses acting as labor market intermediaries, I found that they play critical roles in coordinating the actions of employers, fundamentally structuring the employment relationship in much the same way that formal labor market institutions did historically.

·   ·   ·   ·   ·

In sum, work and employment relations in the trucking industry have been radically transformed. Previously dominated by union influence and very good jobs, industry employers now have increasingly free reign to structure the work truckers do and the terms on which they do it. They do so by creating a supply of labor and tailoring it to meet their needs while suppressing pay, minimizing turnover between companies, and delaying worker exit from the industry. Employers can now produce drivers who are willing to submit to a demanding regime of self-sweating—pushing themselves to work or sacrifice more despite little or no financial gain and significant risk—and who, in many cases, are not in a position to do anything else.

What's happened to employment relations in trucking is happening in other American industries as well. It epitomizes a critical change that is fueling inequality in the US under what's called the "new economy"—an economy with weaker state regulation, little union or other labor influence, and a globalized workforce.[73] Sociologists call these jobs "precarious," because they typically demand much greater flexibility and exposure to risk from workers.[74]

Economists and sociologists generally understand the outcomes of labor markets to be increasingly determined by a set of ideas and policy prescriptions known as "neoliberalism."[75] Neoliberalism encourages reliance on market processes, individualistic solutions, and a reduction in government regulation and ownership. Neoliberal ideology suggests that in natural market conditions the countless individual actions of firms and workers will determine the price of labor and the shape of jobs, based on supply and demand.

Sociologists have long argued that, in fact, markets are socially constructed, and that both formal institutions (e.g., government regulations such as minimum wage; unions) and informal institutions (e.g., norms and worker expectations) establish the patterns of behavior that constitute labor markets. However, beyond acknowledging these most basic forces, the dominant sociological narratives today suggest that firms and workers are guided by institutions that are fundamentally not about collective class action, whether among workers or among employers. Of course, the collective efforts sociologists and economists have previously studied—mainly workers' attempts to raise wages via unions or professional associations—are clearly attempts to structure labor market interactions along class lines, and are recognized as such.

But, beyond such studies, there is an assumption that in free labor markets, there is little or no coordinated action by employers as a group to gain advantage over workers—aside, perhaps, from industry-wide political action by employers aimed at the state, for example to prevent legislative action that would make it easier for workers to join unions.[76] While scholars have acknowledged the role of third parties in establishing new norms of employment (e.g., labor market intermediaries such as temp agencies),[77] or lobbying for favorable regulation, much of this behavior is not viewed as class behavior. Instead the third-party actors developing the labor market norms of the new economy are viewed as self-interested entrepreneurs whose loyalty is not inherently tied to either workers or employers.[78]

Labor markets consisting of only informal institutions, and perhaps third parties, are portrayed as a kind of class-neutral social space, in which buyers and sellers are able to shape their sides of the employment relationship to realize their interests solely on the basis of their individual characteristics and behavior within any given set of market conditions. In other words, the common view of labor market outcomes is that they are increasingly determined by the free exchanges of self-interested individual actors on the basis of supply and demand for particular kinds of workers (e.g., those with particular skills or educations). In the absence of formal labor market institutions that are explicitly structured around group interests, it is assumed that there is an absence of class-based action.[79]

The Big Rig demonstrates that this understanding of labor markets fails to capture a whole range of actions employers take collectively that help explain why deregulated and deunionized labor markets have been so bad for workers, and why and how so many workers end up, and remain, in them for so long.

1 The CDL Mill

TRAINING THE PROFESSIONAL
STEERING-WHEEL HOLDER

WOULD-BE TRUCKERS

Since the 1990s, millions of workers have been trained to drive a tractor-trailer and earned a commercial driver's license (CDL). Like me, many of them have attended large, private "CDL schools," often run by carriers themselves, that each train thousands of new drivers every year. Almost every Monday morning in the US a new cohort of thousands of workers eager for the chance to become a trucker attend their first day of CDL school. On one typical Monday morning before the Great Recession in a midsized midwestern city, I observed a group of trainees at a trucking school run by a company I'll call "Advanced." In all key respects, Advanced is the same as Leviathan, the company I worked for. On the first day, several dozen trainees reported as instructed at 6:00 a.m. to the lobby of the national chain motel where Advanced was putting them up. They had arrived the night before from a half-dozen or so neighboring states.

A sense of excitement filled the motel lobby as the would-be truckers mingled over free cups of coffee. All the informal conversations that ensued followed the same pattern: trainees introduced themselves and then took turns providing a personal account of why they were there. They were there because they wanted to become truck drivers. And it is hard to imagine any other purpose that could gather such a diverse cross-section of the American working class.

There was Matt, a white evangelical Christian in his late twenties from St. Louis, who had a four-year degree in philosophy and had been working for several years as a drug and alcohol counselor. He couldn't stand the stress and negative feelings he brought home from working with street addicts all day. Matt was engaged to be married soon and was hoping trucking would allow him to save up money to begin a family.

Denise, a black woman in her late thirties, was from a poor neighborhood in Kansas City. As a single mom, she had worked a steady string of low-paying retail jobs to support her three children, who all still lived at home. Her oldest daughter was now expecting a child of her own, and Denise needed a job that could meet the added costs to her household.

Dennis, a white twenty-four-year-old, had served in the army in Afghanistan as a helicopter mechanic. After an honorable discharge he looked for a job servicing civilian helicopters, but ended up working for a company that catered in-flight food for a major airline. Dennis's wages were barely above minimum wage, he had no health insurance, and he'd lost hope for a better career in aviation.

Mitch was a white male from Ohio in his late fifties. After thirty years of mounting tires at a Chrysler assembly plant he retired with a union pension and a bad back. A recent divorce had left him in need of a good regular income. He hoped he'd get that and make enough to buy the Harley-Davidson motorcycle he intended to ride in his second retirement.

Rick was a white truck mechanic, "looking at forty," from a small town on the interstate somewhere in Indiana. Married with a six-year-old son at home, he needed more income to pay the bills. After seventeen years, he got "tired of turning wrenches for nothing" and quit. He had seen enough of trucking to know that the time away from his family would be hard, but he needed the money, and he couldn't go back to his old job because his boss had already hired two young guys for "next to nothing" to replace him.

Jackie and Laura were a lesbian couple from northeast Indiana who planned to drive as a team. Jackie had been employed as a temp doing office jobs, and Laura had worked in food service at diners. They had a truck driver friend who let them ride along a couple of times, and they decided trucking would be a great way to make more money and see the country together.

Brian and Beth were newlywed evangelical Christians who had just completed four-year degrees in psychology. They wanted to drive as a team, live frugally, and save up enough money to pay for graduate school and put a down payment on a house.

Joe, a young single white male, had served as an army computer specialist in Afghanistan. He had been working as a forklift operator in a Kraft Foods warehouse for eight dollars an hour. And the recruits just kept coming in: Larry was a black man in his fifties from Detroit who had worked a laundry list of bad jobs. Tyler was a white man in his forties who left his job as a plumber because his benefits "went to shit." Bob was non-union factory worker looking for better pay and job security. John and Mike both worked at Home Depot and weren't happy with their annual twenty-five-cent per hour raises. Bill was a white twentysomething who had worked on a highway maintenance crew in rural Indiana. Shane was a black male in his thirties from Chicago who had worked a series of low-end retail jobs.

Alone among the group in having ever been behind the wheel of a tractor-trailer was Tim, a white male in his thirties, who had been driving locally, apparently without a commercial drivers license. Any discussion with Tim quickly turned to how much money he thought he could make as an over-the-road driver and then to the virtues of his lifelong home of Youngstown, Ohio, and the prospects of the Cleveland Browns in the upcoming season.

All the other trainees had similar stories of financial need and nontrucking jobs that were, in one way or another, bad. With the noticeable absence of Latinos, the group was diverse in terms of race and gender and had a very wide range of work and educational experience.[1] All had steady work histories, though a few had been suffering from unemployment recently. They were all there because they believed trucking was the best job opportunity available to them in terms of pay and benefits. And they were hopeful about it, extremely so. But what most of them did not yet understand is that they were not really there for job training. Advanced had not hired them, it had only offered them a spot in truck driving school. And Advanced wouldn't hire many of them—these workers were basically there for an extended job interview that the company was charging them hundreds of dollars per day to attend. This is the way that most workers become truckers today, but it wasn't always that way.

WHERE TRUCKERS USED TO COME FROM

Prior to regulation, many over-the-road drivers were part-time or former farmers looking for a way to get their produce to urban markets cheaply, or to supplement or replace farm income. During the regulatory period, farmers and rural workers continued to supply a significant portion of the industry's workforce. Many nonfarming truckers learned to drive as part of another job, from family members or through military training, but most truckers ultimately entered the industry through on-the-job training programs in union-controlled companies.

Most importantly, trucking was for most a lifetime career. This was especially true for Teamsters members, who enjoyed high wages, good working conditions and job security. There were few, if any, jobs that drew such workers away from the trucking industry, and this resulted in little need for companies to recruit and train new labor. When such labor was needed, hiring was heavily influenced by the Teamsters, and workers were likely to be trained by union members on the job. For nonunion operators, experience with heavy equipment and trucks on farms or through a family member remained a primary means for learning to drive a truck.

Deregulation completely disrupted these traditional sources of labor and the ways labor was trained. In the decade or so after deregulation, the rapidly growing TL segment employed the multitude of drivers displaced by bankruptcies and firm restructuring. But as competition forced firms to continually lower wages and degrade working conditions, this more experienced labor left for better jobs with less-than-truckload, private, or niche firms, or exited the industry altogether.

As this preexisting highly trained labor force dried up, companies were forced to develop a number of strategies to recruit and retain drivers. These strategies have all depended upon bringing new people into the industry who increasingly have no experience at all driving a truck.

Though truck drivers are not considered skilled labor by government record keepers, being a safe and efficient driver requires numerous skills. Achieving basic competence in these skills takes several months, mastering them takes years. As TL companies began to suck huge numbers of inexperienced drivers into the industry, safety became an increasing concern. Within a few years of deregulation, the federal government began reregulating the trucking industry to ensure safety under the auspices of the Federal Motor Carrier Safety Administration (FMCSA). This agency is tasked with setting the key work rules for truckers, as will be discussed in the next chapter, but the first major change instituted was to require all tractor-trailer drivers to have a CDL. The need to license new drivers and provide initial training rapidly spurred the development of truck driving schools.

By the mid-1980s, many carriers were increasingly dependent upon truck driving schools to recruit and train labor. Schools, even those not run by carriers themselves, quickly began tailoring training to carriers' interests. In 1986, the Professional Truck Driver Institute was formed by carriers to set standards and began certifying schools shortly thereafter. By the late 1990s, one of the founders of this organization estimated there were around fifteen hundred CDL schools in the US.[2] By this time many large firms were running their own training schools as well.

Thus, by the beginning of the 1990s there were plenty of opportunities for potential drivers to learn the "rules of the road." But before truck driving schools or carriers can train workers, the industry needs to convince them that trucking is a good job.

GETTING WORKERS TO TRUCKLOAD'S REVOLVING DOOR

Recruiting new workers is a massive undertaking that can cost large firms tens of millions of dollars annually. For instance, companies like Schneider National, a leading TL firm similar to Leviathan with about fourteen thousand trucks, decline many applicants based on motor vehicle records, criminal history, or spotty work histories. In 2004, Schneider reported fielding 320,000 inquiries about jobs and sending out 112,000 applications. It got about two-thirds (74,200) of these applications back, and interviewed about half (37,700) of those workers. Just twenty-seven thousand passed Schneider's interviews. Only 9,959, less than three percent, of those who inquired that year were ultimately hired.[3]

In other words, for each one of the almost ten thousand drivers it hired in 2004, Schneider needed to generate initial interest in the job from thirty-two workers and get eleven of those to actually apply. That's hard to do when you're offering a job that most of these workers wouldn't want if they actually knew what it was like.

The False Promise of Big Money

Most workers who try their hand at a career in truck driving are actually taking a pretty big gamble. Trucking's not a job you apply for one day and start earning money the next. It costs thousands of dollars to earn a CDL and takes several months before you can actually start driving on your own. So new truckers generally consider the pros and cons of truck driving as a career seriously for at least several months before they enter the industry. But many of these workers have little sense of what trucking will really mean for themselves and their families. Partly this is simply because it is difficult for workers to know what truck driving is actually like. But the industry's success at recruiting large numbers of people despite the risks for workers is also the result of would-be truckers' misconceptions about the job. These misconceptions are directly promoted by carriers, for-profit CDL schools, and recruiting firms and, in some instances, indirectly endorsed by publicly supported CDL schools and government agencies, such as state unemployment offices.

While some of the truckers and trucking recruits that I spoke with over the course of my research told me that they went into trucking because they believed they would have greater autonomy at work, or job security as truckers, virtually all new truckers share one belief about the job that ultimately drew them to the industry: that they will earn more money trucking than in any other available job. Some companies, including Leviathan and Schneider, provide a relatively realistic portrait of what kind of pay they offer, but many companies mislead workers about the income they can expect starting out, and what they can expect once they have some experience. And virtually no one tells would-be truckers what the job requires in terms of hours worked and time away from home.

To get a sense of how trucking was portrayed by carriers, I looked at recruitment magazines distributed at truck driving schools, highway rest areas, truck stops and other locations (e.g. major retailer stores such as Wal-Mart). These publications are gazette size and may be a hundred or more pages long. Most feature short articles on trucking, but the bulk of the content is job ads. These ads frame trucking jobs in diverse ways and typically make a range of claims about everything from income to the quality of carriers' trucks. Most ads use a variety of rhetorical approaches to focus on "values" and portray carriers as everything from a family to a travel agent.

To get a sense of how accurately companies represented the key thing that draws workers to the job—income—I coded income claims in jobs ads geared toward the recruitment of new or inexperienced drivers from twenty issues of four common publications published from the fall of 2004 through the fall of 2008. Most of these ads suggested that truck driving provides high incomes, but did not provide specific numbers beyond pay rates per mile. Every couple of pages, however, I found ads with claims about annual income.

Ads for a dozen different TL companies presented "average" or possible incomes specifically for drivers in their first or second years. These ranged from a low of $36,000–39,000 for a "student driver" to $60,000 for a "first year driver." The average of the figures advertised for inexperienced drivers was almost $48,500. These same companies claimed that their "average" driver earned even more, with an average advertised salary of about $57,000. Suggested salaries of "top" drivers averaged roughly $71,500.

Given that the median wage-earner in the US earned around $26,500 in 2006,[4] it is easy to understand why workers in service and blue collar jobs would find such salaries attractive. Unfortunately, these numbers are gross misrepresentations of what truckers actually earn. I recorded annual incomes for thirty-one of the company drivers (out of thirty-nine) that I interviewed who had worked the full previous year and did not report unemployment. Those with less than two years experience earned an average of $30,200. That is 38 percent less than the pay advertised for such drivers. Drivers with two to nine years experience reported an average income of $43,300, about 25 percent less than advertised for "average drivers." Drivers with ten or more years of experience reported an average income of $51,200, almost 30 percent less than what was advertised for "top" drivers.

The incomes my drivers reported are consistent with other sources, but this doesn't prevent the industry from advertising wildly inflated salaries. It is not just a handful of unscrupulous firms that mislead would-be truckers. Trucking schools,[5] and even the industry's leading trade association, the American Trucking Associations (ATA), make claims such as the following: "Long-haul truck drivers with two or more years of experience usually earn at least $50-$60,000/year." The ATA also claims, "For more specialized driving, such as being part of a sleeper team, a driver can make $100,000 per year."[6]

Nearly all the workers ATA's recruitment website actually attracts to the industry will work for at least a couple of years for a truckload dry van carrier, like Leviathan. The ATA's own benchmarking survey in 2011 found an average pay per mile at such companies of thirty-six cents.[7] The National Transportation Institute (NTI), an industry benchmarking firm that conducts a quarterly survey of 350 major carriers, reported the same average pay per mile for that year.[8] The number of miles the average over-the-road driver in this segment drives per year can vary depending on freight volumes, but at a typical large firm a driver who has enough experience to reach full productivity will get paid for somewhere in the neighborhood of 2,200 miles per week on average, or 110,000 miles annually, if they work fifty weeks. That works out to $39,600 in annual earnings. The average starting pay rate at TL dry van firms was thirty-one cents per mile. Typically drivers are initially given the lowest rate for six months to a year. These drivers will be lucky to drive 100,000 miles in their first year, giving them a first-year income of around $31,000 (this does not take into account the months they spend training at little or no pay). At many companies drivers will earn several percent of this base mileage pay for non-driving work and possibly bonuses for fuel efficiency or safety. These additional payments can raise total earnings by several thousands dollars for many drivers.

Would-be truckers might get better information about trucking jobs from a state unemployment office, as several of my interviewees did. Many of these provide US Bureau of Labor Statistics (BLS) data on trucking wages. BLS reports that general freight truckers earned an average of around $41,000 in 2008. However, the agency also reports such drivers earn about $19.72 per hour, based on forty hours of work per week. Unfortunately this dramatically underestimates the hours truckers work, as I will explain in the next chapter.

Who Gets Recruited

The truckers I interviewed came from extremely diverse working- and lower-middle-class backgrounds. They had job experience ranging from computer programming to migrant farm labor, and educations from eight years of total schooling to four-year college degrees. Their experiences cut across broad occupational categories. One way to explain how workers with such diverse backgrounds ended up in the same occupation is to understand the reasons these workers gave for becoming truckers.

Approximately one-third of my interviewees I would describe as "falling" into trucking, one-third were "pushed" into trucking, and the final third were "pulled" into trucking. Those who fell into trucking did so as a result of farming, family members in trucking, or military service, or were already involved in the freight transportation industry. These workers had job experience that made trucking seem like a natural choice. This group includes one former farmer and several former farmworkers, who had operated heavy equipment or driven trucks in the course of their work. Others were servicemen who had learned to drive trucks in the military. Still others went into trucking right out of high school with the help of a family member who was a trucker. The remainder of this group had worked in trucking or warehousing as dispatchers, mechanics, or freight handlers. Drivers who fell into the industry tended to be older, more experienced, and better paid than my other interviewees. With the exception of one white woman, these were all native-born white or black men.

Another third of my interviewees were pushed into trucking because of the loss of another job they preferred. Most of these had been blue-collar workers in construction or manufacturing. They often reported having been laid off or unable to continue at their previous job because of physical injury—like one former carpenter who was "getting too old to carry materials and kneel for long stretches." The rest had been low-level managers, small-business people, or educated white-collar workers. In some cases these individuals had college degrees and had been working as skilled laborers, for example, as a chemistry lab assistant at a university. Several of the most educated of this group were male immigrants unable to find work in the US in their previous line of employment. For former white-collar workers, trucking was often a desperate last resort for a paycheck that they hoped would allow them to maintain previous levels of income from better jobs.

The final third of my drivers were pulled into trucking in search of higher pay. Like those pushed into the industry, they had diverse work histories. They had been, among other things, store clerks, day laborers, and service workers. They often struggled with the long hours of trucking, but were the happiest with the income it provided. This group was the least educated and the most racially and ethnically diverse.

For those workers who were pushed or pulled into trucking, income was universally *the* attraction. They came into the industry expecting to make significantly more from trucking than they could in other jobs. Although there is little publicly available data about workers attracted to trucking, information about the 895 workers trained by Federal in 2005–2006 that Hoffman and Burks studied suggests that my less experienced interviewees were similar to other trainees. The trainees at Federal were slightly younger and more educated than other blue-collar workers in the US. About 96 percent had a high school degree, about a third had some college experience, 14 percent had a junior or technical college degree, and 8 percent had a bachelors' degree or more. The average age of the trainees was thirty-seven. Ninety percent of the trainees were men. Importantly, the trainees at Federal had poor credit scores, and more than 70 percent reported household incomes of $30,000 or less.[9]

TRAINING NEW TRUCKERS

Virtually all of the inexperienced drivers who enter the TL segment will get their initial training at a CDL school run by a for-profit company, a public vocational school, or a major carrier. Noncarrier schools typically have an ongoing relationship with carriers who hire their students. Eighty-six percent of the TL carriers in a recent ATA survey had a formal relationship with at least one noncarrier CDL school. Seventy-two percent of those with such a relationship had one with a publicly funded school, and 88 percent had a relationship with a private for-profit school.[10] Publicly funded schools are typically associated with community colleges. The National Association of Publicly Funded Truck Driver Training Schools, a nonprofit organization that represents some of these schools and the employers who hire their graduates, estimated that its 110 members graduated about eighteen thousand students in 2005.[11] An organization called the Commercial Vehicle Training Association (CVTA) represents for-profit truck driver schools. CVTA claims that its fifty-plus members, which include at least fifteen carrier schools, operate more than two hundred training locations nationwide. These locations have the capacity to train more than fifty thousand new drivers per year.[12] Carriers use their own CDL schools and recommendations from private schools as a way to weed out workers before they hire them. They then use the financial obligations incurred by workers during their training to coerce workers into staying in their jobs longer than they want to. Carrier-run schools tend to be very large and can train thousands of workers per year. Leviathan's schools, for instance, can easily train ten thousand new truckers per year.

Large carriers have developed a way to turn the debt incurred by workers into a hedge against turnover. In the 2011 ATA benchmarking survey, 91 percent of carriers that hired inexperienced drivers offered reimbursement for training tuition, and 95 percent of those required the driver to stay with the company for a specified period (on average more than a year) to get the full reimbursement.[13]

The recent research on Federal has revealed how much firms can benefit by tying length of employment to reimbursement for training, or charging workers for training and offering to forgive the debt if the worker stays with the company. This research found that 73 percent of the drivers hired by Federal were trained directly by the company. Half of these drivers left within eight months of being hired, despite the fact that they spent on average six weeks or more in training and had agreed to pay thousands of dollars back to the company for the cost if they quit in less than a year. In fact, the likelihood that a Federal driver will exit the company spikes dramatically six to eight weeks after they are hired, right around the time when a typical new driver finishes Federal's on-the-road training and begins actually doing the job on their own. The next most likely time for a driver to exit the company is just after one year, when many of these workers are no longer required to pay back the cost of training.[14] Hoffman and Burks (2013) analyzed the quit rates of 895 newly hired drivers trained by Federal. These drivers were trained at five different company facilities under different contract conditions, which varied because the company was exploring the optimal contract requirements (length and fee structure), and because of different dates of requirement implementation due to state approval processes. This variation allowed Hoffman and Burks to compare the quit-rates of drivers who were under no contract with drivers under a twelve-month contract to pay training costs of $3,500–4,000 and drivers under an eighteen-month contract to pay training costs of around $5,000. Hoffman and Burks concluded that training contracts reduced quitting by 10–20 percent and were critical to ensure the profitability of training for Federal. Based on Federal's estimated cost of $2,500 per worker, they calculated that the firm would lose about $200 per truck annually without a contract. But when workers were required to sign either a twelve- or eighteen-month contract, training workers produced more than $4,000 in estimated profit per truck per year.[15] In other words, training contracts designed to keep workers from quitting because of the debt taken on may be necessary for companies using almost entirely inexperienced labor, like Federal, Advanced, or Leviathan, to be profitable. Thus, many of the workers who try out trucking every year do so under a modern form of debt peonage.

The need to train new workers has segmented truckload employers into those firms that recruit and hire inexperienced drivers and those that do not. Large firms have a strong incentive to recruit and at least partially train new truckers, because this allows them to have wages and working conditions that don't attract enough experienced drivers. While small- and medium-sized firms are unlikely to hire drivers with less than one or two years of experience, due to the cost of training and insuring them, the largest firms are self-insured and have established training programs that allow them to hire drivers with no experience at all.

Operating a training program and possibly a CDL school is a major undertaking and key part of the business model of many of the largest

TL companies. These programs are one of the major components of the billions of dollars that turnover costs the industry in a typical year. Firms with their own schools spend thousands of dollars per new driver to maintain the equipment, staff, and facilities for training, which involves classrooms, trucks, and, in some cases, multimillion dollar driving simulators.

To rely primarily on inexperienced drivers also requires carriers to provide additional resources to shepherd these drivers through their first few months on the road. In addition to money, as an academic article looking at the costs of turnover put it, this means that "companies must spend a great deal of their management capacity replacing, training, and indoctrinating new drivers."[16]

The Cost to Taxpayers

The cost of training new drivers presents significant risk to firms if they cannot ensure that these drivers will remain with the company long enough to make the firm's investment worthwhile. In 2007 Ray Kuntz, then president of the ATA, said that the "biggest problem our industry has always faced is training new drivers. We spend millions of dollars trying to steal each other's drivers, but few spend that kind of money on driver training." Kuntz's firm was still training new drivers as the Great Recession took hold, while his competitors had stopped. He wryly noted the consequences: "I train them, they hire them. It makes us a real popular neighbor."[17]

As ATA president, Kuntz sought to defray the cost to carriers of training drivers by seeking more state and federal funding, such as the $315,000 grant his own firm received in 2007 from the Montana Department of Commerce to train sixty-three new drivers. In addition to such programs, workers interested in training to become truck drivers can draw on a wide range of state and federal funds that range from Pell grants to the GI Bill to Workforce Investment Act (WIA) funds, which is federal money intended to support state-run training programs for displaced or underskilled workers. According to CVTA, up to 60 percent of the fifty thousand students its members' schools train are funded by WIA funds.[18]

In other words, taxpayers are subsidizing a significant share of the cost of the industry's high turnover.

LEARNING TO TRUCK

CDL school is just the beginning of the training workers need before they can really drive a truck on own truck. After CDL school inexperienced drivers need to complete additional training in "finishing" programs that only the largest carriers operate. As a result, whether or not they operate a CDL school, a few dozen large companies serve as gatekeepers for the industry's labor force, because they are the only place new drivers can complete the last stages of training and gain initial employment.

In order to explain how this works and the consequences of the process for the way workers understand the industry and behave as drivers, I will explain my own experience, which was typical for a new driver trained entirely by a carrier. Like all workers new to truck driving, my training was a multistage process. Before beginning training, I had to obtain a learner's permit and pass physical and drug exams. In the first formal stage, at a school a day's drive from home, I learned basic operation and inspection of the rig, recording of work hours in a federally mandated logbook, how to plan trips, and various aspects of the law and driving routines. At the end of the first stage, which took about two weeks, I was hired by Leviathan. In the second stage, I learned to drive in heavier traffic, slow maneuvering, and how to use the company's communications equipment. In the third stage, I hauled actual loads across the eastern half of the US while constantly supervised by a trainer. The fourth and final stage involved preparing for and taking the state CDL driving exam.

I moved through the training and licensing process about as quickly as it can be done. From my first contact with the company, it was about ten weeks before I hauled my first load unsupervised. Of this, four weeks were spent studying for and taking DMV exams, completing drug tests and physicals, filling out paperwork, and waiting for company responses and a space in the initial phase of training. The other six weeks were intensive full-time training at company facilities or on the job training that precluded other kinds of paid work—a typical worker will spend somewhere between eight and ten weeks to complete this training.

Pretraining

In early February 2005 I called Leviathan to apply for a job after seeing an ad in a local newspaper. I was immediately routed to a phone tree of automated questions about my age, criminal record, and driving record. Since I was over twenty-one with clean records, at the end of the questions a recorded message announced: "Congratulations, you meet our minimum requirements!" I was then connected with a recruiter, who gave me a basic description of the job. I would be on the road for about two weeks at a time and paid twenty-five cents per mile. We also discussed where my home operating location would be and where I would be able to park the truck while I was at home.

The recruiter then explained the tasks I would need to complete before the company would schedule my formal training. I would have to pass the written portion of the CDL exam and the physical examination required by my state. I also needed to pass a company required drug test and submit a paper application. The recruiter then assigned me to a second recruiter, who would track me through the application process over the next month or so. I was told that if I completed all of the tasks assigned to me within twenty-five days, I would receive a $250 bonus.

I studied for the CDL exam using a study guide provided by my local Bureau of Motor Vehicles (BMV) office, an online study guide, and a printed guide I bought on the internet. From these sources I learned basic information about the operation of the truck and the laws governing commercial vehicles. The CDL exam tests different sets of information for each class of license. There are Class A, B, and C licenses depending on the size of vehicle and whether or not it carries passengers.

I was required to have a Class A license, which allowed me to drive an articulated vehicle (tractor and trailer rather than a "straight" truck) with a gross vehicle weight rating of twenty-six thousand pounds or more. Leviathan also required me to have an endorsement on my license to haul hazardous materials. For this, I had to pass a test on how to label hazardous loads, specific requirements and precautions for these loads, and basic information on what to do in case of an accident or spill. To get this endorsement, I also needed to submit fingerprints and $125 for a Department of Homeland Security screening.

After a week of study, I paid sixty dollars and took the written test at a local BMV office. I had to pass several different sections individually, one on general knowledge of driving a commercial vehicle, one on air brakes, one on driving an articulated vehicle, and one on hauling hazardous materials. Most of the drivers I interviewed did not report much difficulty passing the exam, although it was not uncommon to hear of someone who failed it on their first try. I missed several questions, but still passed easily. I was immediately presented with a learner's permit that allowed me to drive under the supervision of a Class A license holder.

I then took the physical exam required by the state. Doctors must be certified by a state Department of Transportation to administer a physical examination for CDL license holders, and by coincidence my doctor at the University Health Center was certified because he handles occupational health and injuries for the university's maintenance staff, some of whom hold CDLs. I passed this examination without a problem. I took the opportunity to interview my doctor during the exam and was told that the physical represents a very real obstacle for some drivers. He told me that diabetes and high blood pressure were the primary reasons workers failed the exam. Vision and hearing were also rigorously tested. Occasionally, limits on physical mobility would disqualify someone. The more common ailments his patients suffered from, such as joint problems, back injuries, and carpal tunnel syndrome, were typically not severe enough to disqualify workers.

Once the company received a copy of my learner's permit, along with results from my physical and a separate company drug test, my recruiter called to schedule my training, which started in a couple of days. In fact, I barely had time to get my personal affairs in order and buy the clothes and equipment required for the thirteen days, including travel. The students I trained with came from all over the region, at least ten states, to a Leviathan CDL school in the Midwest, one of a number that it operated around the US at that time. The company provided transportation by shuttle from the nearest company facility or by bus.

CDL School: Learning to Drive the Truck

Like that of Advanced, Federal and other large companies, the initial training provided by Leviathan wasn't job training, it was a CDL school run by a trucking company. Despite the fact that the students were all there because they were recruited for the job and the training was required, it would become apparent within a couple hours, when school staff explained the terms of the training contract, that the company had no intention of hiring all or even most of us. Despite this and the fact that, with interest, we could owe the company more than $4,000 if we didn't work for them for a year—if we were in fact hired—everyone signed the contract.

We would wake early, usually around 5:30 a.m., and wrap up the day at the terminal by around 5:00 p.m. After that we would return to the hotel, have dinner at one of the many fast food restaurants within walking distance (paid out of pocket), spend an hour or two completing homework assigned by the classroom instructors, and then pass out.

Our trainers lived within commuting distance of the facility and had at least a couple of years of long-haul driving experience, though most had much more than that. Each trainer was individually responsible for training four students to actually operate the truck. These four students were split into pairs that spent either the morning or the afternoon in the truck.

Each day in CDL school was equally divided between classroom and driving exercises. While half of the class trained in the trucks, the other half was split between two adjoining classrooms. The classrooms were set up with tables in rows. It was obvious from the comments of many students that the classroom environment made some uncomfortable and that many trainees considered themselves to be generally poor or out-of-practice students. The classroom work covered topics ranging from equipment maintenance to laws of the road. The three most extensively covered skills were trip planning, map reading, and recording work history in logbooks, as required by law. The classroom time was quite boring for students who picked up these skills quickly. Fortunately, the classroom instructors labored diligently to keep our attention with jokes and antics that we eventually realized they repeated week after week (leading to a fairly tight performance). Only a few students seemed to struggle to learn the classroom material; driving, however, was another matter entirely.

The first day of driving consisted simply of trying to learn to move the truck forward. The immediate challenge was learning to shift using a "double-clutch" method. In order to double-clutch, you push in the clutch to get the transmission out of a gear, release the clutch, then depress the clutch a second time and shift simultaneously into the new gear, then release the clutch. This process may sound like shifting a car with a manual transmission, but tractor transmissions are not like car and light truck transmissions. A tractor's gears and engine speed must be manually synchronized, so you must slow down or speed up the engine an exact amount, or you simply cannot get the truck into gear—a critical problem, particularly at busy intersections and on hills. The matter is not helped by the fact that each failed attempt to get the truck into gear is accompanied by a horrible noise, as the temporarily incompatible gears are ground into each other. If you are successful in getting the truck into gear, but the engine speed is lower than optimal, the motor will "lug," and the engine's high torque will cause the tractor to rock violently side to side as the tractor hops forward. While a circle of two dozen or so tractors coasting to unintended stops and violently lurching forward intermittently around a parking lot filled with the constant din of grinding gears appeared comical to trainers, the situation was desperately serious for trainees.

We drove without a trailer in circles around a large paved training yard, until our instructors decided we were ready to menace the industrial park that surrounded the facility. In most cases we could do this after an hour or two behind the wheel, but most students wouldn't get that much time in the driver's seat until the second day. By the end of the second day, some students were ready to couple to a forty-eight-foot-long trailer (which is shorter and much easier to make turns with than Leviathan's more common fifty-three-foot trailer) and pull that around the yard and industrial park, while others were still working on basic shifting. In the end, it would be two months before the average student would be ready to haul freight unsupervised, and we would still be just rookies with plenty to learn about how to operate a truck efficiently.

It is difficult to describe how challenging and intimidating learning to drive a tractor-trailer is. Since I was a boy, I have been a quick study with everything from basic power tools to heavy equipment, and confident I could operate any machine at least competently with the right instruction.

That is, until I got behind the wheel of a tractor-trailer. Even with my wide range of experience operating tools and equipment, the truck intimidated me. But even more than intimidate, the truck frustrated me. Despite my best efforts for days, even basic competence seemed to elude me. From the classroom instruction I knew *what* I needed to do to, but that didn't mean I knew *how* to do it. There were general guidelines to follow—allow rpms to drop four hundred to shift from third to second gear—but to actually do it you needed to physically embody that knowledge. You had to develop a feel for the changes in the machine, hear them, figure out what the truck wanted to do. If the blue-collar manual workers I trained with were intimidated by the equipment, as I was, none of them admitted it. But they seemed equally frustrated by it. Those without such work experience struggled even more, and few of them seemed to have reservations about expressing actual fear.

Adding to the frustration and fear was the constant surveillance and evaluation by trainers. Our trainers evaluated us daily and informed us of our progress. Occasionally in this stage and in later stages, we were evaluated by other trainers, to ensure that our assigned trainers were properly instructing us. Over the course of my six weeks of CDL and company-specific training, dozens of written evaluations of my performance (that I was aware of) were performed by six different trainers and two training supervisors before I took the CDL road test. Though a summary of our evaluation was typically given to us verbally by trainers, I was never shown the actual evaluations and did not know the range of information they contained.

Within a few days, the sense of insecurity among the students was palpable whenever we gathered as a group. Underlying it was the threat of failure combined with the steep price of the training. Students would often be visibly shaken, frustrated, or saddened by their last stint behind the wheel. The frustration of learning the new skills we would need was heightened by the constant evaluation of trainers who were documenting our progress after each session. Despite a strong sense of camaraderie, we constantly compared ourselves to one another and discussed our latest evaluations in an attempt to assess if we were ahead of or behind our peers—and, of course, what the evaluations might mean for our chances to be hired by Leviathan. We were given new goals to reach every day, and

Leviathan!

rarely if ever did we achieve them on the day we were supposed to. The scheduling of the goals seemed deliberately set to make them impossible to meet. This provoked great insecurity in trainees, but little sympathy from trainers.

Soon it became obvious that having to pay back the training was the only thing keeping some of the students there. Only about half of the workers I trained with would complete the initial portion of the training and be hired by the company. Several were given the option of staying on with the next week's class to work on the skills required to graduate—though it was never clear that graduating would automatically lead to being hired. A few were forced to leave because of drug or criminal histories not previously disclosed to the company. A few others were advised to leave because of poor performance in operating the truck. The atmosphere was so intimidating and coercive that several students snuck away in the middle of the night, as if escaping some kind of forced labor camp. Their roommates would dutifully detail the escapee's grievances over meals the next day. If adequate details were not available, the remaining trainees would speculate based on previous conversations. Each day was filled with at least one or two stories of trainees who were either forced to leave, stole away in the night, or negotiated a release—perhaps, it was speculated, at a discounted rate.

On graduation day Leviathan hired about half of the original fifty-eight trainees. We had a short graduation ceremony, during which our names were announced and we received a certificate. I received a pair of steel-toed boots and was officially hired by Leviathan. I was then bused home for the next phase of training at the company facility closest to my residence.

AN "ELEVEN-DAY JOB INTERVIEW"

The fact that we were not employees during CDL school was evident in the way the program was structured. It felt more like boot camp than job training. More than being trained, we were being tested. While the CDL school was a necessary step for the carrier to prepare workers for the job, the company got far more out of it than simply teaching workers how to operate a truck. It allowed the company to assess workers' attitudes, potential, and commitment as they negotiated an exhausting and intimidating training regime over eleven days under near-constant supervision. The company wasn't just testing students' ability to learn the self-discipline and self-direction required to safely and efficiently drive a truck in unfamiliar environments, they were testing that ability as the trainees grew increasingly fatigued.

Trainers understand this well. As one experienced trainer explained it to me, his job was not to train people to be truck drivers, but to figure out who should and who shouldn't be behind the wheel of a truck, who the company should invest in putting on the road. Sure, he admitted, with enough time, you could probably train lots of people to be good drivers. But this program wasn't designed for that. That could take months and months, and chances are a driver like that isn't going to stick around long enough to make the investment worthwhile. Of course, he wanted to teach as much material as possible about how to be a truck driver during CDL school. But CDL school is less than two weeks long. It would take most students at least a month, probably two months, of additional training before they could go out solo. This training wasn't intended to give people the skills they would need to be truckers. Instead, he said, "it's an eleven-day job interview."

The trainees who did not complete the initial training had wasted their time and gone into debt to *apply for a job*. The firm had weeded out undesirable workers and foisted much of the cost onto them or the government programs paying for their training. It had also indebted the workers it hired with a high-interest loan for a year, which would deter them from quitting. This is how most new long-haul truckers are introduced to the truckload industry.

Finishing Training

After CDL school I completed three more training phases. I did phase two at what would be my "home" terminal (about forty miles from my house). This phase covered company procedures and driving skills. It was organized much like the first in terms of the split between classroom and driving, but we were not assigned to specific trainers. We were again put up in a motel near the company facility. Over the course of a week we learned about communicating with our supervisor through the satellite-linked computer, how to fill out reimbursements and other company paperwork, etc. And we spent lots more time in the truck honing our skills in basic operation and backing.

The biggest difference now was that we were company employees, and the stress of worrying about whether we would "make it" was gone. It was clear that the company was now committed to training us until we were ready to go out on our own. Most of the trainers were now supportive and treated us like fellow employees, which was a welcome relief after frequent feelings of indifference and even antagonism from trainers during CDL school.

For phase three, I was assigned a road trainer, who supervised me constantly as I delivered real loads. This training is what companies refer to as "finishing." My trainer was paid a bonus per student trained in addition to his normal mileage pay for the loads we delivered. I spent ten days with this trainer. Normally this part of the training lasts twelve to twenty-four days, though some drivers take up to three months. Leviathan, like other companies, pays trainees a set amount of money during this time, typically between $250 and $350 per week in 2005.

Drivers really learn how to do the job by working alongside an experienced driver. I learned how to handle the day-to-day challenges of scheduling up to fourteen hours of work per day to maximize my pay, deal with shippers and receivers, and efficiently manage truck maintenance and paperwork. This portion of the training ended when my trainer decided I was ready to start final preparation for the CDL driving exam and then drive on my own.

After completing road training I returned to my home facility, where I spent four days training to pass the CDL driving tests. One of these tests involved a series of tasks including, among other things, backing the truck at various angles, parallel parking the truck, and driving in reverse through an obstacle course. Another required that I list about a hundred parts of the truck, show how to inspect them, and describe what might go wrong with each. The final test required properly driving a preset route around the city. My trainers also acted as the state examiners for most of the CDL tests in the area. In other words, it was a Leviathan employee who decided whether or not I passed the state license exam.

Unfortunately, despite the tailored preparation and evaluation by a Leviathan trainer, I failed my first attempt at the road test. I was paying so much attention to the requirements of a turn in heavy traffic conditions that I missed a sign and sped through a school zone. That was enough to fail me. After failing the test, I spent another day training. On my second attempt I passed all portions of the exam easily and was assigned my own truck that day. After a brief test drive, I headed home to pack up the truck and get on with the work of hauling freight. All told, I had spent several months applying and training for my new job as a trucker. I felt proud that I'd successfully completed what was by all accounts a grueling weed-out process and happy that I was about to get on with the "real work" of driving a truck myself. For all of this, I'd earned less than $1,000, and indentured myself to Leviathan to the tune of more than $4,000, with interest.

WHAT DRIVERS LEARN FROM TRAINING

A whole set of themes, both explicit and implicit, runs throughout training. They range from the ergonomics of sitting for long periods to the undesirability of unions. These themes are repeated by trainers and management at all levels, in both the classroom and the truck. But by far the most consistent and prominent theme is safety. New truckers are taught that, as professionals, they are responsible for the safety of the motoring public, who are largely unaware of the dangers inherent in truckers' work. This responsibility is enormous. A wrong move at any time of the day, too careless a check of your mirrors, losing track of a vehicle in one of the truck's several enormous blind spots, taking a ramp too fast, driving tired—are all potentially life-threatening mistakes against which drivers must constantly guard.

According to the Bureau of Labor Statistics being a trucker is the fourth most dangerous occupation in the United States, behind timber cutters, airplane pilots, and construction laborers. But in absolute numbers far more truckers die on the job in any given year than any other kind of worker. In 2012 there were 104,000 injuries and 3,921 fatalities in crashes involving a large truck.[19] What makes the danger of trucking so stressful compared with most other jobs is that a serious accident can come at any time, and as a result of the actions of people who may have no idea how they are endangering you or themselves.

Understandably one of the primary requirements of training a potential trucker is to instill a healthy respect for the dangers inherent in the job. The primary means of accomplishing this is fear. You are told that honing your skills, planning, and conscientious, defensive driving habits can keep you alive and prevent you from killing others. Instilling fear is both a conscious strategy, carefully planned by the company, and an informal teaching technique of trainers. It is also an increasingly important task for the industry, as inexperienced drivers are less safe than more experienced ones.

The potential for disastrous accidents was conveyed with considerable skill by trainers as a means to draw attention to important lessons. Trainers hammered home safety aspects of the job, often vividly relating personal stories of accidents and tragedies that they had experienced or witnessed.

Beyond driving safely, there are a number of other things workers learn as trainees. Training is an opportunity for the company to introduce workers to the job as they prefer it to be done. Workers trained by companies like Leviathan take for granted many of the features of the job that are only found at particular companies or in certain industry segments, such as GPS tracking and pay by mile. In addition to these, new drivers are trained to accept the large corporate structure that depersonalizes the process of determining load assignments and monitoring driver behavior. These issues are particularly salient for experienced drivers, but inexperienced drivers are unaware of any alternative.

In general, training is designed to maximize the productivity of workers while reducing the costs of managing them. Achieving this goal required a classroom focus on developing planning skills that would allow drivers to independently maintain a consistently productive schedule. Employees were also encouraged to allow the requirements of the job to encroach on their (extremely limited) home life. For instance, drivers were taught to manage their body both on and off the job. We watched videos on sleep, diet, and exercise. We watched one entire video on how to manage sleep at home so that we would be prepared to work our next shift. We were encouraged to tell our families to cooperate by respecting a sleep schedule that would allow us to catch up on sleep missed on the road. We were also encouraged to do things like cut out daily caffeine, so that it would be more effective when we needed it to maintain alertness at the end of a work rotation.

The training also explicitly dealt with issues beyond job performance. The company repeatedly introduced us to various aspects of the industry in formal ways. This education included very specific ideas about how we should understand our company relative to state and federal governments, customers, competitors, and unions.

The two primary outside actors most often discussed in training were the government and customers. The government was presented as the ultimate creator and enforcer of most workplace rules. In fact, it was often unclear as to whether something was company policy or state or federal law. Aside from the government there was one other reason given for rules: customers. The competition for customers and the need to keep costs low—and thus Leviathan's prices competitive—was used to justify some of the worst abuses we would face as drivers, such as sitting unpaid at docks. While Leviathan claims to be a "top trucking company," "the best," and "an industry leader," when it comes to customers and the law, it portrays itself as a servant and obedient subject.

Leviathan explained the specific organization of the work of trucking through a historical account of the industry. This history began with the deregulation of trucking, which was explicitly explained to us as an effort to increase competition and to remove the negative influence of unions, which prevented companies from operating efficiently. We were told that monopolistic companies and unions could not survive after deregulation, because they did not appeal successfully to customers or drivers. This theme was addressed repeatedly in Leviathan's training. Trainers played a video in CDL school arguing that the only reason unions would want Leviathan drivers is because they are "a business," and their business is recruiting members who pay dues. And when unions need revenue, they try to organize at new companies. We were instructed, "Before you sign anything, understand what it is."

Unions were formally addressed again in the second stage of training by a terminal manager, the highest-ranking employee to be formally involved in this phase of the training. He gave a thirty-minute presentation in which he welcomed us to the company and discussed the conflict resolution procedures available to us. He explicitly drew contrasts between these procedures and the way that unions functioned, arguing that unions would take away our ability to be treated as individuals, and that we would be subjected to bureaucratic rules instead. He argued that unions were driven out of the TL segment of the industry after deregulation because they were no longer effective organizations, and that they were antithetical to the ability of companies to survive in the current competitive environment. He said that if Leviathan drivers were to unionize, the company would not survive, and we would lose our jobs.

While the company certainly succeeds in shaping the views of workers regarding their company and the job, it is not universally successful in convincing all drivers to follow its rules completely or to blindly accept its reasoning. Even before the end of the training, it is clear the company is far from the collegial atmosphere of cooperation suggested by management and company literature.

We learned during training that the industry has a reporting system that companies use to blackball workers who break company rules. These reports are called DAX reports, after the name of company that sells them, and they are checked by companies before hiring a driver. This report was never formally discussed in the classroom, but it was raised by several of my trainers, who made it clear that quitting the company before I completed a full year would make it difficult, probably impossible, for me to get another trucking job. There was also a company reporting system that allowed drivers to report accidents involving their fellow workers. If the driver involved in the accident did not self-report, the reporting driver would be entitled to a portion of the cost of the damage done to the equipment. There were posters promoting this program, and we were explicitly encouraged by trainers to use the system.

Though we had been told about how happy Leviathan drivers were, the existence of these programs, and other small indications here and there, began to suggest otherwise even during training. Perhaps the biggest problem for the company was that it had to rely on former drivers to train us, and there was obvious discontent among these trainers. I was able to develop some working hypotheses about the company partly because many trainers deliberately tipped the company's hand to us as fellow workers, rather than treating us as trainees. There were a few trainers who were "lifers." They were said to "bleed blue," the company's main color. But most trainers alerted us to the fact that these trainers were a bit too "by the book," by making jokes about how loyal these drivers were to the company. Several of these drivers, recognizing how they were viewed by their fellow trainers, would introduce themselves by explaining how loyal they were and why, as if apologizing ahead of time.

It became obvious fairly quickly that at least some of the trainers wanted to tell trainees what they really thought of the company but could not, because there was always the possibility that a trainee would turn them in for improper behavior. We were given the opportunity to evaluate our trainers several times during the training, and we were explicitly told twice by more-senior trainers that we should report any trainer who broke company rules or suggested it was okay to do so. The trainers themselves are particularly vulnerable, because they do not enjoy the labor market freedom of other truckers. They had chosen to leave long-haul driving for various reasons, and none of them wanted to return to the road full time.

Despite trainers' vulnerability, they taught several important lessons the company probably didn't want its drivers to learn. They taught trainees that the company has all kinds of rules, and it is not in your interest to follow *most* of them. The government will also give you all kinds of rules to follow, they said, and it is not in your interest to follow *any* of those, with two critically important exceptions: 1) don't get caught breaking a rule that the company presents as important or which you will lose your license over; 2) follow the rules important for safety and have a healthy respect for the dangers inherent in the job.

Company and government rules are so routinely violated by drivers that it was difficult for trainers to present them as if drivers actually followed them to the letter. The first time a rule is presented in training, everything about it is portrayed as ironclad. But once trainers had stressed the need to pass the CDL exam, the importance of safety, and the consequences of getting caught breaking significant company rules or the law, they tended to focus on what *they* thought was really important. Occasionally we were told by trainers that we would need to unlearn what we had been taught in previous phases of training. We had learned that stuff to pass tests; now we had to learn how to really do the job.

THE LARGER CONSEQUENCES OF CHURN

Truckers used to enter the industry as the coworkers of those who trained them. And most often those coworkers were Teamsters. Today, many truckers enter the industry as debt peons seeking a better job. To get one, they have to commit to a company before they understand the job and the differences between companies, and before they have any sense whether they are capable of dealing with the tremendous physical and personal tolls of the job. At every stage, the tremendous advantages carriers have over workers is virtually unchecked by any collective efforts of workers. The end result is a continual flood of cheap and inexperienced workers, most of whom will only be in the industry for a matter of months. For the most part, these workers learn the history of the industry and how they should do their job as their employers want them to.

Many experienced drivers I interviewed believed large company control of training and recruitment was the single biggest problem facing truckers and the industry more generally. They believed "CDL mills" produce poorly trained, poorly paid, desperate drivers that allow large firms to drive down the pay rates of better employers and cause constant turnover, which affects safety and the image of more experienced drivers. According to experienced drivers, these companies can and do take in anybody who can "fog a mirror" and turn them into "professional steering-wheel holders." And there is little that experienced drivers believe they can do about it.

For drivers who have been in the industry long enough, CDL mills are tied directly to deregulation, and large companies undercutting rates by exploiting new drivers and transforming labor market institutions, such as training. Here is one driver explaining the changes he has seen over his career.

A lot of those guys are trapped . . . they have to go to school . . . when they put you through school, you sign an agreement that you will work for two or

three years and then they pay you crap, but you are locked in . . . I didn't
have to go to class [I was trained on the job for free] . . . I think [deregula-
tion was] terrible, I think it should be regulated to get rid of some of these
companies that undercut. That is something that the big companies, like the
High Techs and the Big Reds and the Leviathans, they will come in and haul
a load, and lose money on it, just to move their truck. It shouldn't be allowed.
It just undercuts the whole industry and that keeps going down, down,
down, gets cheaper and cheaper . . . one and two truck operations can't
afford to run. The big companies will drive them all out of business, I guess.

Experienced drivers cited high turnover and the constant stream of
new drivers as the biggest obstacle to drivers doing anything about their
problems, such as overcoming employer resistance to unionization.

My training appears to have been typical of nearly all new drivers,
based on my interviews. This training and recruitment provides key
advantages to the firms that can carry it out. These advantages result from
a tremendous asymmetry in class power. A very few carriers, by virtue of
their size, almost completely control worker access to the industry. In
response to labor market conditions after deregulation, carriers have
developed systems to process huge numbers of workers to maintain a
steady supply of labor that cannot be retained for long at the wages and
conditions these companies offer. Unlike the highly unionized LTL segment, carriers can hire who they like and structure training as they please.

The power asymmetry in the economic relations of recruitment and
training is astounding. It is particularly evident in the initial training
period, before you have actually been hired. During this time you never
have a clear decision point to reject or accept the company, while the company is evaluating you as a potential employee for several weeks and
charging you for the opportunity to apply.

Providing training also allows carriers to coerce workers into staying
with them for a year or more—they are essentially in debt peonage once
they begin training with a company. For the workers that I trained with
and those that I interviewed from large TL companies, the cost of training
and the interest that would be charged if they quit were very strong incentives to continue working for the company that trained them. Control
over recruitment and training provides other advantages. Carriers get to
choose workers and shape their initial understandings of the work and the

industry. As I explain in the next chapter, they create a set of expectations and beliefs about the industry that persist and influence the behavior of drivers over the next several years of their career. They also shape the way workers think about and behave in regard to various aspects of the organization of work that are relevant to contracting.

In many ways, workers continue to chase for years the promises made to them in their initial recruitment. Large companies' control of recruitment and training also hampers class action among truckers. Companies are able to write the history of the industry as they see fit, and in training and recruitment they do just that. This discourse about the industry, and behaviors learned in the initial recruitment and training, undermine awareness of and support for alternative ways of organizing the industry and the labor process.

2 Cheap Freight, Cheap Drivers

WORK AS A LONG-HAUL TRUCKER

In order to understand what makes trucking jobs so bad, we have to understand in some detail the work truckers do, the challenges they face in doing it, and the ways they overcome those challenges. First I will explain what drivers experience by describing some of the good and bad days I had while trucking. Truckers' experience of both good loads (i.e., lots of miles with little waiting time) and bad (i.e., few miles and wasted days with little pay far from home) leads them to play a "miles" game, in which every decision they make prioritizes driving paid miles.

Inexperienced drivers are almost always paid by the mile. Like other "pieceworkers," or workers paid based on the units of work they produce, truckers try to find the most efficient ways to organize their tasks in order to increase their pay. Sociologist Michael Burawoy argued that managers purposefully design the labor process to allow pieceworkers autonomy within a narrow range of options that ensure profitability. In response, pieceworkers treat management's demands as rules to a game in which they strategically invest effort where it returns them the greatest compensation. By playing the game, workers consent to management's rules and end up working *harder* (i.e., producing more) than they would under more coercive and costly methods of control, while still experiencing a greater sense of control. The game thus shapes both what workers *do* and *how they understand what they do.* Burawoy's concept of the game perfectly captures the way the pay-per-mile system shapes the experience of truckers.[1] In the long run, the intense self-sweating (i.e. voluntarily working harder despite little economic return and/or in the face of significant personal discomfort or risk) that results from the miles game causes truckers to focus on getting more control over the loads they haul. Thus they consider becoming contractors, because they believe contractors have such control. Truckers draw this conclusion despite the fact that there are other, much better, trucking jobs available—two of which I also worked during my time as a trucker and detail below.

A GOOD DAY OF TRUCKING

It's Tuesday, June 28th, and I have just begun the second day of a twelve-day work rotation. Yesterday, June 27th, I arrived at my truck at 8:00 a.m. and received a series of text messages on my satellite-linked computer. The messages were filled with some of the many abbreviations I've come to know well over the last few months: PU (pick up), MT (empty trailer), MLS (miles) LVLD (live load), LVULD (live unload), APPT (appointment) and DEL (deliver). Here is what the text looked like:

PU MT TRL: W32475	MLS: 12
Wal-Mart DC	Marcy, NY
LVLD: W32475	MLS: 106
Keystone Paper	Natural Dam, NY
APPT: 6/27 12:30	Estimated Load Time: 4 hours
LVULD	MLS: 936
US Paper	Neenah, WI
DEL APPT: 6/29 12:00	

To the uninitiated, these messages might not seem like they contain much information, but based on them and a couple sets of local driving directions written by other drivers, I knew exactly what Leviathan wanted me to do for at least fifty-four hours. A similar series of messages will direct my work for the nine days that follow. Unless there is a problem on the customer's end, or my driver manager decides he wants to "just check in," formulaic messages like these, and those I send in return, will be virtually all of my communication with Leviathan while I am on the road. I won't need or want more.

As the text messages instructed, yesterday I drove to a Wal-Mart distribution center (DC) in Marcy, New York, twelve miles away from my home parking location. I waited in a line of trucks for the security guard to record my truck number and reason for entering the DC. After fifteen minutes or so of creeping amid row after row of hundreds of nearly identical fifty-three-foot trailers owned by Leviathan and several of its nearest competitors, I found trailer W32475. After a brief inspection, I coupled up to it, signed out at the guard shack, and hauled W32475 to a paper mill about 106 miles away.

I was at the mill by noon. By 4:30, W32475 had been loaded with six giant paper rolls that were due in Neenah, Wisconsin, by noon on Wednesday. I had used the waiting time to take care of paperwork, organize my gear and food, and clean and thoroughly inspect the truck. I also planned in detail my entire trip to Neenah. Before I left I knew exactly what I would be doing every hour along the 936-mile route until I arrived at the delivery location forty-three hours later—an acceptable thirty minutes early for the delivery. I knew exactly where I would stop for bathroom breaks, food, fuel, and sleep and within fifteen minutes or so of when I would pass through Buffalo, Cleveland, Chicago, and Milwaukee to avoid rush-hour traffic.

I drove four hours from the paper mill to a large truck stop in western New York. This truck stop has hundreds of parking spots, and it offers a wide range of services, including a barber shop, wireless internet, a free movie theatre, and a decent twenty-four-hour restaurant with a salad bar. But there was no time for such amenities last night. I chose this location for my Department of Transportation–mandated ten-hour break last night only because of its ample parking and the fact that it is located one full legal day of driving (on paper, at least) from a Leviathan terminal near Chicago. As soon as I arrived, I fueled the truck, checked the oil, cleaned the windows, and parked for the night. Minutes later, I was asleep in the bunk of my truck.

I wake at 6:00 a.m. I head into the stop to use the bathroom, brush my teeth, and wash my face. I am greeted by a poster touting the best chicken-fried steak this side of St. Louis, complete with a two-foot-tall image of this "king of steaks" swimming in a sea of plastic-looking, light-brown gravy. I file away another mental note about the constant temptations of life on the road.

After completing my morning routine, I return to the truck, which the early morning sun has already heated to an unbearable temperature. I put the key in the ignition and make sure the truck is in neutral by flipping the range selector on the shifter up and down rapidly with my thumb. I hear the familiar *click-pissst-click* of air pressure changing the transmission controls from low- to high-range and then back again, telling me for certain that the truck is not in gear. I turn the key and the tractor shudders to life. The motor is a Detroit Diesel Series 60, a no-frills workhorse. The six-cylinder D60 only puts out about 375 horsepower—about twice what my family minivan does—but, as required of a tractor motor, it generates a massive 1,450 pounds-feet of peak torque. So while some trucks pass me on hills like I am standing still, this truck is more than capable of the job of hauling freight, and can easily idle out of a stop at its maximum legal gross weight of eighty thousand pounds.

Within a few seconds, the D60 is idling smoothly at about 700 rpm. I flick up a switch on the dash to engage the high-idle speed of 1,000 rpm, which ensures enough oil pressure to lubricate all the motor's parts. Then I "adjust" my air conditioning, which means using the highest temperature and fan settings in recirculation mode—the only combination that actually *cools* the truck at all. Ahh . . . the truck would be uninhabitable without it. My truck is a seven-year-old Freightliner Century Class with more than a million miles on it. It's no luxury vehicle, but to me it's become an oasis in a world of work consisting almost entirely of concrete, asphalt, and dirt lots filled with clouds of dust and diesel exhaust. With the air conditioning on, an extra pillow, and earplugs, I sleep like a baby in the lower bunk—day or night. I outfitted the cab at my own expense with a small twelve-volt refrigerator, a lunchbox style stove, and CB and satellite radios. Since I just left home with clean sheets and clothes and decent food, life on the road is comfortable—at least for a little while.

After an extended moment in front of the air conditioning, I move to the back of the truck and sit on the lower bunk. I pull a sliding desk out of the cabinet behind the passenger's seat. I use this desk for filling out paperwork, in this case my logbook. I record the date, vehicle numbers for my tractor and trailer, the name of the shipper, the type of cargo, and the load number. I report that I spent ten hours off duty, even though I did not. Ahead of time, I record the next fifteen minutes as "on duty not driving." I also record that I inspected the tractor and trailer. With my logbook updated, I then fill in a form message on the truck's satellite-linked computer with my legally available hours to work over the next day and week and send it off. I don't know where this message goes, but I assume it goes to Leviathan's load planning department, which will use it to schedule my next load.

Now it's time to inspect the truck. Federal law requires that I perform safety inspections of the tractor and trailer at several points in a typical day and record the time and location of each in my logbook. Though it is legally required, I am not paid to do this work. A full legal inspection after a ten-hour break can take thirty minutes and tests everything from brakes to windshield wipers. No one does the full inspection. Some drivers don't do any inspection at all, but I do a fairly thorough version every morning.

I am proud of the modest skills I've developed operating my truck, and I often feel a sense of almost seamless integration with it when I am driving. During training I found the truck's movements and sounds foreign and, more often than not, a source of fear rather than useful information. Now the truck's movements, vibrations, and sounds provide confirmation that all is well, or alert me to problems. And the truck is not just a tool, it is home for twelve to nineteen days at a time. Most of those days I will spend all but an hour or two in it. I've named the truck Mavis, and we have a special relationship. But as much as I love my truck, I know any sense of oneness is a potentially life-threatening illusion. The power, size, and weight of my body and those of the truck are measured on vastly different scales.

In the few short months I've been trucking, I've witnessed the physical carnage my truck and I could cause. While I was training I saw the remains of a tractor that had been run into a bridge embankment at more than 60 mph. It was hauled into a company terminal and loaded in one piece into a dumpster of scrap metal. On impact, a load of metal coils tore through the thin sheet of aluminum at the front of the attached trailer and obliterated the tractor's cab and its driver. All that was left on the tractor's undercarriage were the eight driving wheels and a mass of fiberglass, aluminum, and plastic that been crumpled around the steel of the engine block—like a piece of tinfoil around a toy truck. As I looked over the wreck I wondered how much of the driver was there as well. I realized then that, while the shell of the tractor cab looked substantial, it offered zero protection against the lethal threat of forty thousand pounds of freight just a few feet behind me as I drove mile after mile. I never heard the cause of the accident. Maybe it was something the driver could have avoided, or maybe it wasn't. All we heard was that there was no sign that the driver was braking before impact. No personal details about who that driver was were shared with us.

I can't control what is going to happen around me on the road today. I inspect the truck because it's something I can control. I want to make sure that there is nothing wrong that could cause an accident. I also want to know that the truck will be able to give me its best performance if I have to respond to unexpected hazards—most likely a four-wheeler on a cell phone who races in front of me, only to then slam on the brakes.

I start the inspection by turning on my hazard lights and headlights and supplying air pressure to the trailer brakes. I hop out of the truck and grab a hammer and leather gloves from the storage compartment on the side of the cab where I keep my emergency equipment, spare parts, and tools. The company supplies things like emergency triangles, flares, and spare light bulbs. Per company recommendations, I supplied three sets of gloves, insulated and uninsulated leather and a rubber-coated pair for fueling and checking oil. Also as recommended, I carry my own set of wrenches, screwdrivers, and a few specialized bits required for parts on this particular truck. I have a three pound short-handled sledgehammer and a long-handled wrecking bar for more complicated problems—like the time I needed to slide a trailer's eight "tandem" wheels forward to properly distribute weight across the truck's axles (that and gross weight are what those scales you've seen at state borders are checking), but the spring-action steel pins holding the tandems in position were rusted in place and under the weight of forty thousand pounds of beer.

I take several minutes to circle the seventy-foot-long truck, looking for any damage or blown lights. Along the way, I visually inspect the walls and treads of the tires, particularly the tractor's two steering tires. I strike the sixteen nonsteer tires with the hammer and listen for the characteristic thud of a flat. I take special care looking over the release mechanism and gap of the "fifth wheel" (the plate and pin that connects the tractor to the trailer), and the hoses and cables that supply air pressure and electricity to the trailer. During training we were told stories of trailers that detached from tractors with deadly consequences. If averages hold, well more than a dozen Leviathan drivers will kill themselves or others in accidents this year; I don't want to be one of them.

I climb back into the cab through the passenger side and strategically arrange the things I might need throughout the day on the dash, the floor, the passenger seat, and in various small storage compartments. These include: a hefty set of laminated trucker's maps, a guide to truck stops, a guide to interstate exits, an apple, a pear, a can of almonds, two bottles of water, my satellite computer keyboard, a six-cassette history of World War I, my sunglasses (in their case), my wallet (with plenty of cash for tolls), my cell phone, and my logbook. My most faithful companion, my XM satellite radio, is already mounted so it's just off my right knee when I am driving. This arrangement, and my routine of stretching exercises while driving (Leviathan trained us in these), are attempts to combat repetitive-stress injuries. I suffered from excruciating pain in both my left knee (from operating the clutch) and right upper back (from reaching for controls on the dash and repeatedly scanning satellite and CB radio channels) within a few weeks of driving. I have developed strategies to keep this pain to a manageable level and assess signs of any developing injuries, particularly to my back and hips.

Satisfied that I have forgotten nothing vital, I climb into the driver's seat, being careful not to bump the oversize shifter into gear. I start repeatedly pumping the brake pedal to drain air pressure from the braking system. Soon the clanking racket of an air compressor rises above the low-pitched rumble of the motor. I stop pumping and carefully listen, while watching gauges indicating pressure in the primary and secondary air tanks that supply the tractor and trailer brakes. I want to make sure the compressor is running smoothly and tank pressure is building steadily. The compressor is the yin to the motor's yang, and if the former can't balance the latter, I want to know about it while I'm parked, because at

60 mph I need more than a football field to safely stop this truck *under good conditions.*

The compressor cuts out around 120 pounds per square inch, as it should. I hold the brake pedal down for a full minute to make sure there are no leaks in the system. Then I depress the clutch all the way to the floor, engaging the clutch brake. Next, I release the tractor brakes by depressing a large bright yellow knob on the dash. I push the shifter straight upward and it falls smoothly into second gear. After that, I release the brake pedal, and briefly lift up on the clutch—just a hair and no more—while leaving the trailer brakes applied, to "tug test" the connection between the tractor and trailer and the trailer brakes. For a moment the left side of the tractor's hood heaves upward violently, as the torque of the motor strains against the resistance of the trailer brakes. I can feel the tractor's frame contorting beneath my seat and feet, like a giant steel towel being rung out by the powerful motor. Finally, I test the tractor brakes. I am now convinced the truck is safe to drive, and take it out of gear.

I fasten my seatbelt and fill three air bags in my seatback for lumbar support (I have already permanently set the other twelve seat adjustments). I draw a line on my logbook indicating that I am "on-duty driving" and using up the precious legal hours in which I can do the only work I will really be paid for: driving. I depress the clutch and check my flat mirrors, taking note of how close the trucks on either side of me are. The J. B. Hunt truck to my left is only three feet from me and has pulled too far forward in his spot—rookie! An owner-operator truck, a yellow Peterbilt loaded with chrome—a real beauty—is a good distance away on my right.

When I started driving trucks I couldn't even get one into gear. Now I know can drive one through an obstacle course in reverse—if I ever needed to. While backing into tight spots still requires some careful thinking on my part from time to time, pulling out of them is now routine, and assessing what to do is largely an unconscious process. I don't *think* about distances and *decide* how to pilot the truck much any more, I *see* and *feel* what I need to do. I carefully scan the area in front of me from far left to far right for two seconds, put the truck in second gear, and then release the clutch. At eight feet high and six feet in diameter, the paper rolls I'm hauling are bulky and thus maxed out the volume of the trailer, which means I am lightly loaded (less than sixty-five-thousand pounds gross). At this weight the truck inches forward smoothly without any use of the accelerator. I scan left to right again as I give the engine a little fuel. Then I give the wheel a quick quarter turn to the right to take advantage of the space between me and the owner-operator. I will need it to clear the front of J. B.'s truck. Then I check my distance from the trucks on each side again in my flat mirrors. I have now covered about two-thirds of the distance between my parking spot and the trucks in the row in front of me. Using a hand-over-hand motion, I steadily crank the oversized twenty-inch steering wheel to the left. My fifty-three-foot-long trailer will significantly "shortcut" the arc of the tractor, so my attention is now focused in the flat and convex (spot) mirrors to my left to ensure that the end of my trailer does not hit J. B.'s front right mirror or fender. I stare into the mirrors as I complete the turn, taking time twice to glance in front to ensure I also have enough clearance to keep the arc of the tractor from intersecting with the trucks directly in front of me. I can no longer see the owner-operator in my right mirrors, but I know I left enough room to ensure that as the back of my trailer kicks out at the end of the turn it will not clip his front. Once I am sure the trailer will clear J. B., I focus my attention in front. The D60 is running at about 1,100 rpm, adequate to shift to third gear, so I depress the clutch and pull the shifter down out of second and into neutral, release the clutch, allow the engine to drop to 800 rpm, depress the clutch again and pull the shifter down into third, release the clutch, and then give the engine more fuel. I continue to scan in front of me and occasionally check my mirrors as I accelerate, shifting from third to fourth, and then fourth to fifth. At no point in shifting like this do I need to look at my tachometer; I can tell by the sound of the engine and the movement of truck how it wants me to shift.

I am now moving at about 15 mph. I slow slightly without braking or shifting at the end of the row. The motor begins to lug slightly as the truck's speed drops too low for fifth gear. I begin a sweeping left-hand turn toward the exit, and focus on my left mirrors to make sure that my trailer will clear the truck at the end of the row. I apply more fuel and take another left at the exit. I then flip the range selector on the shifter upward to access the high range of gears, shift into sixth (the same space occupied by first gear when the range selector is down), and proceed straight through a stoplight directly into a toll plaza for the New York State Thruway (I-90).

I have an EZ-Pass, so I slow to an idle in sixth (a little more than twice the posted speed limit), the light turns green and, eyes alternating between my left flat and convex mirrors, I head across the lanes toward the west-bound ramp quickly to prevent any four-wheelers from getting on the side of me and forcing me to slow and downshift. I apply fuel and shift from sixth to seventh, and then to eighth. The ramp is posted at 25 mph. I take this information seriously, as cloverleaf interchanges are notorious for causing truck rollovers, and my load is tall, which raises the trailer's center of gravity. I slow the motor to 1,400 rpm and downshift into seventh. My speedometer has not worked for the last few weeks. After several attempts to get it fixed at company terminals resulted in nothing more than driving unpaid miles and wasting time, I memorized a table of gears, engine speeds, and corresponding road speeds. I know that 1,300 rpm in seventh gear is roughly 25 mph, and I keep the engine there. I glance at the tach to double-check the engine speed. Just before the ramp straightens out, I hit the accelerator and shift to eighth, then ninth, and prepare to enter traffic. Now, as I apply fuel after each shift, a high-pitched whine from the turbo-charger rises over the low rumble of the motor. I don't know why, but I love that combination of sounds. Maybe I've been conditioned to like that chord because it marks the start of a long, high-speed road segment after the stress of less desirable—and unpaid—work. Maybe that chord tells me that I'm in control and getting paid.

Even though I am lightly loaded, I still have to run the truck hard to get up to interstate speed. I enter the slow lane at about 50 mph, continue to accelerate, and shift into tenth, the truck's highest gear. I immediately turn on the cruise control and use a lever on the dash to get the truck up to its maximum governed speed of 63 mph. I then begin the visual scan of my surroundings that I will try to continue uninterrupted until my first stop, which will be five hours from now. To avoid tunnel vision or "high-way hypnosis," I was trained to move my eyes every two seconds while on the open road. And, as trained, when checking my mirrors I try to move my head rather than just my eyes, to keep myself as physically active as possible. Every few minutes I begin a new "scanning" pattern of looking ahead (near and far) and checking gauges and mirrors. A pattern might be: check traffic in right flat mirror—scan right to left in near front—left convex mirror—scan horizon left to right—right convex mirror—check a gauge—near scan left to right—left flat mirror—horizon scan. I repeat and repeat and repeat patterns like this. This constant scanning is the physical embodiment of the rules I follow for defensive driving on the interstate, just as my ability to now go five hours without stopping is the outcome of disciplining my muscles through stretching and posture, and my bladder by cutting out my morning coffee and carefully regulating when I drink water. When I inevitably find myself simply staring ahead, daydreaming too intently, or slouching in my seat, I know I need to assess my alertness. Maybe it's time to do one of my in-seat stretches or drink a Coke. If I realize that I don't remember where each of the cars around me came from, maybe I am "zoning out" or "microsleeping." It's probably time for an unplanned stop to stretch, eat, or walk and, if needed, climb in the bunk for a short nap.

For the next five hours I need to maintain just the right balance of alertness and relaxation. If am not alert, I could be slow to recognize stopped traffic ahead and be unable to stop in time. This situation, which most truckers fear more than any other, is sometimes called "the moment." The moment is the instant you consciously recognize you cannot stop in time to avoid a crash. The possibility of it terrifies me, as it should. I imagine cruising along at full speed and having the brake lights of a minivan stopped three hundred feet ahead in my lane suddenly catch my eye. In that moment of mortal terror, what should I do? What *can* I do? With a lightly loaded trailer, if I slam on the brakes will they lock up and jackknife the truck, sending me into an unrecoverable spin? If I try to steer myself off the road, will I lose control and nosedive the tractor into a ditch, bringing it to sudden halt and sending whatever I am hauling flying toward the thin sheets of aluminum and fiberglass separating me from the freight? Unfortunately, stopped traffic is just the most obvious hazard. If I am not alert, I might allow a four-wheeler to slip into one of my blind spots unnoticed. I try to keep track of the makes and colors of cars that disappear into my blind spots. It is often impossible to keep track of them in heavy traffic, but if I am not confident that my blind spot is clear, I might second-guess myself if I need to change lanes quickly. Twice since I began driving I've seen four-wheelers in sparse traffic and perfect road conditions lose control and spin out right in front of me without any warning or apparent cause. Both times I was maintaining a safe distance and knew I had space to move into other lanes or onto the shoulder, but fortunately I didn't need to, since the cars ended up spinning safely to the side of the road. When you are on the highway for ten or more hours a day, day after day, you will eventually find yourself in circumstances like this that you simply *can't see coming*. Maintaining good defensive driving habits is absolutely critical. Big trucks have serious limitations in terms of stopping and turning, and you will at some point find yourself in a situation that even quick thinking and skilled driving can't get you out of. If you fall into bad habits, the chances of that happening increase exponentially. As a trucker, you can't just get on the interstate, crank up some tunes, sit back, and relax. This isn't a road trip, it's *work*. Keeping track of every vehicle around you and "always leaving yourself an out" require constant mental alertness. At the same time, you can't be tense and worried, because stress will both cause fatigue and make it harder to recognize the subtle cues that tell you fatigue is setting in.

So I need to constantly monitor my mental and physical alertness, while at the same time occupying my mind enough to prevent the monotony of staring out at hundreds of miles of white and yellow lines and an endless procession of cars and trucks from putting me to sleep or driving me insane. No one is there watching me. No one else will tell me my driving is getting sloppy and I need a break. At the same time, I want to maximize my productivity. I am responsible for balancing that productivity with safety, and I now embody this balancing act through rigid planning and a set of mental and physical self-disciplining practices.

Yes, today will be a very good day: 630 paid miles, no shippers, no receivers, and no loading, unloading, or waiting. The route can be a little boring, but I love seeing the morning sunlight reflecting off Lake Erie and the sunset over the otherworldly landscape of Lake Michigan's steel plants. Even though the most efficient route and schedule are essentially determined by the locations and time requirements of the load and, to a lesser degree, by the law, I can stop when and where I want along the way. Only Ohio's 55 mph truck speed limit will slow me down. Yesterday I planned the entire trip so as to avoid rush hour in Buffalo and Cleveland today and Chicago and Milwaukee tomorrow. This morning I will drive five hours and then stop at a rest area on the other side of Cleveland for a half-hour lunch break, much of which will be spent parking the truck, filling out my logbook, and walking to and from the restroom. I will then drive about seven hours and stop near Chicago for the night. I will break up this second bit of driving with one stop to use the restroom and stretch my legs. When I reach Leviathan's terminal, I will fuel the truck, check the oil, clean the windows and mirrors, park, complete my logbook, and send another form message updating the company about my hours. I will report eleven out of my actual twelve driving hours and eleven and one-half of my actual thirteen hours of total work. When I go off duty around 8:00 p.m. local time, I will use the terminal's exercise room for about twenty minutes, take a shower, and then eat dinner in the truck. I will be asleep in the back of the truck a little after 9:00 p.m. I'll wake at 4:30 a.m. tomorrow, start driving around 5:00 to beat rush hour in Chicago and Milwaukee, and be in Neenah a little ahead of schedule. Hopefully I'll get a load from there down to the Gulf Coast.

If you ask a long-haul trucker what they like about their job, they're likely to tell you about a day like this. On such a day you feel free from direct supervision and in complete control of your work. If you plan wisely you can safely maximize your pay within the spirit of the laws governing trucking and feel a deep sense of accomplishment for a job well done. Operating an expensive and dangerous piece of heavy equipment requires skill and constant alertness, which drivers explicitly say correspond to a masculine work ethic and identity they find satisfying. Drivers will talk about these feelings and the fact that the overall income the job provides is more than they can earn elsewhere. Unfortunately, these are not the only kinds of days truckers can talk about.

THE BAD DAYS

I delivered the paper rolls in Neenah by noon on June 29th. I then hauled more paper rolls from Neenah to Beech Island, South Carolina. In Beech Island, I picked up a load of facial tissue headed to East St. Louis, Illinois. From East St. Louis I hauled a load of Gatorade to a grocery warehouse in Tipp City, Ohio. In the first seven days of my rotation I hauled four separate loads and drove more than 3,400 miles. I was paid for the number of miles Leviathan charged the shippers: 3,183. At my standard pay rate of twenty-six cents per mile, that worked out to $827.58. I received $170 in bonus pay for unloading a trailer and "excessive" waiting time, for total gross pay of $997.58 for that week. For a forty-hour week that works out to almost twenty-five dollars an hour. But I didn't work a forty-hour week. I spent ninety-seven hours on duty to earn that pay—almost fourteen hours a day on average. That works out to about $10.28 an hour (of course, I also wasn't paid for all the off-duty time I spent waiting and sleeping at truck stops while out on the road). Nonetheless I considered this a very good sequence of loads, and I was happy.

On Monday, July 4th, things turned bad. I spent the morning performing the unpaid work required to drop the trailer of Gatorade in Tipp City. After I backed into the dock for live unloading by warehouse staff, I immediately sent in a form message via the satellite computer prematurely reporting that the load was complete (a strategy I regularly employed to try to reduce my waiting time while being assigned another load. Essentially I was telling the load planning department that the trailer was already unloaded so they would immediately give me another load). I began doing paperwork. After fifteen minutes, I still had not received a new load assignment. This was not a good sign. I sent a text message asking for a new assignment to the unknown "third shift" workers who would be covering my dispatch over the long holiday weekend and waited. Several hours later, long after pulling out of the dock empty but still sitting in the warehouse parking lot, I received my next load assignment. I needed to drop the empty trailer, and bobtail (drive without a trailer) 170 miles to Louisville, Kentucky, pick up a preloaded trailer of automotive glass, and haul it 210 miles to a factory near Columbus, Ohio. The glass was scheduled for delivery on Wednesday at 12:30 p.m. I did a trip plan for the load and realized I would be thirty miles outside Columbus that night— Monday night—at 6:00 pm. That meant I would be sitting unpaid for more than forty-two hours. In the previous week I earned an average of more than $130 a day. For Monday's driving I would earn a little under one hundred dollars. Tuesday I would earn nothing. And Wednesday I would be lucky to earn fifty dollars by the time I dropped the glass and picked up another load. I texted third shift about moving up the delivery time and was told nothing could be done until the next day—the customer was closed for the holiday.

After a hard week on the road, my physical and mental state are being tested by the cumulative fatigue that results from a string of long days and the boredom of staring out at thousands of miles of interstate pavement. My clothes and bunk sheets reek of raw and burned diesel fuel. My supply of homemade frozen meals and fresh fruit has run out. I'm now faced with eating overpriced truck stop food for the next four or five days. So on July 4th I find myself outside Columbus, Ohio, sitting atop a concrete parking barrier, looking at a fallow farm field and eating what is undoubtedly the worst Chinese fast food I've ever tasted. My wife calls to tell me everyone at the family barbeque back in New York says hello. Friday is her birthday and our fifth wedding anniversary. She asks whether we can plan on going out Friday night. I tell her I'm hopeful I'll be home Friday evening, but I won't know anything until I get my next load assignment on Wednesday. Even then I may not know for certain whether I will be home Friday, Saturday, or Sunday. As we say goodnight, the tone of her voice tells me the report does not please her. Time apart is difficult for truckers and their families, and I'm no exception. What I have going for me, as a relative who drove trucks for a few years told me when I started this research, is that I know I'll only be doing this for a few months. But the temporary nature of my life as a trucker is little comfort as I sit for another half hour and watch the glow of fireworks on the horizon.

I've been on the road solo for three months now. In the beginning I enjoyed driving new roads and seeing new places. But the novelty of the work has worn off. The only part of the job that is still fun is blasting the air horn for the kids on the side of the road furiously pumping their clenched fists up and down. Good days on the road blend into one another now—they are just a blur of endless highway miles. Bad days, on the other hand, stick out. On bad days the work is frustrating, even insulting. And you remember the details. I remember the frame of the window through which a shipping clerk chastised me for arriving an hour early and then made me wait two hours to get into a dock. I remember the fence surrounding a grocery warehouse I stared at while the workers inside took four hours to load twelve pallets onto my truck with a forklift. I wasn't allowed inside and so had no idea when loading would be completed. The shipping clerk wouldn't give me a time. If I'd known it was going to be four hours, I would have taken a much-needed nap. I also remember the time

I skipped lunch to arrive on time for a 2:00 p.m. appointment only then to be told the load wouldn't be ready until 8:00.

So, I remember July 5th. I woke at 7:00 a.m. and by 8:00 I had a text message from my driver manager. He told me the shipper was willing to move up the delivery appointment the next day by two hours but had no space in the warehouse to take the glass any earlier than that. I texted back that I was not happy sitting so long. He responded that he was sorry and would try to arrange some way to get me another load, but because I was due home in three days, the options were limited. He said that since my delay was more than twenty-four hours, he would request that I get layover pay of eighty dollars. I thanked him, even though I knew the gesture meant nothing to me financially, because the company guarantees a salary of $500 for a full week spent on the road, and I would definitely earn less than that this week even with the eighty dollars.

Now certain that I was stuck at the truck stop for the entire day, I took the free shower I was given for purchasing 150 gallons of fuel the day before. After that I read a little in my bunk. But after long stretches of driving and working alone, I wanted to interact with people. So by early afternoon I headed into the truck stop's driver lounge and watched the apparently endless parade of crime dramas available on cable TV. Over the course of the afternoon, I pondered which *Law and Order* series is the true linchpin of American culture, as a steady stream of drivers came through the lounge. Many lingered in front of the TV waiting for showers to free up or for the dead time between load assignments to end. Conversations about everything from the current NASCAR standings to the ongoing wars were struck up easily, and typically ended just as abruptly, with either the *Law and Order* theme or a name and shower number called over the PA system. None of the participants in these conversations would likely ever see each other again. We were all just trying to fill the difficult time between work sessions, when most truckers simply try not to dwell on what they are missing at home.

Like decent food. Late in the afternoon, I moved across the stop to the restaurant. The buffet is by no means good food, but in addition to heaping piles and simmering pots of unhealthy calories—some of which can only be identified because they have labels—it has a decent selection of hot foods, like roasted chicken, and, more importantly, whole, unfried vegetables (a true luxury on the road) in the salad bar. Most importantly, it only costs fifteen dollars, including tip. The buffet is the only real meal I'll have all day and is the best consistently available food option I have found while driving. I just can't eat fast food regularly—I promised myself I would not ruin my health doing this research. Unfortunately, bad overpriced food is a serious workplace hazard most truckers can't easily avoid. It's difficult to pack enough fresh food to take on the road, and there is rarely the time to search out decent food. Even if you could, and you're confident you can find a place that you can safely park your truck, the company is going to count the out-of-route miles against you when they figure your quarterly bonus. Therefore, many truckers pay the costs of eating at truck stops in higher rates of heart disease, obesity, and diabetes. After loading up at the buffet, I considered exercising, but decided there is probably a net health negative to walking in circles around a parking lot filled with idling trucks. So I headed back to the TV lounge for a few more episodes of *Law and Order* and then out to the truck to read and sleep.

Days like this tell you something as a trucker. They say: your time is not important. Your paycheck is not important. Whether you are home with your family for special events and holidays is not important. *You* are not important.

As I write this, years after the experience, I can still remember how I felt. How angry I was. I knew what I was angry about—I was wasting a day of my life sitting at a truck stop. But who was I angry with? It wasn't my driver manager's fault. He didn't plan this load for me, and his brief text messages suggested he was genuinely troubled by my plight. What about the load planners? They don't know me from Adam, and they only have the loads to assign that the salespeople send them. And the salespeople can only sell my services for loads that need to be hauled. Leviathan would certainly have given me the day off if I was close to home, but I wasn't. I was seven hundred miles from home, and they certainly weren't going to pay $300 for fuel to get me there.

So it was nobody's fault, at least no one that I could reach with a text on the satellite-linked computer. And that is how it is supposed to work. As a trucker I was paid for a little more than half the time I worked. I sat unpaid with nothing to do for hours, sometimes days. One week I would earn almost $1,000, the next $500. My July 5th wasn't a mistake, it was a predictable, routine outcome of the way the work of truckers is organized. This organization has other outcomes. First, of course, it leads to worker dissatisfaction and contributes to turnover. Second, it makes workers desperate for ways to gain more control over their work. Third, it fundamentally shapes the way they understand the business of trucking and the kinds of jobs available to them. Before I explain how this is so, we need to understand the system that produces good days and bad days like these, and how it differs from other ways to organize the work of truckers.

LOADS: THE GOOD, THE BAD, AND THE UGLY

Drivers just starting out are likely to average about eighteen hundred miles per week at a company like Federal or Leviathan. It takes the average new Federal driver more than six months to reach weekly productivity of somewhere in the neighborhood of 2,200 paid miles per week.[2] These drivers were probably averaging about six days per week on the road working a twelve-days-on, two-days-off schedule. Once drivers have developed basic planning skills, load characteristics determine how hard they work and how much they earn. All drivers recognize better and worse loads. Essentially, good loads involve more driving time and less unpaid work and loading time. Generally there are just a few load characteristics that determine this. The first is how soon a driver can start hauling it, and whether it needs to be live-loaded or is preloaded. The second consideration is how many miles the load is to be hauled. All else being equal, long loads simply mean a greater amount of driving relative to unpaid work. The third major consideration is the geographic area the load requires a driver to traverse, and whether it is mountainous, urbanized, etc., which determines among other things driving speed, how long it might take to find parking, and, of course, how far the driver is from home.

Drivers focus intensely on load quality, since it determines nearly every aspect of the job, from how many hours they work and when, to how much waiting and unpaid work they do, to what kind of traffic conditions they encounter, to when they will be able to return home, and ultimately the size of their paychecks. For instance, I tallied up my hours, miles, and pay for what I considered to be one of my best work rotations in terms of loads. I spent a little over nineteen calendar days on the road. I averaged 475 paid miles driven for every twenty-four hours on the road. I drove 8,938 actual miles and was paid $2,403.64, or 26.9 cents per actual mile driven.[3] At about $800 a week, this was roughly equal to an annual salary of $40,000. But that calculation obscures the reality of how many hours I worked. I received just $9.46 per hour I spent working.

I had five days during that rotation where I had no stops to make, no waiting time, minimal unpaid work to perform, and did not have to worry about driving hard only to wait for delivery appointments. On those days I averaged 553 miles per day while working an average of 12.1 hours and earning about $12.30 per hour. On the other full workdays of that rotation I averaged 430 miles, 13.6 hours of work, and just $8.54 per hour. In other words, on a good day I earned about thirty dollars more than on the other days, while working 1.5 fewer hours, or almost four dollars more an hour.

A typical bad day might be working a thirteen-to-fourteen-hour day in which one to four of those hours was spent delivering the load I had on the truck overnight, another hour was spent waiting to be assigned a new load, and then another four or five hours were spent getting my next load on the truck. On a day like this I could easily spend ten or more hours simply waiting and doing unpaid work. If I was already fueled, didn't have to scale the new load, and could deal with personal needs, like bathroom breaks, food, and showers while I waited, then I might be able to sneak in five or six hours of driving, though I might break the law by exceeding the fourteen-hour rule. If I was lucky I could get 250 miles in on a day like that and earn about sixty dollars, or less than four dollars per hour worked. I tallied up my hours, miles, and pay for a bad rotation that had two such days. On those two days I was on duty for a total of twenty-seven hours but drove only 370 miles and was paid for no non-driving work—I earned about $3.70 per hour.

Unfortunately, when drivers get a bad load at a company like Leviathan, there is little they can do about it except complain to their driver manager or ask to be reassigned. One driver, John, recounted such a scenario to me, which happened early in his driving career:

> I was scheduled to be home in New York on Friday night, but was dispatched on a load that made two deliveries in Chicago at 5:00 and 7:00 a.m. on

Thursday. I told my driver manager Tuesday that I needed to be home on Friday for personal reasons. She said she would make sure of it. [After the deliveries in Chicago] I expected to be dispatched on a drop and hook from Chicago to New York to get me home on time. But after my first delivery in Chicago on Thursday, I was dispatched on a new load with two live load [stops] in Chicago and headed to Maryland! I was looking at getting home on Sunday at the earliest. I called my manager to complain and she said "okay, lay into me," when I told her that I was upset about the way I was dispatched. *I didn't want to blow off steam or verbally abuse someone, I wanted to get home!*

This driver manager's use of the phrase "okay, lay into me" struck John as evidence that his manager did not understand his problem nor what would rectify it. John did not know it, but he had just encountered a common company strategy to handle driver discontent over bad loads. Companies train their driver managers to invite drivers to "lay into them," in the hope that getting things off their chest will help drivers to feel that their concerns are being taken seriously, without requiring that the company actually address them. "Lay into me" was likely part of a script, either the manager's own or provided by the company, intended to facilitate this process by giving the driver authorization to state his concerns frankly while maintaining supervisor authority. According to driver managers I interviewed, such scripts allow them some emotional distance from the intense verbal altercations that can occur between upset drivers and managers.

In most cases, driver managers have little power to change things, and only infrequently will they exercise what power they do have. The load planning system is the boss. Most of the problems a driver manager deals with are not aberrations, but frequent and expected outcomes of the organization of the labor process. A driver manager's primary task is to make drivers feel better about complying, when the system does its job correctly and drivers pay the price. In general, driver managers tell drivers they have to take the good with the bad and that every driver gets his share of bad loads. They may also justify bad loads by suggesting that they are required in order to set up drivers for really good loads in the near future, or that bad loads are the result of the company's attempt to get them home, which prevents them from sending the driver on long loads far from home.

It was clear from my interviews with both drivers and managers that, in general, a driver manager will only request a change in a driver's work assignment from load planners when they cannot convince the driver to take a bad load in exchange for things like a small payment for multiple stops or excessive waiting, an extra day off, or, most commonly, the vague promise of better assignments soon. Furthermore, before asking for a reassignment, the driver manager can simply tell the driver that no better load is available and present him with the option of waiting, which drivers rarely accept. As a result, lacking information and fearing that they could be informally punished in future load assignments, drivers accept nearly all assigned loads. It is better to drive a bad load and get paid poorly than to complain and possibly get paid even less in the future.

Productive drivers, however, don't respond to bad loads by simply accepting an inevitable drop in productivity; they speed themselves up. Most will try to run as close as possible to their average number of miles despite the challenges presented by a bad load. To do so, they exert greater control by intensifying the miles game, perhaps by deciding to break laws in order to work faster and longer. While this response can be stressful, fatiguing, and dangerous, overcoming a bad load every few work assignments gives drivers a sense of control and a sense of satisfaction—"that load didn't slow me down!" In other words, as Burawoy's theory expects, the game drivers play is what companies achieve through pay-by-mile. When faced with a bad load, in order to maintain their productivity, safeguard their take-home pay, and assert control, drivers decide to work longer and harder, sometimes by punishing their bodies and minds. In response to a lack of control, they achieve a sense of autonomy, a feeling many drivers I spoke to contrasted to the subjugation they reported feeling in other jobs. Here a driver (who now works as a road trainer for extra pay and thus deals frequently with easily fatigued rookies who get in the way of his game) describes the benefits of the job and how intensely he plays the game:

SV: What's the best part about driving, what do you like about it?

Driver: The freedom while I am driving by myself, there is no one else around to bother me, I am driving the truck, knowing that I am doing it. I guess that is the ... it is almost like owning your own business, but not. When I was driving solo, where I could run, run, run, and you have your sleep time and your down time. Didn't have anyone in the truck, I could turn the radio up on whatever station I wanted to. When I was solo, it was more enjoyable ... As long as you are getting miles, it is okay ... You have got appointments. If you take the job seriously, which some people say I take it too seriously, [your attitude has to be] I have got to be there on time. "Let's go!" They say, "You are too energetic, man, chill out, man, *we will get there, we will get there*." I want to get there, if we can, *early*, 'cause then you can drop [the load]. If you can't deliver early, maybe you can drop it at a drop-yard or terminal. Trainees don't like handling it like that, but it is the only way that you are going to make money out here.

However, while drivers feel autonomous and in control of their work, their ability to do more than simply compensate for bad loads through self-sweating is minimal. This is because the game cloaks the value of a driver's labor relative to unpaid work, miles, and self-sweating. Despite having read everything I could find on trucking and sociological studies of piece-rate systems, I too was taken in completely by the game. I did not realize its true effects on compensation until I systematically compared my logbooks, paychecks, and field notes long after I had finished my driving.

Let's return to the "bad" rotation I mentioned above. I analyzed this rotation, because I vividly remember the sense of frustration that I felt about the delays I was experiencing. My field notes are filled with complaints, expletives, and the occasional rant about my poor load assignments, company inefficiency, and the consequences of the game I was enduring. I abused my body and took risks to compensate for my bad loads. By the end of this rotation I was extremely fatigued and disappointed.

I vividly remember the "good" rotation described above as well, but for much different reasons. The bad rotation directly preceded the good one and I was determined to not have another frustrating rotation. As a result I decided, much to my wife's displeasure, to stay out on the road for three weeks rather than two. My driver manager had told me that the short loads I got during the bad rotation were due to my need to get home, and that the longer I stayed out, the further I could go from home, and the longer the hauls I would get. So I stayed out three weeks, and I could not have been more pleased with the results. I drove from New York to Wisconsin to

South Carolina, back to Wisconsin, down to Mississippi, back up to Wisconsin, down to Pennsylvania, back up to Illinois, down to Pennsylvania again, and then home to New York. Along the way, I also delivered loads in Ohio, Tennessee, North Carolina, Kentucky, Alabama, and Indiana.

I did not feel stressed during this rotation. I felt in control. I had few violations of the eleven- and fourteen-hour rules (these rules are explained below), which tend to produce the most acute stress, since they can be easily discovered and more often require immediate sleep deprivation. I was, however, in violation of the seventy-hour rule 90 percent of the days I was out and suffered from significant cumulative fatigue. Despite the sleep debt I had built, I was quite pleased with the result.

And what did I earn that made me feel so great? About five dollars per calendar day and thirty-six cents per hour worked more than I earned in the previous bad rotation. At the time I thought I was earning lots more per hour worked. But I wasn't. In reality, better loads and staying out longer dramatically lowered my stress but only marginally improved my overall earnings. I hadn't done any systematic analysis while I was driving. All I thought about was the $1,000 paycheck I received in the middle of the good rotation and the $500 one at the end of the bad one. My experience told me there were two things that determined whether you made good money as a trucker: staying out longer and getting good loads. But, as it turned out, that $500 check represented better pay per hour than my $1,000 check. Because of my bad loads, I had received $74.16 in guaranteed minimum pay to get me to $500 for the last five full days I worked. Because of this pay, I actually earned twenty-seven cents more per hour worked and eleven cents more per hour on the road than I did in what I considered the far better rotation. At the time I couldn't see that; all I saw was that I did not drive as many miles.

This focus was the result of the way that the work is organized across much of the industry.

WHERE TRUCKING'S LEVIATHANS CAME FROM

Under regulation, the average trucker's wages and working conditions were either directly set or heavily influenced by the collective bargaining agreements of the IBT. In part, the better work routines for general freight drivers of the past came from the fact that general freight tended to be hauled by LTL carriers. The use of terminal systems made it easy for companies to get drivers home often and give them regular schedules. Drivers were often able to "bid" on regular routes based on seniority within the union. And, of course, when problems arose on the job, the worker had both the contract and the union to turn to.

That didn't mean, however, that Teamster leaders failed to consider the effect of labor costs and work rules on market share for trucking overall. Like Hoffa, powerful Teamster leaders were generally advocates of efficiency even when the costs to Teamster drivers were significant. For instance, by the 1960s railroads began to compete with long-haul truckers through "piggybacking"—loading truck trailers onto railroad cars for long segments. Hoffa recognized that efficiency gains were critical to maintaining the competitive position of the industry overall.[4] He allowed companies to rapidly expand, partnering with railroads in order to piggyback trailers. He made long-distance hauling cheaper by supporting the use of sleeper cabs, and by negotiating a small premium for driving while in a team but with no pay when not driving. He also favored the use of double trailers as a labor-saving device. All of these positions either came at the cost of jobs or were unpopular with the rank and file, but Hoffa was able to minimize resistance to them, build them into contracts, and then ensure contract enforcement. He demanded that companies pass some of the savings of these innovations on to drivers through higher wages, but he was motivated overall by concerns for industry competitiveness.

That sort of cooperation between labor and employers regarding the way truckers worked came to an abrupt halt when the industry was deregulated. As suggested in the introduction, overcapacity caused freight rates to plummet after deregulation. With higher costs due to terminals and Teamster labor, most general freight, less-than-truckload companies were quickly driven out of business, as private and for-hire truckload carriers and owner-operators began hauling previously regulated freight from point to point.

Within a few years, an even lower-cost model of trucking was setting the competitive standard and gobbling up market share. A new set of trucking companies, referred to by some at the time as advanced truckload firms

(ATLF), were employing nonunionized employees and undercutting rates while returning significantly more profit. These companies used sophisticated load planning processes to focus on specific freight corridors and achieved much higher rates of asset utilization, a key for success after deregulation. For instance, ATLFs drove only 8 percent of their miles empty versus 15 percent for firms using contractors.[5] But this system required drivers to accept whatever load was assigned to them and go wherever that load needed to go, in a random pattern that could send them far from home for long periods of time.

That's what most long-haul truckload drivers still do today. Drivers for private firms and less-than-truckload carriers still enjoy significantly better working conditions than truckload drivers. The typical private or less-than-truckload driver is home much more often and servicing regular locations. In a 2011 survey by the ATA only 6 percent of truckload and only 2 percent of dry van truckload companies reported that their drivers got home more than one a week. In contrast, 83 percent of less-than-truckload carriers and 18 percent of private fleets reported getting their drivers home daily.[6]

HOW LEVIATHAN WORKS

Although it also hauls refrigerated trailers, flatbeds, and other more specialized trailers, Leviathan's primary business is hauling general freight using dry vans. It hauls just about anything that can be loaded into those vans, from steel coils to baby diapers over distances ranging from several hundred to thousands of miles. Its drivers typically stay out on the road for two to three weeks at a time. They do not need specialized skills, such as those required to load fragile cargo or care for live animals. Loading and unloading is usually done by the firms shipping or receiving the freight. Most of the freight is moved on pallets by forklifts or by hand-operated pallet jacks. The only service Leviathan drivers provide to customers is to simply transport a trailer from one loading dock to another within a specified amount of time.

How companies like Leviathan organize this work is important for a number of reasons. First, they are responsible for training and/or employ-

ing the vast majority of new over-the-road truckers. As a result, they influence how these workers understand the work of trucking and the ways it
can and should be organized. Second, their organization of the labor process, low wages, and economies of scale set competitive standards for the
industry. Finally, these firms dominate the American Trucking Associations,
which is the most influential voice of the industry with regard to safety
regulation and other matters.

Leviathan has well over ten thousand tractors and more than forty
thousand trailers. At any given time, the vast majority of these trailers are
either attached or assigned to a truck, or are being loaded or unloaded by
customers at one of the more than ten thousand customer locations
Leviathan regularly services. Leviathan also hauls thousands more shipping containers that use detachable chassis to and from rail- and ship-
yards every week. Leviathan trucks are monitored by satellite and on the
move across North America twenty-four hours a day, 365 days a year. This
mobile juggernaut is fed loads from the company's headquarters in a
medium-sized US city.

Leviathan's headquarters has none of the flash one might expect in the
headquarters of a Fortune 500 company. Set within a large complex of
minimally landscaped parking lots, it consists of a single massive low-
slung building detailed with the distinctive Leviathan blue. The building
has a utilitarian appearance in which concrete trumps glass. Beyond the
spacious entry, after passing reception and security, visitors can go around
the building in one direction and pass the obligatory offices of human
resources, benefits, finance, and a wing of executive offices with a separate
reception area.

In the other direction is "the field," a several-acre room of cubicles that
contains the workspaces of about one thousand sales personnel handling
interactions with the company's customers. Here workers find loads,
negotiate contracts, and manage accounts. Almost every conceivable kind
of freight for thousands of small and medium-sized firms and two-thirds
of the Fortune 500 are handled in the field. The field looks and sounds like
a bustling stock exchange. Large groups of cubicles are delineated by signs
carrying the names of the largest customers, such as Wal-Mart, Johnson
and Johnson, Kraft, and Proctor and Gamble. Low freight rates and the
work done in the field are what allow Leviathan and companies like it to

dominate the general freight market, much to the dismay of small firms and independent truckers.

The loads contracted in the field are sent to a load planning department that assigns them directly to individual trucks. Even though drivers are not paid for the vast majority of waiting they do, idle trucks are capital investments that bring in no revenue. Leviathan wants to keep those trucks moving. The key to success is finding the most profitable immediately available load for each truck, while minimizing the number of miles a truck travels empty (known as deadheading) to reach that load. In small companies, this can be accomplished by looking for loads once a truck's delivery point is known. This involves the time-consuming task of searching Internet load boards or calling brokers and known customers looking for loads that might be available when and where the truck will be available.

Large companies like Leviathan, on the other hand, know that one of their thousands of trucks will essentially always be close to a load when it is ready to move, and can gobble up huge numbers of profitable loads whenever they are available, often working out bulk contracts with large shippers in advance. Leviathan actually contracts to haul up to fifteen thousand loads a day—thousands more than its trucks can move. After their load planners assign loads to all of Leviathan's drivers, partially with the aid of sophisticated software, in ways that optimize the company's resources, several thousand loads are usually left unassigned. Leviathan then subcontracts the remaining loads to small companies and independent contractors and takes a significant percentage of the load price as a brokerage fee.

Leviathan's approach is the most profitable way to behave in the general freight market. It requires not just size, but great flexibility in terms of drivers' work schedules and geographic range. Loads are identified, contracted, and assigned with no input whatsoever from drivers. The only considerations relative to drivers are that they have sufficient legal hours available to drive (as self-reported by the driver into a central system daily through the truck's on-board computer) and that they be routed home during a window that recurs typically every two or three weeks for "home time."

Drivers do not know what work is available, who assigns work, how it gets assigned, and, consequently, what latitude there is to change work assignments. All that drivers are told is that there is little flexibility, it is costly and difficult to change load assignments, and that load planning is done systematically and with the greatest possible efficiency and fairness. This system is known as "forced dispatch," because it requires drivers to accept whatever load is assigned to them.

Once loads are assigned to Leviathan's drivers, any problems they encounter are handled by driver managers at more than twenty company facilities strategically located along major freight lanes throughout the US. Leviathan's drivers and driver managers are organized into units called "boards," housed at the terminal closest to their homes. Leviathan's smallest terminals have only one board, with a hundred or so drivers and three or four driver managers assigned to it, while the largest have several boards, dozens of managers, and more than a thousand drivers. Driver managers report to a board manager, who in turn reports to a terminal manager, the most senior employee outside company headquarters.

Driver Management and Monitoring

A driver might see his immediate manager in person just a few times each year. The average driver will receive a handful of personal text messages from a manager and talk by phone with them once or so over the course of a few weeks. In fact, since they perform most of their work either on public roadways or at customer locations, drivers rarely interact with *any* workers from their own company while on the job. Though drivers pass through terminals once every two or three days, they generally use them only for fuel, food, and a parking spot, both while on the road and when they take home time.[7] The chances for any interaction with coworkers, or supervisors who would be involved in or aware of the specifics of the driver's work, are extremely unlikely.

Satellite-linked computers allow managers to text drivers and automatically collect data about the truck's location and operation. Every few hours, Leviathan driver managers "pull"—check the location of—their drivers to ensure they are on track for an on-time delivery—drivers do not know when or how managers check on them. Truck computers record the average fuel economy of drivers, the number of miles they drive, the number of times they exceed company-set speed limits (which with governed trucks can only be done going downhill), and the amount of the time that the truck idles (an enormous waste of fuel and source of significant additional cost). These are the metrics a company will use to determine a driver's productivity and bonuses, which can add several percent to a driver's pay.

The capacity of Leviathan's system of organizing the constant movement and productivity of tens of thousands of pieces of equipment is nothing short of astounding. Leviathan's roughly twenty thousand employees can move almost half a billion pounds of freight over five million miles to and from thousands of locations *in a single day*. On a typical day, not a pound of freight will get lost and relatively little will be late by more than a few hours. All of this is achieved despite the fact that the company's employees will contend with every rush hour, interstate accident, and major weather system in the US and lower Canada. Indeed, systems like this are the main arteries moving the physical goods of modern capitalism and are a wonder to behold. It is systems like Leviathan's and a handful of similar companies that have dramatically increased the speed and decreased the cost of moving freight by truck. But, as economist Michael Belzer has suggested, it has turned many trucks into sweatshops on wheels.[8]

THE TASKS OF A DRIVER AND OBSTACLES THEY FACE

Leviathan drivers are paid according to the miles that a shipper is charged for a load, which is determined by the distance between post offices in the zip codes of the customer locations. This payment system is critical to how workers understand the labor process. The long-haul trucking game produces a fetishistic obsession with mileage that often obscures other possible considerations, such as the number of hours worked or the consequences of neglecting sleep. The basic strategy of the game requires prioritizing driving over everything else in pursuit of miles. Personal tasks, from bathroom breaks, to eating, to showers, to haircuts and shopping, are fit into unavoidable downtime between loads, after work hours, or during time at home. The most successful drivers develop a routine that tailors every waking moment toward achieving the highest productivity, analyzing every task, however small, to determine when nondriving tasks can be done without diminishing the number of paid miles driven.

Of course, these are the things that truckers can control. Many other things that affect truckers' pay are often completely out of their control, and they are forced on an almost daily basis to absorb the resulting costs through lower pay, unpaid labor, longer and unplanned work hours, less time at home, and personal and physical inconvenience and risk. Traffic and weather cause drivers to lose lots of paid work time. Drivers quickly learn to meticulously plan hours or days in advance in order to avoid traffic congestion or bad weather. But customers are truckers' biggest problem. Shippers and receivers typically have little, if any, incentive to use drivers' time efficiently, and do little to get drivers in and out quickly. In fact, it can be in customers' interest to deliberately waste truckers' time. Customers may tell truckers to be available far in advance of when a load is likely to be ready, so they are there the instant freight can be loaded and hauled. Or customers may deliberately delay the delivery of loads to use a trucker's trailer as free storage space until scarce warehouse space and/or labor is available. Larger shippers that trucking firms can ill afford to say no to, like Wal-Mart, can systematically turn trucking companies' trailers and the unpaid time of truck drivers into free additional warehouse capacity.

A 1999 survey found that dry van drivers spent an average of 33.5 hours *per week* waiting for loads or loading and unloading. The average driver spent two hours waiting to load or unload per stop, 1.1 hours per stop loading, and 1.2 hours per stop unloading.[9] For the typical pay-per-mile driver nearly all of this time is unpaid. In several months of driving I was only paid twice for excessive waiting. In the instance described above, I was nominally paid a couple dollars per hour while waiting to deliver a load over the July 4th holiday. But since I received the weekly minimum of $500 for that week, the fact that I was credited for waiting didn't actually change my pay.

Typically, when I arrived at a customer location I had either a fixed appointment time or a loading window of a few hours. If I was simply dropping a loaded trailer off or picking up a preloaded trailer (know as a "drop and hook"), I usually performed at least an hour of unpaid labor dealing with shipping clerks, handling paperwork and other communications, and finding, inspecting, and attaching a trailer. I worked feverishly to minimize this time and get back to driving. More often I would wait while my trailer was "live" loaded or unloaded, which took anywhere from an hour to almost five hours. Given their powerlessness to reduce the time required to load and unload, drivers quickly realize that a key strategy is to take care of unpaid work (like trip planning, recording work hours, organizing the truck, etc.) and personal needs while they wait.

Besides taking care of all possible nondriving work during unavoidable down times and careful trip planning, the other key to maximizing productivity for drivers is managing the logbook in which they must record their work. Employers determine what work truckers do, but they do not control the most important rules for *how* truckers work. Those rules are set by the Federal Motor Carrier Safety Administration, which decides the basic nationwide regulations, known as Hours of Service (HOS), for over-the-road truckers. HOS require truckers to record their work in a logbook, which is essentially a month of charts and tables. Each chart represents a twenty-four-hour period. Truckers must record on these charts one of four different statuses (off duty, sleeper berth, driving, on duty not driving) in fifteen-minute blocks for every day of the year, including the days they do not work. Drivers must record duty status changes as they occur on these charts, which means that a driver's logbook must be up to date at the moment it is viewed. Whenever drivers change duty status to or from "driving," they must record their location by city or interstate mile marker. Logbook tables record the number of hours spent in each status per day and running counts of on-duty hours over the last seven and eight days. Enforcement of HOS is handled by state DOT officials at truck scales and roadside checkpoints and by police. The immediate accuracy of the logbook is the driver's legal responsibility.

Logbooks must be completed in pen, and drivers must acknowledge that they are true and accurate by signing each page as it is completed. Drivers found in violation can be fined thousands of dollars and have their commercial license revoked. Companies can be fined or even shut down if they do not ensure that drivers, including contractors hauling loads under the company's authority, are in compliance.

HOS rules have been the subject of more than a decade of contentious legislative and court battles between safety groups, the insurance industry, trucking industry groups, and regulators. Debate over the rules has been further complicated by the more recent question of whether logbooks should be replaced by onboard computers for recording and enforcing HOS. A detailed explanation of these debates is beyond the space available here. For our purposes, what matters is how truckers understand the rules and how they respond to them. When I drove, there were three basic HOS rules drivers recognized as important. First, drivers were allowed to spend no more than eleven hours actually driving without taking a ten-hour mandatory break (the eleven-hour rule). Second, if fourteen hours had passed since the end of their last ten-hour break, they could not drive any more, though they could continue to do other kinds of work (the fourteen-hour rule). So if a driver came on duty at 6:00 a.m., he could not drive after 8:00 p.m., regardless of how much time he had spent actually driving during that period. Third, drivers could spend a maximum of sixty hours over seven days or seventy hours over eight days on duty before they needed to stop driving (this rule is called the seventy-hour rule, because most drivers spend eight or more days on the road at a time). Work hours were reset to zero under the seventy-hour rule if a driver took an uninterrupted thirty-four-hour break, known as a "restart."

The CB term for a logbook is a "comic book," and it is common knowledge that HOS rules are routinely broken by most drivers on a daily basis. Most drivers simply believe HOS make no sense given the flexibility required by their work environment and schedules. For instance, drivers classify time they spend dealing with a shipper or consignee, filling out paperwork, or waiting while their truck is being loaded as off-duty hours, even though these should be "on duty not driving." Most drivers also don't count driving into or around facilities, backing into docks, or hooking or unhooking trailers as on-duty driving time. These practices add significantly to the number of hours they can drive under the seventy-hour rule. In fact, these practices are so engrained in their routine that most drivers don't consider them "real" violations at all. Knowing how to log to maximize productivity without creating obvious logbook violations, and gaining the confidence to do so, takes some experience. Truckers must coordinate all of the times, mileages, and required geographic makers recorded in their logbook so they seem reasonable given the impact of traffic patterns, weather, and the work performed. While some drivers committing regular serious violations consciously think about how to avoid detection, for the vast majority of drivers, daily regular violations of HOS are both justified and a routine part of doing the job.

Like four-wheelers who regularly drive 72 mph in a 65-mph zone, the vast majority of drivers commit only small violations, none of which they believe affect safety. But as experienced drivers know, these small violations add up to huge differences in productivity. Many drivers' strategy for HOS is to simply take the number of miles they drove, divide it by sixty, and then record the result as the number of hours driven over a particular period. This is partly because a driver may update a logbook before they leave a facility to start driving, but may not update it again until they are in a dock unloading. In between, there may be a lot of slow-speed driving, backing, and nondriving work. The rationale behind this is that an average of 60 mph will always be a defensible number, and a driver definitely does not want to needlessly reduce the hours available to them to work. But 60 mph grossly overestimates the speed at which drivers can perform the overall work. I detailed all of what should have been logged as driving time, relative to paid miles driven, and in a typical week I averaged roughly 40 mph.

I only had two interviewees who claimed that they logged according to the technical requirements of the law. I worked and logged like most of my interviewees. In a typical rotation I would log less than 65 percent of the hours I worked. This figure will seem outrageous to many familiar with the ongoing contentious debates about HOS regulations. But it is quite simple to explain and entirely consistent with other data, such as truckers waiting thirty to forty hours per work week at customer locations. While electronic onboard recorders can monitor the activity of trucks while they are driving, only drivers can know what they are doing when the engine is off. The fact is that drivers don't log waiting time as they should, as "on duty not driving." Though the law requires them to record this time as working, I never met an experienced trucker paid by the mile who did so. A typical driver stops counting time as "on duty driving" the minute he is off public roads. Time spent waiting in line, talking with clerks, waiting for a dock to open up, backing into a dock, waiting as the truck is loaded, closing up the trailer, pulling out of dock, etc., doesn't fit easily into the fifteen-minute blocks of a log book, so drivers don't log it accurately. If they spend two, three, or four hours at a shipper's location, they might, *might*, log one fifteen-minute interval at the start and another at the end of that period as "on duty not driving." The rest is logged as "off duty" or "sleeper-berth."

Not logging hours is not simply the result of deliberate misrepresentation; truckers really don't consider a lot of their work as stuff that should be logged as the law requires. As a result they will report working sixty-five or seventy hours a week, when according to the law and most people's definition of work—physically being on the job and performing required tasks as needed—most actually work closer to ninety or one hundred hours, as I did. I kept detailed records on the road of what I actually worked and what I logged using common practice. It is difficult to know exactly what the consequences of logging accurately would have been for my productivity, but simply assuming I would have had the same sequence of loads and spent the same number of days on the road, logging legally would probably have reduced my pay by at least 25 percent in some weeks. In the end, truckers know logging driving and nondriving time accurately would cost them a lot of miles, so there is significant economic incentive to view the unpaid work and waiting they do as "not really working." Truckers themselves, like their employers, diminish the importance and extent of this work when they think about their jobs and pay.

Although companies are supposed to ensure that drivers comply with HOS, how strictly they monitor drivers varies dramatically. All companies are required to review driver logbooks and store them for random audits or review in the case of accidents. A very small number of drivers told me their company encourages or forces them to commit serious violations. At the other extreme were a few drivers working for well-paying niche companies, which typically pay by the hour, that demanded perfect compliance with HOS, including nondriving hours.

However, with these few exceptions, most companies enforce the rules loosely and permit drivers to violate them as long as their logbooks appear legal and the violations are not egregious. Nearly all large carriers have quite sophisticated means to monitor drivers independent of logbooks, such as satellite-linked computers. But it is not in a carrier's interest to enforce HOS too strictly, unless the demonstrable costs in terms of safety are significant. Most large companies schedule loads according to the legal hours a driver reports having available to use, as registered in central computer systems.

Once a load is assigned, if a driver is delayed and needs an extra hour or so to get a load delivered on time, most companies let him have it. So if a driver drives twelve hours instead of eleven or drives after fourteen hours on duty, driver managers routinely let it slide. But if a driver drives fourteen hours instead of eleven or takes a six-hour mandatory break instead of ten, driver managers might verbally reprimand them. If such egregious and obvious driving-hour violations continually occur, a driver will eventually be fired by most companies. But company enforcement is almost always limited to actual time that a truck is moving on public roads. I never once heard of any company questioning the recorded hours for nondriving work, or the waiting time of a driver paid by the mile, something they have far less interest in monitoring.

Even though many large companies are moving to electronic logs, the widespread falsification of driver logs continues. In fact, because electronic logs can be edited and require drivers to manual enter on duty nondriving time, drivers employ the same basic strategies to falsifying electronic logs as they do paper logs. Electronic logs typically do not capture much of the slow-speed driving truckers do, and don't record what they are doing when not driving.

Comparisons to the Miles Game: Dedicated Routes and Driving for Wal-Mart

Not all truckers play the miles game. Drivers in niche markets are often paid by the hour. And more experienced drivers paid by the mile deintensify the game by working on a dedicated account that services a large shipper. While truckers hauling for these dedicated accounts may haul nonaccount freight several times during a rotation when account freight is not available, they tend to be assigned regular shipments to just a handful of locations.

Such an account has many advantages. First, the driver can become familiar with customer locations and driving routes and thus avoid predictable problems. Second, large shippers prefer to preload regularly scheduled shipments to save warehouse space, thus saving drivers the work and time associated with live loading. Third, regular routes most often mean regularly scheduled home time, as frequently as once a week and occasionally more. Finally, these accounts may be for relatively long loads.

I was randomly assigned to a dedicated account for a large consumer products manufacturer for one rotation. I hauled raw materials from suppliers to manufacturing plants, and finished products to customer stores and distribution centers. I was only out of compliance with HOS on one day during this eleven-day rotation. I earned $10.73 per hour worked, roughly $1.27 more than I averaged while playing the miles game. In terms of my pay per day, I earned $4.48 more per twenty-four hours than I did during the good rotation described above, and $10.78 more per twenty-four hours than I earned during the bad rotation.

I earned this greater pay without any significant self-sweating and very little stress compared to other rotations I worked for Leviathan. The load assignments were so much better that I could earn more for less work with less risk. My interviews with drivers working on dedicated accounts suggest that there is much less of an opportunity to self-sweat. These drivers still play the same basic game in terms of self-disciplining and planning in order to reduce problems and delays, but the constraints of these accounts limit the benefits of intensifying the game through greater self-sweating. The loads available under these accounts are limited, and trucks are assigned according to predetermined and relatively consistent volumes. It is unlikely that a driver on such an account will be dispatched on more loads and thus be able to drive more miles by delivering more quickly. In most cases, there is already a regularly scheduled load to which he will be assigned.

Another way out of the game is to work for private fleets. My experience driving within Leviathan's pay-per-mile system was put in stark contrast when they hired me out to Wal-Mart for five days. My job at Wal-Mart was to replace a regular company driver who was taking vacation time. Though I made pickups and deliveries more frequently than I did when dispatched by Leviathan, I was expected to run only one or two routes per day. Wal-Mart stores receive several regular truck deliveries a day from the nearest distribution center. A single route might involve picking up a loaded trailer at a distribution center and delivering to one or two stores. I would then pick up an empty trailer from the store or merchandise from a supplier and return to the distribution center. I did this around the Northeast. Several days I delivered to stores in New York State and was sent to my home parking location at night, allowing me to sleep at home. While my loads had all of the undesirable characteristics long-haul drivers try to avoid, such as lots of stops and shorter hauls, I made more money, committed no HOS violations, slept at home several times, and enjoyed the work far more.

I was paid $120 a day while driving for Wal-Mart, almost as much as I could expect to earn during my best rotation under normal dispatching. I earned an average of $11.32 per hour, roughly $1.80 or 19 percent more per hour worked than I earned playing the game. Receiving a set wage and delivering regularly scheduled loads made driving a fundamentally different experience. I wasn't rushing around, constantly trying to gain a few minutes here and a few minutes there. Most of the work was done during regular business hours. But I didn't worry, as I normally did, about what the traffic would be in the city up ahead. I wasn't even frustrated by the behavior of Wal-Mart's dock staff (though they were the least competent I had ever seen). I didn't have to spend time correcting bad directions or paperwork problems. Rather, I was relaxed and the job was enjoyable. I took care in everything I did. I certainly could have sped up the work to earn my pay in less time. But it just wasn't worth the stress. I talked with experienced drivers paid by the hour, and they reported similar kinds of behaviors and attitudes, as I will demonstrate in later chapters. There is little point in rushing and cutting corners when you are paid by the hour, or when the work available to you is essentially fixed.

OUTCOMES OF THE GAME

The trucking industry is as diverse as the freight hauling services needed in the American economy. Different products, production processes, and supply chain systems can require vastly different freight services. While general freight and similar truckload (TL) for-hire segments, such as refrigerated and flatbed hauling, are the largest employers of new and inexperienced drivers, dozens of other large and small labor markets, ranging from private fleets to expedited parcel services to bulk hazardous material hauling, employ a majority of truckers—roughly nine hundred thousand— in the US. Many of these segments provide much better wages and working conditions—for the right kind of drivers. Experienced drivers see themselves as workers dependent on companies for jobs, but as free to exercise control over the sale of their labor. They are confident that with a clean driving record and a solid work history they can easily find good jobs. This approach to the labor market comes from a fundamentally different understanding of the work of trucking.

Less experienced drivers take key aspects of the labor process for granted. For instance, in interviews, they *never* questioned the pay-by-mile system or suggested they should be paid for all of the unpaid work and waiting time required of them. Experienced drivers, on the other hand, see pay by mile as *the* critical problem. Out of concern for safety and stress, these drivers, while still breaking less important rules frequently, establish clear boundaries on self-sweating and seek consistent routines that limit the aspects of their game playing to issues of trip planning. In other words, most experienced drivers reject the miles game. They don't want *more miles*, they want better wages and consistent schedules, and focus on total take-home pay rather than miles.

> [I switched to a niche company because my former company's] famous thing was: if you want more money, run more miles . . . That is better? I make more money because I drive more miles? *God damn!* I had my six weeks of college, I know there is something wrong with that! That "more miles" shit is for the birds. It's a stupid mentality . . . If you get more miles, you are not going to get home . . . Just living your life in a truck and the world is passing you by . . . you are out there humping your ass off. It sucks.

And because they reject the miles game, experienced drivers don't see nondriving work as an obstacle to earning a good income. Driving is just one part of what they do, and what they do is just one part of the total business of trucking. Unlike inexperienced drivers, who saw driving as what made their companies successful, experienced drivers emphasized the critical role of things like sales, and firms' ability organize overall service to customers effectively and efficiently by coordinating a whole range of required labor.

For example, I interviewed a driver named Pete, a fifty-nine-year-old white male who was a contractor for six months in the 1980s. For fifteen years Pete has worked for a small company that does niche hauling and warehousing of TL and LTL shipments of food products. He is home most nights of the week and earns $13.50 an hour whether he is driving or not—even for time he spends off duty on the road overnight. He made $45,000 the year before I interviewed him. Here is how he described the way he is paid:

> I might sit at a dock . . . we have had a guy at a dock for thirty-two hours . . . you get paid for all that time . . . [And] there is no comparison . . . I wouldn't work any other way . . . There is so much that you do as a driver if you are getting paid by the mile that you don't get paid for. [I get paid for all the work I do and] if I have a real bad load, [my boss] will tell us to hire a [dockworker to unload the trailer] and go to bed, and we are still getting paid by the hour.

Pete understands the way he is paid as a result of the specific niche market of refrigerated hauling and warehousing that his company does. This service requires greater coordination of his labor activity with that of other workers and demands additional services, such as hand unloading and sorting of temperature-sensitive shipments. Whereas inexperienced drivers oftentimes never even see the freight they are hauling, let alone touch it, Pete is personally responsible for inspecting, handling, and caring for his cargo. His company's customers are willing to pay higher freight rates for this more complex service. Here is how he compared the way his work is organized to that of drivers at large TL companies, who are paid by the mile and provide lower-value services to some of the same companies.

> Everybody wants to pay by the mile . . . you have [companies] like High Tech, Big Red, the big ones, they go into those big warehouses too. But their guys get paid by the mile and they don't touch the freight [they sit unpaid, while they pay someone else to unload it and then the company reimburses them] . . . It's a mess, I don't want any part of it. Basically, they put the inefficiencies on the back of the driver . . . It has been going on forever, the driver has always been crapped on. Trucks are looked at as a source of revenue, free labor . . . [Drivers' shouldn't allow this but] a lot of them, their attitude is, this is your freight, you unload it. When I hired on with Davis Distributing, [the owner] sat down and told me exactly what I was responsible to do, "this is what we do as a company: we give good service, we do this, we do this, we do this. If you are unloading freight, you are getting paid for it, so don't worry about it."

Pete's loads often consist of smaller orders required for just-in-time production and lean inventory processes and, as a result, can be extremely time sensitive. Thus Pete's work is much more tightly scheduled and monitored than that of most over-the-road (OTR) truckers. Yet Pete sees benefits from this monitoring:

> Everything is customer, customer. And the customer . . . order[s] something from Hershey and Hershey says it will be brought out to you by Davis Distributing . . . and they know our website. They will punch it into the computer and find out where that order is and when we are going to deliver . . . [Mr. Davis] has put a lot of money into service . . . He gave us all Nextel cell phones . . . and he can punch my phone number into his computer and it will pop up on his screen with a map, with a little blue line [showing] where I left, the time I left, the route I took . . . And by the same token . . . let's say I got pulled over for speeding, he can punch it in and it can tell him, well, I am at mile marker 212 . . . and he can back it up a little bit and it gives the time of day and the speed, so we could fight it in court. That is fantastic.

Many inexperienced drivers, particularly contractors paid by the mile, deeply resented monitoring like this, often calling it "Big Brother" and seeing it as a potential barrier to the self-sweating they believed was essential for success. They found it insulting to them as professional drivers. Pete is not personally invested in a sense of autonomy in this regard. He embraces the ability of his employer to monitor him. He wants his employer to check in on him, because he knows it will demonstrate the value of the conscientious efforts that make him a valued driver. A driver like Pete follows the rules of road and HOS to the letter. He has no interest in breaking the law in order to self-sweat, and no incentive to do so. Experienced drivers paid by the mile feel similarly (though they are more likely to break minor rules frequently). Here is such a driver, who works a dedicated account for a better-paying general freight company, discussing satellite monitoring:

> I had an $800 logbook ticket [with my last company]. With [my current company] you can't run over your hours, you can't cheat the system. You have got to keep track of your hours on the computer. [With a paper] logbook you can run as far as you want, but you have to [falsify] your logs. [Company HOS enforcement] has kept me out of a lot of trouble . . . it has taken a lot of stress off . . . Before, I would push myself so hard that I would

get myself in trouble. Now I see it this way, it gets there when it gets there. If it is early, it's early, if it's late, it's late. At least I'm not dead and the freight is there safely . . . I still make enough money.

Experienced drivers know they must protect themselves and the value of their labor from risk—that is how their position in the labor market is improved. They see government rules as protecting them. Here is one driver describing why he likes HOS regulations:

> Driver: You can drive eleven hours then you got to take a ten-hour break . . . that is a safety thing for truck drivers [and everybody else] because a lot of people would just keep driving all night and that is why you have accidents and stuff . . . But I [follow the rules] because I have got my wife and three sons at home that I want to go back home to.
>
> SV: Because if the rules weren't there you would feel more pressure to make a little more money today?
>
> Driver: Oh, yeah! But I know my limitations. My wife says, "You know your limitations? Do you get sleepy?" . . . And if you get up in the morning, if you go for a couple hours and you feel sleepy, pull over. You'd rather get the load there in one piece than to kill somebody, and then you are going to jail and you are going to regret something like that. That is a good rule.

This is the kind of attitude that earns these drivers better wages from high-quality companies. A few years of self-sweating on the road teaches these drivers valuable lessons that determine their priorities. In contrast, here is the view of a less-experienced driver discussing the HOS rules:

> [HOS are] a big joke. They are spending money [developing and enforcing them] and no driver can tell you that he drives legally. [If he does] he is not a driver. If you drive legally, you don't make any money. Every driver drives fourteen, sixteen hours a day. They got like five different [logbooks], wherever they go, they fix the books. It is a big joke.

The organization of the labor process causes drivers to play certain games and develop particular habits and understandings of how the job should be done. Different kinds of trucking companies hire or produce very different drivers, with different skills and different outlooks. Drivers for large, general freight companies, like Leviathan, develop a sense of the industry in which the primary constraints are shippers, receivers, government, and the load-planning process. Leviathan and companies like it recruit and train workers completely unfamiliar with the trucking industry. As a result, these workers don't know any other way to truck. When difficulties arise and their company does not bend, these drivers are likely to see problems as inherent in their company, or in trucking more generally, and not as being about the kind of freight they haul, the customers they service, or the organization of the labor process in that segment of the industry. In part this is simply because these inexperienced workers have no experience with any alternative, and the company does not present itself as a *particular kind* of trucking company.

The implicit and explicit messages from companies like Leviathan are that they are the result of market forces freed by deregulation, they are the leaders of the industry, the cutting edge, the future. If you are entering the trucking industry and want to have a successful career, they are *your* future. If there are alternatives, they are not long for this world. *You* need to be flexible, because this is the way trucking is.

These companies produce cheap drivers with limited skills and employ them to handle cheap freight for large customers that require drivers to do little more than back into the dock and pick up the load. The inexperienced truckers I talked to chafed under the load-planning systems of these companies. They resented, sometimes even hated, their supervisors. Their work and their pay were subject to the whims of countless others who were unconcerned about how much money was needed to pay the bills at home or how much unpaid work truckers did. But these truckers found a sense of control in the game of trying to run as many miles as possible, and they played it with great zeal. They thought that if they were stuck out on the road, they might as well work, and when they were working they might as well make as much as they could. Unfortunately, at low pay rates these drivers are rarely satisfied for long with this labor process, given their compensation and the tremendous effects on the rest of their lives and their families. And they begin to look for something better.

If inexperienced drivers are aware of other kinds of driving jobs, when they apply the logic of the game to them, they find most alternatives unappealing. Accustomed to cutting corners, breaking laws, and viewing non-driving parts of the job as obstacles to higher pay that need to be dispensed with as quickly and efficiently as possible, these drivers are incapable of servicing the high-paying customers that are better employers. They have no interest in putting extra time into things like short loads, good customer service, or working under systems, like less-than-truckload, that require more coordination with other workers.

When drivers apply the logic of the game to contracting, however, they will reach a very different conclusion. Their experience tells them that better working conditions and higher pay can only be achieved through more miles. More miles, in turn, require control over the big decision that affects the game: load assignments. After a few months or a year, these drivers understand the critical role played by load assignments, and they want control over them. Firms promise that contracting will provide that control and all the miles a driver could ever want.

A Man's World: A Brief Note on Women in Trucking

In the course of my own time working as a trucker I never encountered a female driver after training. I did interview two female drivers and met several women who had worked as truckers in the past. Scholars have commented on the important role masculinity plays in the work and attitudes of truckers.[10] Yet employers are eager to recruit more women into trucking. There have been a number of efforts by individual carriers and industry groups to attract women to the industry. Some suggest that the industry needs to do a better job recruiting women by changing the way it portrays the job to women and even to girls, by highlighting female drivers and downplaying the traditionally masculine approaches to recruiting.[11] However, while major efforts have been made to promote the job to women, some of them seem to be wildly off the mark, such as *Overdrive's* annual Most Beautiful contest, which allows truckers to nominate and vote on the most beautiful female trucker. *Overdrive's* editors clearly note that "inner" beauty is important, and the contest, modeled after a beauty pageant, is meant to demonstrate that trucking and femininity are not incompatible. Unfortunately, encouraging the objectification of female truckers will, if anything, likely increase the obstacles they face on the job.

In fact, the world of trucking is *hyper*-masculine and is seen that way by drivers—a fact I experienced and deliberately highlighted in the descriptions of my work at the start of this chapter. Interestingly, while they used somewhat different language to describe their feelings, the two female drivers I interviewed took as much, if not more, pride in the masculine aspects of operating heavy equipment and life on the road as the average male driver. However, it was quite clear from talking to these women that there were obvious and important differences between the experiences of male and female drivers. Only 4 to 6 percent of all truck drivers are women. Though companies like Leviathan appear to be able to attract enough women to make up almost 10 percent of their trainees, among solo long-haul drivers, women probably account for fewer than one in a hundred drivers. And, despite the focus on the "image" problems that are often faulted by the industry, the challenges of recruiting more women into the job are numerous and fundamental.

First, women do not often have the kinds of manual blue-collar jobs and experience (such as long hours in construction work or operating heavy equipment) that prepared the most successful male workers for life as truck drivers. Second, and perhaps most obviously from the perspective of gender, as the descriptions of the work above suggest, the routines of truckers are, short of migrant labor, about as family-unfriendly as one can imagine. Indeed, a woman would need to abandon key notions of traditional motherhood in order to work as a long-haul trucker if she had children at home. The difficulty of balancing fatherhood with life on the road was extraordinarily difficult for male truckers, even though some attempted to justify their sacrifice by valorizing the masculine aspects of leaving home and hearth to provide a solid income for their family.[12] In fact, though, many of my male interviewees were deeply troubled by the effects the job had on their relationships with their children and their spouses. Many felt trapped in what seemed like a caricature of the strong father. They reported returning home to a "honey-do" list of male-associated tasks, such as mowing the lawn or fixing things, but also to requests from their partner to discipline children who had misbehaved in their absence. Most felt they were too often "playing the bad guy," and too rarely enjoying quality time getting to know and play with their children in positive ways. Indeed, as an interviewer, it was clear to me that the effects of long absences from home on parenting and romantic relationships were by far the most emotionally challenging subjects for drivers. It is difficult

to imagine how women would negotiate the demands of traditional motherhood with such absences. During the ten years I was conducting my
research, I never met a female trucker who had children still at home.

Even if a woman is attracted to the industry and does not have family
or other obligations that conflict with the lifestyle, trucking is still almost
entirely a man's world. Though some aspects of the job are "dirty" and
require traditionally male work, like dealing with fuel and oil, coupling
trailers, applying chains, etc., there is almost nothing inherent to the job
physically that would make women less able to perform it.[13] Unfortunately,
from what my two female interviewees told me, as a work environment
the trucking industry presents tremendous potential obstacles for female
drivers nonetheless.

Take, for example, the experiences of Cathy, one of the female drivers I
interviewed. She is fifty, divorced, and has three children who are grown
and out of the house. She completed ten years of school and then got a
GED. Cathy had been driving solo for less than a year. She had entered the
industry after being laid off from her manager position at an auto parts
store, where she had worked for seven years. She returned home about
once a month. She was working for the carrier that initially hired her out
of a CDL school associated with the carrier.

Cathy didn't find the job physically difficult, but she found it "psychologically" difficult. She found the job lonely and hated being away from
home.

> Getting home, *forget it!* You tell them what state you live in and that state
> falls off the map for you. Whenever the planner goes to run your route, you
> are laughing because, I am not kidding you, whenever they bring you up on
> that screen, that state has to be in red [on] their computers, because you
> don't go anywhere near that [and] when I request time off I can pretty much
> guarantee that I will be two days late.

Beyond that, Cathy said, was a work environment filled with the constant
threat of sexual harassment or violence. As Christine Williams has argued,
work in all-male occupations encourages outward displays of men's masculinity. Men erect barriers to women crossing over into all-male occupations to maintain their masculinity.[14] In trucking those barriers are
ubiquitous.

As Cathy relates, and as I heard myself, female drivers will often be sexually harassed over CB radio while working and at truckstops.

And the CB, oh my God . . . The people that are on there, they make people online look pleasant. They are filthy, degenerate, there just isn't any way to explain them, it is wrong . . . I get so sick of hearing about fat women. All of their jokes and comments and everything and these guys, it is not like they are beauty queens. Driving down the road I can't even tell you how many times I have had guys pull up next to me and say "show me your tits." Where in life would this happen to you? Would you walk up to someone in Wal-Mart and go, "Hey, did you show me your tits?"

Cathy also felt scared working alone at night, particularly when she needed to pick up or drop off trailers in poorly lit or remote drop lots. After telling me about these concerns, Cathy told me that several times, when she responded to harassment over the radio, she was threatened:

Since I have been in the truck I have been threatened to be killed twice and raped once [over the CB] . . . the guys can say what they want, but God help you if you are a female and say a comment back to them.

Cathy felt relatively safe inside truck stops themselves, but she also limited her activity in rest area and truck stop parking lots as well. Cathy said she had gained sixty pounds since she started driving. She blamed the fact that she had quit smoking and that she couldn't get any exercise. If she walked around the truckstop, she feared being taken for a prostitute working the parking lot (a "lot lizard" in trucker lingo), and harassed:

You can't get out and walk around and exercise. Yeah, okay, when you get out and walk around the truck stop, "lot lizard!," no thank you. I don't need the harassment, I don't need to be harassed by cops. I don't need the harassment of truck drivers.

She said that other male drivers policed harassing drivers, but it didn't change the fact that she had to protect herself:

And don't get me wrong, because there are 90 to 94 percent of the truck drivers out there are going to give those guys that are making comments shit. There is only like 6 to 10 percent that are really truly assholes . . . These kind of people hide behind things, and they're going to harass no matter what you do or how you do it. They are just cowards and degenerates and this is the way that they get their jollies. So there is nothing that you're going to be able to do to stop them . . . You just have to avoid them.

Cathy had already decided she would not remain in the industry much longer. She was only staying because the carrier was paying $150 a month toward the $7,000 she owed for her CDL training. She was considering going back to school to get trained as medical transcriptionist, which she had heard was a good-paying job in high demand. Of course, this is also the kind of office based female-dominated job that will make it much less likely for her to experience the kind of sexual harassment she has repeatedly encountered in long-haul trucking. Attempts like this to escape sexual harassment, of course, contribute to the continuation of occupational sex segregation.

3 The Big Rig

RUNNING THE CONTRACTOR CONFIDENCE GAME

ON A MISSION

If we had to boil it down, long-haul truckers have two main problems: low hourly wages and a lack of control over their work in terms of scheduling and working conditions. Many inexperienced truckers come to believe that contracting is the solution to both those problems.

For example, take Joe, a would-be contractor I interviewed. He is an unmarried, thirty-eight-year-old black male with no children and one year of college. About a year before I interviewed him, Joe left a job as a car-parts salesman and became a trucker because, he said, he liked to drive and wanted to make good money and see the country. He was trained as a trucker at a community college trucking school with assistance from his state's employment office, and had been working since then for a carrier with about one hundred trucks.

Joe was eager to talk to me, and we spoke for more than two hours. I began with the basic questions I used to start all my interviews. I asked Joe how often he returns to Forth Worth, Texas, which he called home. He told me that in the nine months he had been working as a trucker he had not returned home once. I then asked how many miles he was driving per week, a standard measure of productivity for drivers. He hesitated and looked at my questionnaire with a raised eyebrow. I repeated to him that the interview was completely anonymous. He said he was running about 3,600 miles a week. Before I could stop myself, a surprised look crossed my face, and Joe replied with a smile: "Me, I don't go home. I stay out. I am on call 24/7. I have been on the road nine months. I am on a mission, man. I am serious . . . *Yeah, I run.*" Joe was driving himself hard and clearly working far beyond the legal limits set for long-haul truckers by federal law. I did some rough math in my head and realized Joe was probably working more than a hundred hours in most weeks. Living out of his truck, without rent or other regular bills, Joe was happy with what he was earning overall. He knew he could not keep up the intensity of his work routine forever, but he believed he was just beginning to taste the financial success trucking could provide. Joe was planning to become a contractor, and he was convinced it could give him a more sustainable work schedule and a lot more money.

> I am on a mission, man . . . I believe [after five years of contracting], you could be taking money and investing it, I believe in a good seven to ten years you can be a millionaire, if you stay focused, stay disciplined.

Joe was certain he wanted to be a contractor when I met him, but he was still trying to answer some difficult questions and was getting conflicting advice. His current company was offering to lease him a truck that he could buy at the end of a multiyear term and then contract his services on a yearly basis using that truck, a common arrangement called a lease-purchase. Several contractors that he had encountered from other companies had discouraged him from this arrangement because, they argued, it would give the company too much control over him. They told him to save up money and buy a used truck from a dealership instead.

Despite this advice, Joe was leaning toward the lease-purchase for several reasons. He had heard that breakdowns were a common problem for contractors and was worried about the maintenance a used truck could require. His carrier was offering an extended warranty on all major components of the used truck they were offering to sell him. Based on the financial numbers the company had provided him, Joe was sure he could pay off the truck quickly and have more take-home pay. He also liked the idea of staying with his carrier, because they consistently gave him lots of miles, and he figured if they were holding the note on his truck they'd likely continue to do that.

Joe was also concerned about conflicting views he was hearing about how much money he could make as a contractor. It is worth listening at length to Joe talk about these views and what he thinks will make him successful:

> I am getting a lot of feedback as far as what [contractors earn in take-home pay] . . . I have heard people who make this much and some people don't make that much. Some people say, "That is crazy, there is no way that that guy makes that much . . ." I am like, "If those guys have been out here forever, they know what they are talking about." But then how is it this other person . . . [is] saying that they are [making a lot of money]? So I say, "What are these people doing differently?" . . . You know, if you are serious about making your money, and not like everybody says, "Well, I am serious about making it too." But they go off and they do other things with it and they get distracted and they don't do as much work. They get comfortable, they relax, they don't do as many miles. Just different things come into play and then they will use the excuse of, "You can't really make that kind of money because of all of the variables and things." No, it is just because you lost focus. So . . . if somebody says that they can, that you can do it—then I pretty much believe that you can. And not just one person. I said, well, maybe this is just this one person that got lucky, like winning the lottery. Well, let me make sure that this isn't just a lucky thing that happened to this guy. And it is not easy, you know, from what I have heard, it is not easy.

Joe's account of how disciplined effort can determine success epitomizes the thinking of would-be contractors. He wants to realize the American Dream of small business ownership and upward mobility. Joe is hard-working and ambitious—he's already working harder than most readers can probably imagine. In fact, Joe is exactly the kind of hard-working, risk-taking person our economic system is supposed to reward. He's actively trying to figure out the best decision to ensure his economic future. And though he hopes to make it big, he is not looking for a get-rich-quick scheme. He's willing to invest and risk his time and money for years. He's carefully weighing the choice between traditional employment and self-employment, and considering the risks of each by talking to existing contractors and potential employers, and reading trucking magazines and business manuals for contractors. Joe's doing everything he can to make the best labor market decision.

Unfortunately, what Joe and thousands of other truckers like him don't know is that the decision they face and most of the information they will use to make it are carefully crafted by trucking employers and associated businesses to convince them to become contractors, a decision that far too often results in financial and personal disaster.

Just as in the past, bad working conditions and low pay push truckers to look for something better. But today, rather than forming unions, truckers want to become contractors. They become contractors because they don't know what the consequences will be. If the story ended there, we might just chalk the whole thing up to an information problem; workers make employment decisions under conditions of uncertainty, and employers have more and better information than workers. But the story doesn't end there—not by a long shot. The reason that most truckers become contractors is because they are systematically influenced by a set of labor market institutions that favor the interests of employers. The choice to become a contractor is not simply a bad decision that results from carelessness or lack of effort by workers to learn about contracting. Far from it. Most workers consider the decision extremely carefully. But the decision-making process they go through is the outcome of labor market institutions that shape almost everything—from their individual experience on the job, to industry-wide class relations, to the industry's wider economic and regulatory contexts—to favor employers.

DUSTED OFF AND RECAST: THE REBIRTH OF THE OWNER-OPERATOR

After deregulation, trucking firms needed cheap labor and therefore turned to contractors. They also used contractors as a way to avoid the risk of owning trucks in the chaotic and hypercompetitive markets immediately following deregulation. Opportunities available to existing owner-operators and for employees to become contractors increased dramatically.[1] Research suggests that carriers that increased their use of contractors benefited from critical cost savings.[2] Carriers who did not adopt the use of contractors were much more likely to go bankrupt during this period.[3] In other words, in the first years after deregulation using contractors was a survival strategy for many carriers. In 1986, 85 percent of carriers reported that they intended to increase the use of contractors.[4] But the shift to contractor labor was short-lived.

Despite carrier interest, by the mid-1980s this labor supply was declining rapidly, as intense competition and plummeting freight rates bankrupted many contractors. The most profitable companies—the AFTL firms discussed in the last chapter—now made their profits through more efficient use of employee drivers. An academic article on the subject at the time stated that these new companies had explicitly rejected

> owner-operator use as incompatible with the achievement of efficiency and cost goals . . . [They] have found that use of company drivers (non-union) allows them to purchase capital goods (particularly tractors and trailers) in large quantities and achieve discounts of up to 20 percent. They have found the company non-union drivers to be more productive, more reliable and safer than are the owner-operators, based on past experiences.[5]

The article concluded, "There are unmistakable signals that owner-operators may well be driven off into the sunset."[6] Contractors were being squeezed by declining rates and could not afford to invest in their equipment, which resulted in poor customer service and a loss of productivity. The high asset utilization rates achieved by profitable truckload companies that emerged after deregulation required that trucks be dependable, and that drivers accept every load that was assigned to them by the increasingly sophisticated load planning systems that were being developed. Contractors, while appealing in terms of low pay and reducing capital costs and the likelihood of unionization, were seen as unwilling or unable to submit to the dispatching requirements and maintenance schedules required by these firms. Within just a few years, the number of loads hauled by owner-operators dropped dramatically.[7]

From the late 1980s to the mid-1990s, the leading truckload carriers generally favored nonunion employee labor. But deteriorating pay and working conditions were causing the extremely high levels of employee turnover discussed in previous chapters. In an attempt to retain drivers longer and gain the cost advantages of contractors, carriers once again turned to contractors in the mid-1990s. But contractors clearly did not fit with the organizational need carriers had for control and reliability. So firms began consciously transforming labor market institutions to create a new kind of contractor that would fit their needs. Here is how one editorial in 1998 explained the transformation:

> Fleets bent on filling empty driver seats with independent contractors must work to fit square pegs neatly into round holes. It's tough work driving a square peg into a round hole. Unless you have a big enough sledgehammer—or better yet, a fine enough chisel to ensure a clean, smooth fit . . . Only a few years ago conventional wisdom still regarded company-owned and operated equipment as the most efficient and least risky way to haul freight. Owner-operators, so went this thinking, were valuable only as a means to quickly and cheaply grow—or shrink—a fleet. By the late '80s, owner-operators were out of vogue . . . they were written off by fleets as lacking the foresight and capital to keep pace with changing times . . . [But today] The knights of the road are being dusted off and recast as viable entrepreneurs vital to trucking's future. By their own hard work and example, thousands of individuals have helped forge a new identity for the owner-operator as a can-do, can-succeed businessperson. That has helped fleets not to view the use of independent contractors as a "control issue" . . . [T]hese contractors are less likely to contribute to "churn" than company drivers and casual owner-operators, who risk little upon leaving.[8]

The use of the phrases "dusted off and recast" and "forge a new identity" are indicative of the nature of this rebirth of contractors. After deregulation, truckers became contractors seeking control over loads, which they believed would translate into more money and home time. But choosing loads and home time was fundamentally at odds with the way the dominant truckload firms ensured efficiency. Carriers needed to create a whole new kind of contractor, one that saw taking whatever load was offered to them not as companies telling them what to do, but as doing what it takes to meet the needs of their customers and a smart way to run their own small business.

Companies have succeeded in doing that, and today's contractors are very different from those of the past in a number of ways. In the mid-1970s a majority of owner-operators were union members in many segments; virtually none are today.[9] Just before deregulation 33 percent of all owner-operators owned more than one truck, and 16 percent owned more than five trucks.[10] By 1997 less than 14 percent of owner-operators owned more than one truck and less than 2 percent owned more than five trucks.[11] Only one of the owner-operators I interviewed in my initial set of seventy-five interviewees had ever employed another driver. Perhaps most importantly, by 1997 90 percent of contractors received their payments through a permanent lease to haul freight exclusively for a single company.[12] In contrast, only 50 percent of owner-operators were under leases of thirty days or more in the mid-1970's, and most of these drivers retained the right to haul for other carriers. Many were union members.[13] Today contractors are paid a fixed rate per mile. Because they are dependent on loads from a single carrier for all of their revenue, they are very unlikely to refuse loads. Before deregulation, 75 to 80 percent of contractors were paid a percentage of the load revenue, which caused them to turn down loads and wait for better-paying ones.[14] Though carriers now appear to be making a strong push toward percentage pay to shift more risk to drivers (as discussed in Chapter 5), in 2005, only 10 percent of large carriers even offered contractors the chance to be paid a percentage of load revenue.[15]

Today, contractors are the preferred labor for carriers. Nearly all large truckload firms use contractors to haul a significant amount of their freight.[16] Quite simply, contractors are a critical source of cheap and flexible labor. The president of the Truckload Carriers Association explained why in 2004:

> It's pretty clear that truckload companies have been the ones that have struggled the most on what we can offer for labor ... Historically [wage increases] have been used before, but as a whole, I don't think we've found you can raise wages enough for prospective drivers to not take construction or other jobs ... [contractors] have a lot at risk, with the volatility of fuel and the component costs [but] are more of a sought-after resource ...[17]

Exact figures don't exist, and the numbers fluctuate significantly, but as many as two to three hundred thousand of long-haul TL trucking's roughly eight hundred thousand drivers have been working as contractors in recent years. Companies gain four main advantages by using contractors. First, they are legally self-employed and thus do not receive employer-paid health and retirement benefits, nor do they require employer contributions to Social Security and Medicare or worker's compensation and unemployment insurance. This can save firms as much as 30 percent in labor costs. Second, because contractors own their trucks and pay for fuel, maintenance, and insurance, firms can potentially shift significant capital and operating costs to them. Third, though contractors are legally required to have control over their work and be free to choose who they work for, they are generally under greater pressure than employees to accept whatever work is offered to them. This is because they are dependent on that firm for all of their revenue and must work almost constantly to meet fixed expenses and earn take-home pay. Because of their financial vulnerability and the costs involved in switching firms, they feel less free than employee drivers to quit bad firms. Fourth, contractors are seen as less likely and able to unionize. In short, contractors are cheaper and more compliant than comparably skilled employee drivers—that's why firms use them.

Given the benefits for companies, the obvious question is: what's in it for the contractors? Well, the answer to that question depends on who you ask. The trucking industry's employers, lawyers, and lobbyists are quick to point out that truckers voluntarily *choose* to be contractors because they see lots of advantages. For instance, in a letter to the US Government Accountability Office regarding that agency's 2009 study of worker misclassification (i.e., when workers who should be treated as employees are instead classified as self-employed), the American Trucking Associations (ATA) argued that contractors want to start their own businesses and "live out their own version of the American Dream." The letter cited a survey that found contractors feel strongly about their independent status and want control over their time at home and work environments. It argued, "Indeed, given the historical driver shortage in the trucking industry, owner-operators would have little difficulty finding work as employee drivers. However, they *choose* independent contractor status because of the benefits and opportunities" (emphasis in original).[18]

But contrary to the ATA's claims, there is no hard evidence from any study that suggests that contractors do better than comparable employees on any measurable outcome. In fact, as the next chapter will show, once we take experience into account truckers are likely to be far worse off as contractors than as employees. Most contractors enjoy neither economic nor workplace benefits of any meaningful kind. It is no surprise, then, that the ATA defends the use of contractors by citing workers' desires, expectations, and goals rather than data about *real* benefits of contracting. Still, in a sense, ATA's argument is true—workers choose contracting voluntarily because of its *perceived* benefits. The rest of this chapter will explain how those perceptions are created.

CREATING THE CAN-DO, CAN-SUCCEED CONTRACTOR

Before they come into the industry, almost no workers have any knowledge about or interest in contracting. Within a few years, most who remain will see contracting as a realistic possibility. A pervasive set of interconnected ideas that I will refer to as the "contracting discourse" shapes truckers' understanding of the industry and leads many to buy a truck, become legally self-employed, and lease their services to a company. This discourse is part of carefully coordinated efforts that ensure that workers are exposed to these ideas every day on the job through company communications and at truck stops, company trainings, industry trade shows, and in a wide range of print, electronic, and radio media. While carriers are the ultimate beneficiaries of these efforts, they rely on numerous third parties to help them not only to recruit contractors but to manage and retain them for as long as possible.

The Contracting Discourse

The starting point of the contracting discourse is the idea that contracting is the "next step" on the "road to success" for truckers. It is a promotion, a vote of confidence, and a step up from being an employee or worker to being one's own boss—a small business entrepreneur.

The discourse makes contracting seem a natural and reasonable step by focusing exclusively on cost-efficient operation and disciplined work schedules as the keys to contractors' success, things that company drivers already know how to do because of the miles game they play. Beyond the game, inexperienced drivers have a limited understanding of what goes into making a trucking company successful. Most have no sense of what customers pay to ship freight, and little specific knowledge of how and why freight rates vary. The inexperienced drivers I talked to would not even hazard a guess at what their companies charged customers for the freight they haul. They have little or no direct knowledge of the specifics of how new customers and freight to haul are found by salespeople. Isolated from these activities, deliberately so in most cases, these drivers understand the work they do as the most important work in trucking. As far as they are concerned, they do everything important associated with the load aside from negotiating price with customers. As a result, these drivers believe success through owning a truck will result from three things: the right to refuse bad loads, driving lots of miles, and cutting truck operation costs (primarily through fuel efficiency).

The discourse cautions that contracting is "not for everybody," and thus provides an individualized way to understand the negative views of contracting that inexperienced drivers may have encountered. Failure is almost always portrayed as the result of a driver being undisciplined or not managing his money properly. For instance, one director of truck leasing for a major carrier suggested in an article aimed at would-be contractors that his company had great success with the driver "who manages his time and money and truly has a desire to make it work."[19]

The contracting discourse acknowledges the risks but emphasizes that despite these, many truckers have used contracting to become successful businesspeople. Some large carriers point to their own origins as one-truck companies and tout their success as a model for contractors. Such stories argue that success is about hard work, risk, sacrifice, and entrepreneurial spirit—things that often resonate with inexperienced truckers, who are sacrificing much of the rest of their lives and working grueling hours as long-haul drivers. Such drivers would frequently cite the history of their employer or prominent carriers in interviews as justification for their interest in becoming or remaining contractors. Here is how Roehl Transport, a company with $275 million in annual revenue and over seventeen hundred trucks, presents its history as a model to follow in a "business manual" it publishes and makes freely available for contractors:

> In 1962, company founder Everett Roehl began his business, just like you, with one truck. Roehl Transport has continued to grow every year since beginning operations in 1962 . . . And it has a plan to help its owner operator partners grow their businesses and be successful just like the company founder.[20]

As this quote suggests, carriers are not only models for contractors, but also partners eager and well equipped to help contractors realize their dreams. Carriers portray contracting as a business partnership of equals. They promise drivers complete control over miles and home time, the right to refuse loads, and dramatically higher income. At the same time, carriers caution truckers that contracting can be a risky endeavor given the competitive nature of trucking, and they need a business partner they can rely on. For instance, the Roehl manual states:

> For many professional drivers, [contracting is] the most exciting, rewarding trip you'll ever take . . . [W]hen you're good at your job, you will profit from your superior skill and hard work. But like any road trip, you need a good map—a plan that tells you which turns to take and what roads to avoid; one with checkpoints along the way that assures you're heading in the right direction and making progress, yet flexible enough to adjust to changing conditions. In today's tenuous business environment, it helps to have a solid business partner that understands the route. And when it comes to putting owner operators on the road to success Roehl Transport is a partner you can trust.[21]

Independent owner-operating without a carrier partnership, on the other hand, is portrayed as difficult and risky. An independent can fall prey to unscrupulous brokers, who take large cuts of load revenues, take weeks or months to pay truckers for the loads they haul, and may not pay them at all. Contractors need carriers to secure good loads on a regular basis in highly competitive freight markets. Contractors should focus on the job of driving—which is the real revenue generator in trucking, according to the contracting discourse—and leave the activities that support that work up to the carriers. The Roehl manual states:

> The fact is brokers and load boards are not a predictable or reliable source of steady business. And any time you'd spend selling your services to shippers is downtime and a cost to your business—not an income generating activity. When you team with Roehl on the other hand, you don't need to worry about where your next load will come from. Nor will you be in the position of having to take less desirable freight just to keep revenue flowing.[22]

In order to address concerns that carriers exploit contractors, carriers differentiate themselves from "other programs" less advantageous to contractors. An article aimed at would-be contractors stated:

Figure 1

[L]ast December M. S. Carriers began offering an equipment lease /purchase plan to help qualified drivers get into business for themselves. "Unlike other carriers that regard these plans as profit centers," [a company executive stated], "our intention is to help create 'real' owner-operators."[23]

Carriers suggest that contracting is a means to class mobility. Under the headline "Dream," the recruiting ad in Figure 1 claims that this carrier's lease-purchase program helps drivers live the American Dream by becoming successful business owners.

Recruiting magazines are also filled with ads that make deceptive claims about the amount of money drivers can earn as contractors. These ads are often visually structured around income figures suggesting contractors can "make up to" some outrageous amount of money. One ad from a company called Megatrux Transportation claimed first year solo contractors earned $175,000 or more a year and their first year teams

$370,000 or more a year. The ad also stated that the average length of haul for its contractors is 2,100 miles (the average length of haul for a typical OTR driver is now less than five hundred miles), and that the average pay per mile is $1.25 (the average TL driver earns thirty-six cents per mile). Length of haul and pay per mile are the two basic metrics employees use to assess pay relative to the game they play.

Other ads are far more sophisticated. Figures 2 and 3 show two facing pages from one ad that addresses issues of control and class mobility by suggesting that workers can "be their own boss" and "own and operate their own trucking business." The idea of business partnership is promoted by statements that the carrier has everything a contractor "needs to succeed." In fact the ad implies that, just like the carrier in Figure 1, this carrier is not only a firm organized to make a profit, but may be a vehicle for emancipating workers from dependence on the wage relationship: "Since 1934, Dart has been a place where working people make the American Dream come true."

But these ads are far more nuanced than they may initially appear to a nontrucker. The truck pictured in Figure 2 is one that a driver with even a few months of experience would recognize as the quintessential independent owner-operator rig. It is a premier brand, Peterbilt—there is even a magazine for Peterbilt owners called *Pride and Class*. This particular Peterbilt is loaded with a number of expensive chrome accents (e.g. sun visor, bumper, tool boxes, dual straight exhaust pipes) and extra lights, which all clearly suggest this truck is owned by a worker with the right and money to customize it. In contrast, the ad on the facing page, Figure 3, pictures two trucks on the opposite end of the prestige scale. Over the words "You can afford it" are two cheaper brands of trucks typically driven by employees at large low-cost carriers. This page describes the trucks the carrier is offering to lease, *which do not include Peterbilts.*

Why would a company deliberately contrast the less-attractive trucks they are leasing with a premier brand? Because these images visually embody the promise of class mobility in the terms of drivers' day-to-day experience. These ads and images validate truckers' understanding of what will determine success, and their concern about the transition from employee to contractor. A trucker with even minimal experience knows that the Peterbilt shown is likely to be much less fuel efficient, with its

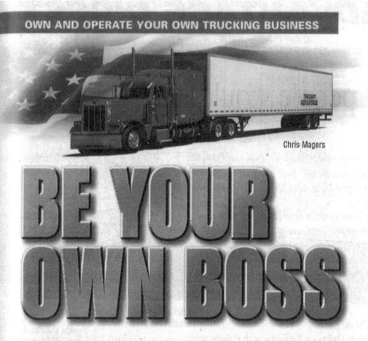
Figure 2

Figure 3

square nose and other nonaerodynamic features. The text in Figure 3 focuses on fuel efficiency as the key to profitability: Dart is offering "high MPG" trucks. This is consistent with the contracting discourse's focus exclusively on cost control per mile, rather than on revenue generation per mile, as the best strategy for success. These trucks aren't fancy, but they are comfortable enough to make a trucker fuel efficient and productive, i.e., the driver can work and live in it for the long periods of time that will be required to run the many miles he will need to succeed.

The Peterbilt will also be intimidating to less-experienced drivers (it intimidates me), because this truck is likely to have a thirteen-, fifteen-, or eighteen-speed transmission. Nearly all drivers at large carriers drive a truck with a ten-speed transmission, as I did. If I were to get behind the wheel of that Peterbilt, my first attempt to drive it would certainly be an embarrassing disaster. Though I have the basic skills to operate it, the truck would lurch, lug, and stall, as I repeatedly ground the gears in an attempt to learn the shifter locations and how to sync these with a more powerful engine.

Inexperienced truckers will also know that the Peterbilt, with all its extras, costs a lot more than the trucks on the opposite page, resulting in far higher weekly payments and requiring a much larger down payment. This truck is likely to have not only a more complex transmission, but a high-horsepower engine. These might make sense for truckers hauling specialized high-value freight, such as oversized loads like heavy equipment—work performed exclusively by highly skilled and experienced drivers, who are far more likely to be independents, not contractors.

The Peterbilt, in other words, represents independent owning, with all of the additional experience, skills, and capital that requires. Together, what the images suggest is: "Go ahead and dream about the day when you will be an independent, but the best move for you right now is to be a contractor. We are not going to try to sell you more truck than you need. You understand the importance of fuel efficiency, so buy this truck, which will maximize your profit. Becoming a contractor feels like a big step, but you have the skills and knowledge you need (you'll be driving the same kind of truck), and as you gain experience you will be able to develop even further." Thus in subtle ways this carrier has reinforced the notion of a career path and the potential for class mobility, while validating at the same time both the concerns and the understanding the potential contractor has about what will make him a successful small businessperson.

SELLING CONTRACTING TO DRIVERS

Truckers may be exposed to the contracting discourse before they even learn to drive a truck. In particular, third-party labor recruiters and private driving schools use the notion of a career path to attract potential drivers to the industry. Carriers may first educate workers about contracting during training, when they provide descriptions of the kinds of arrangements drivers can have in a firm (labor consultants advise carriers that creating the sense of a career path is an important means to retain drivers for longer periods).[24] Some carriers promote multiple stages of employment, ending in contracting, to would-be drivers with no experience at all in the industry (e.g., trainee, then employee, then contractor). Truckers are often then exposed to the contracting discourse extensively on the job. Firms use company communications and terminals to advertise contracting opportunities.

Some carriers promote contracting through more aggressive means. Several drivers told me about their managers' attempts to get them to buy a truck that involved showing them the paperwork for loads that they had actually hauled. These managers stressed the difference between the gross revenue of the load and drivers' pay, suggesting that there was significantly more to be made as a contractor. These drivers told me their managers repeated these efforts several times.

Other firms use a more coercive approach to convert employees into contractors by simply eliminating employee positions, leaving workers with the choice of becoming a contractor or finding a job elsewhere. I interviewed the owner of a company that offered its employees this choice, and more than half chose to buy a truck. Some carriers expand their contractor pool by buying competitors and converting employees, profiting from the sale or leasing of trucks and gaining the cheaper services of contractors. This appears to be a highly effective way to create contractors. For instance, Greatwide Logistics, a major TL refrigerated carrier, claims it converts about 55 percent of new employees into contractors when it acquires a fleet.[25]

While some carriers try to convince their own employees to become contractors, and some simply convert their entire fleet, doing so entails some risks. Legal frameworks that differentiate employees from independent contractors for tax and regulatory purposes often explicitly take into consideration whether a worker has previously been a firm's employee (these issues will be discussed further below). Due to legal and regulatory challenges to independent contracting, companies increasingly prefer to recruit contractors from outside their company. In doing so they are aided by noncarrier partners, which represent themselves as advocates and service providers for contractors.

Nearly all of the drivers that I interviewed who were seriously considering contracting claimed to be researching the opportunity by reading magazines and websites for contractors, and getting information from other sources they considered authoritative and independent, like manuals and DVD guides about how to start a contractor business. Unfortunately, nearly all of these sources are part of an intertwined network of consultants and businesses intended to recruit and manage contractors for carriers.[26] The most important of these portray themselves as news sources and business service providers. A handful of companies dominate trucking media, the most prominent of which is Randall-Reilly Publishing. When Randall-Reilly's services are examined closely, it becomes clear that they are little more than pitchmen, colluding with carriers to convince truckers to become contractors.

Trucking Media

Randall-Reilly owns the most well-known industry magazine: *Overdrive*. *Overdrive* advertises itself to more than ninety thousand subscribers and hundreds of thousands of web readers as "the premier magazine for leased owner-operators and independent owner-operators." Indeed, it has a storied history of advocating for the interests of owner-operators. *Overdrive* was founded in 1961 by Mike Parkhurst, an owner-operator who believed that the Teamsters, regulation, and big corporations had "strangled the healthy growth of the free enterprise system."[27]

As historian Shane Hamilton (2008) detailed in a recent book on owner-operators and trucking deregulation, Parkhurst used the magazine as a platform for an antiunion and antiregulation message. By the 1970s Parkhurst was one of the most influential voices among owner-operators. In 1975, a *Time* article described *Overdrive* as a "muckraking journal," with carefully researched articles and Parkhurst as an advocate for owner-operators. Parkhurst was a self-identified "conservative radical" who, *Time* reported, treated advertisers with "truculent disdain." Parkhurst told *Time* that his goal was "to wake the truckers up to the fact that they're slaves to a monopoly." In the summer of 1979 he was a self-proclaimed instigator of collective actions by owner-operators in response to rising fuel costs.[28]

In 1986, Parkhurst sold *Overdrive* to Randall-Reilly. Like the role of contractors, *Overdrive* has been remade. In the past it advocated *for* owner-operators; today it advocates that truckers *become* owner-operators. *Overdrive* presents its reporting and data as the most sophisticated and accurate available. But the key pieces of information that would-be contractors need are always presented in misleading ways. Here is a typical excerpt on compensation from a regular *Overdrive* column called "Inside Track":

> If you've been in this business a long time, you know things have evolved. Being an owner-operator isn't like it was 20 years ago or even five years ago . . . *Overdrive* has diligently invested to track those changes by commissioning our Owner-Operator Market Report . . . by far the most detailed study of operating methods, buying habits and personal characteristics of the nation's owner-operators. For example, the 2007 report . . . contains facts [such as]: Owner-operators with a two-year college degree who keep detailed records of operating expenses earn $63,700.[29]

Most truckload drivers considering contracting have been in the industry less than five years. In this case, it is likely that *Overdrive's* figure for the average income of an owner-operator with a "two-year college degree who keep[s] detailed records" is almost twice what a typical contractor can expect to earn, as I will explain in the next chapter. Only 4 percent of long-haul drivers have a two-year college degree, and it is not clear what might define "keeping detailed records."[30] Furthermore, like almost all information sources available to would-be contractors, this piece does not make clear whether these owner-operators are contractors or independents, and whether or not they employ multiple drivers.

What would-be contractors don't know is that publications like *Overdrive* are far from unbiased in their portrayals of contracting. They might suspect, obviously, that if a company publishes magazines for contractors and sells ads to their employers, it would want to increase the number of contractors. But such companies are far more intertwined in the promotion of the contracting discourse and allied with the interests of large carriers than would-be contractors ever suspect.

Virtually all of the dozens of recruiting magazines, trucking newspapers, trucking websites, and magazines like *Overdrive* that drivers reported reading regularly are controlled by just three companies.[31] Randall-Reilly Publishing, which describes itself as "the premier business-to-business media company focused on trucking," is by far the largest and most influential.[32] Randall-Reilly produces more than a dozen monthly trucking publications, websites, and national radio shows, and runs several of the largest trucking trade shows in the US aimed at contractors. In 1986, it acquired *Overdrive*, which it describes to advertisers as "the oldest and most respected magazine for independent truckers."[33]

Truckers can subscribe to the print version of *Overdrive* for free or read it online, which is free of charge as well. The tagline of *Overdrive* truckers will see is the same one Mike Parkhurst used: "Voice of the American Trucker." Today there is another tagline for *Overdrive* that Randall-Reilly uses in its promotional materials for advertisers: "Delivering the Owner-Operator."[34] *Overdrive* delivers owner-operators to manufacturers and retailers, but most importantly to carriers.

Randall-Reilly has transformed *Overdrive* from a muckraking investigative journal into a meticulously crafted recruitment magazine designed to turn employees into contractors while appearing to be independent media. In it drivers will find every aspect of what it takes to be a contractor described in detail, and frequent and consistent repetition of the contracting discourse.

As just one example, let's take the question of lease-purchasing that Joe was wrestling with. In lease-purchases, a contractor leases a truck from the carrier for which he hauls. Often this is done through a shell corporation that acts as the lessor of the truck, to suggest that the parent company is not able to use the lease to economically coerce the contractor in the performance of their work. There is no other issue about which my experienced interviewees were both more unified and more passionate. Experienced drivers believe that lease-purchases are a scam carriers use to exploit inexperienced truckers, and that even if a driver is able to stay afloat long enough to make it through his contract, no driver would be able to earn enough to afford the typical balloon payments required by companies at the end of the lease period. They all recommended that drivers who want to become contractors save up enough to independently buy a used truck from a dealership and have enough cash left to repair it if it breaks down. Otherwise the contractor would dramatically overpay for the truck and/or its maintenance and never own it. Most importantly, lease-purchasing means that a contractor can only work for the carrier selling the truck (even if the actual lessor is a shell corporation). Experienced truckers see this arrangement as a kind of debt peonage. If things don't work out, you lose any down payment you made as well as the truck, because you can't drive for another carrier.

Magazines like *Overdrive* often anticipate negative views on contentious topics. Here for instance is the presentation of the issue of lease-purchasing a truck in an *Overdrive* article entitled "Hard Financial Choices":

> Finding the bottom line for two paths in a financial matter can be as murky as driving through fog ... Few owner-operators lease a truck. All things being equal over enough years, buying leaves you with more in your pocket ... On the other side of the buy-lease debate ... leases, which have a buyout at the end, have their proponents. Many carriers, for instance, *structure leases to favor novice owner-operators with little to no truck-buying history or cash for a down payment* (emphasis added). "We're not seeing a lot of folks who have that kind of money and can afford a big down payment," says Steve Crear, Schneider Financial's general manager.[35]

Proponents of contracting are well aware that would-be contractors are bound to hear at least some horror stories about lease-purchases and contracting more generally. In order to counter these stories they frame each debate as one of individual choices, priorities, and situations. According to them, there is no one best way to do anything in trucking.

Here is the beginning of another *Overdrive* article on the subject of lease-purchasing, entitled "Another Way to Buy":

Lease-purchase plans aren't for everyone, but they can work—and work well—as long as you get favorable terms. In the early 1980s, Jeff Warta had made 46 payments on his four-year truck lease-purchase. With only two payments remaining, the carrier's lessor went bankrupt. "My truck was repossessed by the bank to help pay the carrier's creditors," says Warta, who lost both his truck and the $51,000 he had sunk into it, though he later completed a lease-purchase with another carrier.[36]

After acknowledging that a commonly heard horror story can, and did, actually happen, the article goes on emphasize that there are other, positive stories, too:

For every horror story such as Warta's, there is a success tale, too. Among owner-operators driving a truck that has been paid off, 9 percent acquired their rig through a lease-purchase, according to the Overdrive 2003 Owner-operator Behavior Report. Many of them used such a program to begin their careers or to bounce back from financial hardship.[37]

As with almost everything presented on contracting by these companies, the figures above are constructed to mislead. Very few owner-operators have their trucks paid off. Of my interviewees, only two owner-operators had a working truck paid off. One was an independent who inherited his business from his father. The other started off in a lease-purchase before deregulation. According to this driver and several others, lease-purchases were not uncommon before deregulation, but had much more favorable terms for drivers. However, the article doesn't stop with simple misleading figures. It goes on to make it clear that lease-purchases exist because certain types of truckers—those without a lot of cash or good credit (the vast majority of would-be contractors, of course)—need them:

In some instances, though, lease-purchases, as well as straight leases, are often looked upon with skepticism by prospective owner-operators ... Truck leasing generally appeals to two types of truckers. The first is the aspiring owner-operator with little money who is attracted by leases that typically require little or no security deposit. The other type is the experienced owner-operator whose credit suffered after falling on hard times.[38]

As this quote illustrates, the contracting discourse anticipates the negative stories and advice that inexperienced drivers may have heard about contracting, and explicitly frames lease-purchases as in the interest of what in reality is nearly all would-be contractors—those who couldn't buy a truck any other way. "It might not be the BEST choice, but it is the best choice for YOU," is the message.

In 2008, Randall-Reilly was purchased by Investcorp, which at the time owned two major trucking carriers and other trucking media companies. Since that time Randall-Reilly has become quite explicit about its role in creating contractors—at least with advertisers. In its 2010 media guide for advertisers, the company explains that it has "a new two-pronged editorial focus: Analyzing how trucking issues affect drivers/owner-operators and assisting company drivers as they transition to running an owner-operator business." As part of this new focus, it added a regular column in each issue, "How to Become an Owner-Operator." *Overdrive* tells advertisers that this column is intended to help "company drivers prepare to become truck and business owners."[39]

Randall-Reilly suggests that advertisers take advantage of their "closed loop" of services, which include recruiting services and research on contractors. They report that their publications "include industry news, safe driving tips, pay and benefit package information and profiles of successful carriers. Each publication is distributed monthly [free of charge] at 1,400 premium truck stops nationwide."[40]

Additional services are an increasingly important source of revenue for Randall-Reilly. The company now has a Market Intelligence Division that uses *Overdrive* and its other publications and websites to conduct research such as its Owner-Operator Market Behavior Report, which it promotes as "the definitive source of information about the owner-operator market."[41] This report typically collects information on more than eighty thousand truckers annually. Drivers who participate are offered a chance at a $2,500 grand prize for submitting a survey. A few years ago, Randall-Reilly's CEO said this data business represented about 25 percent of the company's revenue, "but moving forward, the focus will be on data, online and event development 'for the same reason Jesse James robbed banks . . . because that's where the money is.'"[42]

While *Overdrive* presents its Owner-Operator Market Behavior Report to drivers as part of its journalistic mission to provide owner-operators with the information they need to be successful, sales to advertisers and carriers drive the collection of such data. Here is how Randall-Reilly's CEO explained this to a business magazine editor in 2006:

> Editor: Randall-Reilly is one of the few examples of a [business to business publisher] succeeding with rich data. Many publishers, particularly small to mid-sized, are having trouble getting their arms around it. What advice do you have for them?
>
> CEO: Rich data is a pretty big term. If we just look at the data we're collecting off our [circulation audits], there's already a lot of data that you're already paying for that you can sell to your advertisers. Years ago we were asking, what type of freight do our readers haul? I asked my publisher, 'How do we use that? If we don't use it every question you ask is costing us money. Is there a way you can sell that to somebody?'[43]

Today, Randall-Reilly doesn't ask truckers what kind of freight they haul or what their major concerns are about the industry. It asks them about things like what brand of oil they use, where they buy it, and whether price, brand, or quality is most important to them.

Cracking the Ethnic Code

As the industry runs out of the traditional sources of contractors it has relied upon, primarily white and black men, employers have explored new sources of labor and ways to reach it. As yet the industry has had little success recruiting women, unless they are working with a husband or partner. The industry has, however, had increasing success recently recruiting immigrants, particularly into local driving jobs. A number of the long-haul drivers I interviewed were Mexican immigrants, but most had not immigrated recently. More recent immigrant populations present additional challenges, including language skills and cultural differences, that may make them difficult to recruit, license, and retain, but they may also present significant advantages for carriers. First, some immigrant men may move without families, may have no home life in the US to return to, and so may be willing to work constantly. I met a recent Thai immigrant who was doing just that. Paul had immigrated to Portland, Oregon, and entered the industry through a CDL school run by one of the largest companies. After a year as an employee, and then a failed attempt at a lease-purchase, Paul had moved to a better-paying job he found through other Thai immigrants. His new carrier was small, with only a dozen or so drivers, all of them Thai immigrants who drove regular coast-to-coast routes. Paul's wife then came to the US and was riding along in the truck with him. They had initially rented an apartment when she immigrated, but had stopped returning to it and gave it up months ago. Now they just traveled back and forth across the continent continually, living out of the truck and "seeing the country." Paul was considering buying his own truck through his company as an investment in his future.

Some carriers have developed relationships with particular immigrant communities, like Paul's carrier has, as ways to recruit labor. In ways that resemble the *padrone* system, common in US cities with large immigrant populations in the early twentieth century, carriers hire more-established and respected members of immigrant communities as recruiters. It is not just the flexibility of this labor that interests carriers, but the potential entrepreneurial ambitions they may have, and the community resources they can draw on to finance trucks. An influential consultant in the industry described the potential of these relationships at an industry roundtable:

> [We] know one carrier that . . . had 29 owner-operators . . . they now have 249, in just about a year, and what they did is they managed to crack the ethnic code in the Somali community, and the commonality is, these guys all wanted to be in business for themselves. [This carrier doesn't] even offer a finance program. This is the amazing part, these guys all scraped the money together to put a truck on the road . . . it's great, [the carrier has] gone from 39 [sic] to 249 in 12 months and haven't even financed a truck . . . [What the carrier] told me was, "you have got to build some trust, we found somebody who was a recognized person in their community, we signed him up as a recruiter, we got him bringing a few people in, we got them talking up their story, 'they make money, we treat them good' and now it is gravy" . . . I think it is important as an industry that [we crack that ethnic code].

Indeed, if the industry continues to chew up and spit out workers at the rate of several hundred thousand per year, it will need to figure out how to tap into new sources of labor, and increasingly this will mean recruiting immigrants. Of course, the fact that immigrants are even less familiar than native workers with the contracting practices of long-haul trucking will allow employers to introduce them on their own terms to trucking's version of the American Dream.

BUYING IT

Three quarters of the drivers I interviewed were current or former contractors or seriously considering contracting. Most of the remaining quarter had either seriously considered contracting in the past or were very new to the industry and will probably consider it if they decide to remain in the industry.

Only eight of the seventy-five drivers I initially interviewed said that they had never and would never consider contracting. Four of these cited the negative experiences and advice of family or close friends who had either tried contracting themselves or had extensive experience in the transportation industry. These sources provided trusted information that allowed these inexperienced drivers to feel confident drawing conclusions about the right course for their career based on the experience of others. The other four drivers had one or more of three different work experiences: 1) driving for a unionized carrier; 2) driving in the LTL segment; 3) dispatching or sales for a TL carrier. These workers, with broader knowledge about the business of trucking and alternative ways that trucking can be organized, considered contracting a means for carriers to shift risk to workers while paying them less.

With the exception of those like these eight drivers, who had access to very different sources of knowledge about the industry than the average trucker, contracting is the subject of a conscious decision-making process for nearly everyone who makes a career in long-haul trucking. This is despite the fact that workers enter the industry with little sense of what contracting is. Within a few years most see it as a realistic and possibly desirable alternative to standard employment relations.

Of course, given what a bad situation contracting is in general, there are plenty of drivers who have tried their hand at contracting and have failed—miserably. However, a few cultural norms surrounding trucking in general and contracting in particular keep this point of view from influencing would-be contractors. The experienced and former contractors I interviewed were scathingly critical of the carrier discourse of ownership discussed above. But from my hundreds of hours of observation in truck stops and numerous informal conversations with groups of truckers, it is clear that experienced drivers are reluctant to discuss these issues with less experienced drivers. In fact, speaking negatively about contracting is almost taboo, because of the heated debates that drivers fear can result. More experienced drivers who do speak negatively are frequently in the midst of troubles with their carrier and are angry. They are likely to be viewed by would-be contractors as disgruntled and/or responsible for their own failure.

Inexperienced contractors, on the other hand, are generally known for speaking too loudly about their success and often provide positive stories of contracting that support carrier discourses. Experienced drivers, including contractors, frequently ridiculed such drivers in interviews suggesting that they were fools trying to impress novice drivers or out for a referral bonus, which most carriers pay drivers who successfully recruit a new contractor.

All drivers considering contracting told me of hearing about fantastic gross incomes from some contractor they had met. And, even if they are not trying to recruit drivers, existing contractors may contribute to some would-be contractors' misunderstanding of how much income contractors earn, simply because giving gross revenue is the norm when contractors discuss "how much they make."[44]

Beliefs about Success as a Contractor and the Contracting Relationship

Would-be contractors see trucking as a career with a relatively clear set of steps on the way to becoming an independent trucker or, perhaps, owning a trucking company. These workers may be dissatisfied with their current carrier and see contracting as a way to avoid bad jobs and be rewarded for their skill and effort with increased financial benefits and, possibly, status. They believe contracting will transform their class position and make them a more self-reliant person.

These would-be contractors are likely to focus almost exclusively on the efficient operation of the truck in relation to the miles game as the key to profitability. Most of them have no sense at all of what freight rates are or how they vary. Though they have little sense of how freight to haul is found and the sales end of the business, they believe that freight markets are highly competitive, but fair. Believing they don't have the knowledge and capital to compete in freight markets directly, would-be contractors think their success will result from three things: the right to refuse bad loads, driving lots of miles, and cutting fuel consumption.

Here is a would-be contractor discussing how to be successful:

> SV: What do you think the key to success is going to be when you have your own truck? Will you do anything differently than you do now as a company driver?
>
> Driver: No. I don't believe so. It is basically the same thing [as being a company driver]. You're just going to have to manage your money and try to keep your fuel down as low as possible.

Here is an inexperienced driver who was considering contracting explaining why he thinks he could be successful:

> I run on a tight truck, a tight ship, my logbook, paperwork, my truck is in good shape, everything is in good shape and I think I have the potential to do it, but I'm just scared [right now because of the spike in fuel prices], afraid that I will lose my butt and get even worse in debt. I don't know, I suppose if somebody came up to me and said, there is a truck over there, make these payments and I'll pay you so much money and all this, I would probably do it.

Would-be and inexperienced contractors believe that they may be able to make more through fuel savings by idling the truck less and may be able to increase fuel economy through load selection (e.g. by taking lighter loads or avoiding congested cities). As employees, they used company-defined bonus goals (e.g., a driver might get a bonus if the time their truck is idling accounts for less than 10 percent of all the time the truck's engine is running) as metrics for efficient operation, and they knew that they often did better than these. Here is one new contractor explaining how he viewed efficiency in his decision to buy a truck.

> SV: Why did you decide to buy your own truck rather than be a company driver?

Driver: Because as a company driver, a majority of what you see, when I started out . . . it was twenty-eight cents a mile [at my company]. A majority of what I see in Class A is thirty to thirty-five cents . . . [After fuel I can get] like forty-nine cents, the money is way better as an owner, because you can control more of what money gets wasted, instead of *the money* controlling what money gets wasted and giving you what is left.

For would-be and new contractors, owning a truck and being responsible for its costs constitutes running a business. These drivers often refer to everything that they earn above expenses to be profit—exactly how profit is defined in the contracting discourse. In contrast, more experienced drivers, whether contractor or employee, defined profit as *additional income above and beyond the market value of their labor as an employee* to compensate for the additional risk and responsibilities taken on by contractors. Would-be and inexperienced contractors don't even consider the possibility that they won't earn more than they would as employees, at least in the long-term. They all want to be contractors at least partially because they believe they will make more money.

Would-be and new contractors recognize that some contractors fail, but they attribute such failure to moral flaws, poor money management, lack of self-discipline, or family constraints. Note how this new contractor, in explaining why contractors fail, thinks the key to success is to behave like the best, most disciplined, "adultlike" company driver:

SV: And the ones who don't make it work as contractors, what are they doing wrong?

Driver: They don't know how to manage their time. It is like when you are a kid, fourteen, fifteen years old and your dad gives you permission to go out and you abuse it. They don't have nobody to control them. They can sleep longer, they can get their fill . . . they can take two days to get there, they can go home every week. He don't want to work Monday or Tuesday, he's going to turn in Wednesday. You have got to keep doing the same thing you do [as an employee]. Discipline, because now it is for you and your family.

And another would-be contractor:

SV: What you want to get out of owning?

Driver: More pay, more of my own decisions [about] home time, and how long I want to stay there, that sort of thing . . . I would really like to be out for two weeks and take a week off, be out for three and take a week off. Something like that.

SV: Do you think that you will make more money?

Driver: Oh yeah. Because I drive. There are a lot of guys who don't like to drive. I usually drive my legal limit and I stop. These guys will drive three or four hours and they think they are tired. That is not me.

SV: So if you run hard, there is money to be made?

Driver: Even if you don't really, and you are just not lazy . . . If you are willing to drive, you will make it.

Would-be and inexperienced contractors refer frequently to the importance of hard work and sacrifice. They see intense competition and risk as valorizing their sacrifice and self-sweating. They take pride in their struggles. Struggling to "make a profit" or bringing home less than they did as employees is temporary and part of a process of investment or "building their business" through which they will eventually reap great financial returns.

In making the contracting decision, truckers assess how their relationship to other economic actors, each with his own set of interests, affects what they can and should do. Would-be and inexperienced contractors view contracting as a mutually beneficial partnership. The worker gets experience running a business and extra pay, and the carrier gets a more committed and experienced driver.

While some held out hope for it in the long term, no contractors brought up independent owner-operating as a realistic near-term option for them. When they did, they contrasted its risks with the benefits of partnering with carriers. Almost universally, these drivers were uncertain about what kind of work would be required to operate without the help of a carrier. They were unsure that they could find good loads consistently and that they had enough money to survive the problems they might encounter.

Independent operation also increased the risk that contractors would fall prey to an unscrupulous actor. They are concerned about fly-by-night companies, about which they have heard horror stories, particularly load brokers. These drivers believe that becoming an independent owner would only heighten the risk of being taken advantage of:

There are brokers and load boards. But the instant that you do that, now you are in accounts receivable risk. Meaning if you haul, who is going to guarantee that you're going to get your money on time? And what are you going to do if you don't? You can make a hundred phone calls and threaten to sue and do all this stuff and meanwhile you're pounding ten thousand miles a month. A guy like me, I am not hiring a lawyer because somebody owes me $732.

Thus such drivers see contracting as making them *less* likely to be taken advantage of than independent owner-operators—contracting protects them from the market. Despite their need for companies, contracting is seen as a step toward self-fulfillment. Here is a driver describing why he wants to become a contractor:

> Driver: Well, it's not my *dream* job, but it is a step in the right direction
>
> SV: So you want to make a little more money and . . .?
>
> Driver: Be my own businessman, which I think is everybody's dream. You ask anybody out here, it is their dream to own their own truck, or be able to work for themselves.

These drivers believe they have the ability to move from being a worker to being a small businessperson. Some of them even view it as a key step in a path that could lead to owning a trucking company that employs other drivers. As a new contractor told me, "Who knows, the possibilities are *endless*."

There are two very specific beliefs that all would-be contractors have that lead them to believe contracting will be better for them: the amount of take-home pay they will earn and the control they will have over their work.

Beliefs about Income

Most of those who become contractors were fairly satisfied with their overall income in their first few years as employees, particularly when they considered it relative to what they made before they entered the industry. Some had made a move or two to slightly better-paying carriers as employees, but many only worked for one company before trying their hand at contracting. While income for employees typically increases several thousand dollars over the first five years or so due to pay increases, additional years of experience typically add very little to annual earnings. ATA data from 2011 suggests that median starting pay for long-haul drivers at large companies was 32.5 cents per mile, the median highest pay was 40.7 cents, and the median time for drivers to reach the top pay scale was six years.[45] In other words, the typical driver is likely to earn about one cent per mile, or around $1,200 more in salary, for each additional year of experience for six years; from then on they will get little or no return on experience. As a result, truckers become dissatisfied with the opportunities they see as employees and frustrated by the lack of return they get on their experience.

Would-be contractors believe that contractors make significantly more money than employees—*a lot more money*. Here is a driver who was planning to become a contractor within a few months of our interview:

SV: What are you looking to get out of owning? Why do you want to do it?

Driver: Just more income.

SV: More money.

Driver: More income, and you can control your time off, if you want to.

SV: You are making a pretty good wage relatively for your experience right now, how much more do you figure you can get by owning?

Driver: Probably another $50,000 a year.

SV: Is there anything that you're worried about with buying your own truck?

Driver: No.

This driver had four years experience and made a little over $40,000 in the previous year. He believes by becoming a contractor he can more than double his income.

Drivers recognize that the figures they see advertised are likely to be estimates of gross revenue, but these drivers find it *inconceivable* that the typical gross revenue for contractors of $150,000 or more would not provide them with substantially more in take-home pay. Here is an exchange with one driver who was considering becoming a contractor:

SV: So you're pretty sure that you want to own your own?

Driver: I told my wife, I really want to, but I only looked at it from the aspect of since I'm getting up there forty-two, forty-three years old, I didn't want to do it when I'm sixty-five . . . So I thought if I bought a truck . . . I could bust my butt for ten years and just get out of it and retire. Because you probably could make enough money, like the guy out there this morning [pointing to the truckstop's parking lot] told me that he made $212,000 last year, and I don't know how much his expenses are, gross and net look a lot different when you own your own truck. But if I did that for ten years, you bust your butt, you should be able to live comfortably. I don't need a zillion dollars. I don't need that kind of money. Some of these guys *I don't know what they do with it.*

The belief that contractors make more money was universal among would-be contractors. This has been an attraction of the position, at least since the mid-1990s at the "rebirth" of the owner-operator. General freight contractors were asked why they became contractors in a University of Michigan survey in 1997. They ranked in importance several reasons on a scale of 1, not at all important, to 5, very important. When asked how important "making more money" was to their decision, 100 percent of these drivers responded with a 3 or higher. More than 60 percent of drivers gave "making more money" a ranking of 5. Drivers who become or want to become contractors have *absolutely no doubt whatsoever* that contractors make more money than employees.

Beliefs about Control

One of the reasons that would-be contractors overestimate what they will earn as a contractor is that they believe they will be able to choose better loads and drive more miles without negative consequences. As one driver considering contracting told me:

Driver: [When] you are a [contractor], whatever company you [lease to], you are free to do whatever you want to do. If you don't want to take a load, you just tell them no, give me another one. A company driver [has] to take it.

Would-be contractors believe they can substantially increase their pay by picking and choosing loads that have the longest mileage on interstates, or the lightest gross weight, or have the quickest turnaround time. Here is a very new contractor explaining his decision to buy:

> SV: So, when you decided to buy your own truck, what were you looking to get out of owning?
>
> Driver: I figured I could get it paid off in three years.
>
> SV: So did you think you would make more money?
>
> Driver: Yeah, because then you can pick and choose what you haul.

Not only do would-be contractors believe they can use their control over loads to make more money, they believe they will have complete control over when they go home, and most plan to use that control to be home more often. A driver about to become a contractor with a company in a matter of weeks summed up his reasons like this: "With my own truck I would make more money, and I will be home with my family." Though the contracting discourse has to put a lot of pieces together to get workers to see how contracting is good for both carriers and contractors, in the end this is what drivers must ultimately believe.

REMAKING LABOR MARKET INSTITUTIONS

Using their position as employers, carriers disseminate a discourse to their employees, sometimes from the moment they are recruited and trained, that encourages them to become contractors. Third parties, often represented as businesses acting in the interests of workers, legitimize this discourse and aid carriers in their goal of turning employees into contractors. I will discuss the reality of contracting in the next chapter, but let's briefly consider why the contracting discourse has such a profound effect on the expectations and understandings of workers.

First, the contracting discourse resonates in powerful ways with the experiences and desires of drivers. It is highly crafted to build upon the understandings drivers have developed through their work of both their abilities and the business of trucking. Second, and perhaps most interestingly, the discourse redefines common concepts in novel ways that support particular kinds of class and employment relations. There are some broad concepts, such as the American Dream, freedom, and autonomy, that provide larger frameworks for grounding the discourse, which remain amorphous. But other concepts are explicitly and implicitly defined in ways that seem clearly different from what we might expect. Take, for instance, two of the most important: small business and profit. The discourse defines small business ownership as consistent with: 1) signing a contract to work for a single employer at a fixed rate of pay for at least one year; 2) being told what work to do, when, and where. Would such a definition resonate with truckers' experiences of nontrucking small businesses? An alternative framing of small business might include engaging in regular market exchanges, in which one tries to, say, seek the highest price for one's goods or services, or attract and retain customers. The contracting discourse, in fact, specifically suggests that this sort of activity is risky and unproductive for contractors, who should instead focus on driving more miles and cost reduction alone.

In tandem with the definition of small business, profit is defined as the difference between gross revenue and net, without consideration for the value of one's own labor. It might alternatively be defined as a premium beyond the value of one's labor that rewards a contractor for taking on additional risk (as more experienced truckers define it). Instead, as I will discuss in Chapter 5, what workers are encouraged to do, quite literally, is evaluate the compensation offered by a carrier in terms of their operating costs and what they spend at home (i.e. how much they need to reproduce their labor power).

What carriers and the third parties working for them have done is create a nuanced and deeply resonant portrayal of the class relations of production that corresponds to their interests. Workers become small business owners. Employers become business partners. Income becomes profit. Lower incomes and unpaid time become investments. Carriers have been able to use this discourse to legitimize changes in the labor process, some of which have been profound (e.g., getting contractors to give up the right to refuse loads; requiring long-term contracts at a fixed rate). What all of this means is that employers have been able to advance their interests by radically altering the informal labor market institutions that shape the expectations, beliefs, goals, and behavior of workers. And these things lead workers to believe, at least for a while, that contracting is a good idea.

4 Working for the Truck

THE HARSH REALITY OF CONTRACTING

LISTENING TO CLAUDIO

I met Claudio in the lounge of the truck stop. He looked tired and a little disheveled. He had a couple days of stubble on his face, and his wavy black hair was standing up in the back. His maroon T-shirt was wrinkled where it wasn't pulled taut over a slightly rounded belly. I know exactly how he ended up looking like that. When you work twelve to sixteen hours a day and sleep in the back of a truck, after a couple days the chances are your hair will be a little messed up and your clothes a little wrinkled. You want a hot shower at the end of each day just to wash the diesel exhaust out of your hair and off your skin, but you only earn a free one for buying fuel about every other day. And every morning you wake up in the bunk in the back of your truck, pull on some clothes, grab your toiletry bag, and walk through a truck stop to the bathroom. If it is a real truck stop, there will only be truckers there. But increasingly stops have mixed services for cars and trucks. So a couple of times each week you find yourself in a convenience store among four-wheelers at the start of your day. Every so often, you just can't help feeling like people are keeping their kids a little closer as you come in to wash your face, brush your teeth, and maybe grab a cup of coffee. Sometimes, as someone gives you a wide berth, you catch a look on their face that makes it clear what they're thinking: *dirty trucker*. And you really want to say something like this: "Hey, brother, *I'm working here*. Do you just roll out of bed in the morning with your suit on and head to the office?" Instead, you just smile and say, "Excuse me."

Though Claudio looked like a typical driver in the middle of a hard work rotation, I immediately sensed something was different about him. He was tense—*really tense*. I explained my research and he agreed to participate without hesitation. We shook hands and sat down across from one another at a booth. He immediately began asking me questions in heavily accented English about my experience in trucking: Did I ever drive? Did I like it? What did I think about the pay? How did my family handle me being on the road? I could see he was deeply interested in my answers.

I never talked about my own experiences as a driver at the start of an interview to avoid influencing how drivers responded to my questions. But something told me Claudio was not going to be influenced by anything I had to say. Claudio had an important story to tell and I immediately knew he was evaluating me, deciding whether I would "get it." I told him I did enjoy parts of the job and didn't mind the lack of routine or the long work hours. But, the pay was too low, the waiting was frustrating, and the long stretches of driving were boring. I told him I doubted I could endure for long the personal sacrifices that life on the road required.

Apparently Claudio decided I would get it because once he started talking, he didn't stop for almost an hour and half. Unfortunately, though it would take me several more years before I really understood them fully, I had already heard stories like Claudio's from other interviewees. He was another victim of contracting. What was different about Claudio was that he was, at the exact time of our interview, hitting contracting's rock bottom, *and he knew it.*

Claudio had worked as a trucker in Mexico to pay his way through school, eventually earning an associate's degree in Chemistry. He then immigrated to the US in the late 1980s to work as a technician for a chemical company in Texas. When that company went out of business during the recession of 1990–91, Claudio was forced to take whatever jobs he could. He fell into kitchen work, first washing dishes, then working as a line cook, and then managing a kitchen. After he married and had children, cooking wasn't paying the bills, and Claudio wanted to provide more for his children than he saw available to most first-generation Mexican Americans in South Texas. He wanted to ensure that they could finish college and get the white-collar jobs that were, despite his education, beyond his reach.

So, Claudio went back to trucking. He worked for several different carriers over two years and maintained a clean driving record. He then landed a long-haul job pulling a flatbed trailer for a small company. With this new carrier Claudio worked hard, driving about three thousand paid miles a week, and earned about $40,000 a year—almost twice what he earned from kitchen work. But, like many long-haul drivers, Claudio was on the road for twelve days at a time and then home for two. His wife and his three children (who ranged from five to fifteen years in age at the time of our interview) hated him being away, and the emotional strain was difficult for all of them. After he and his family endured this schedule for two years, Claudio decided to buy his own truck and become a contractor in the summer of 2004. He was sure he could make more money as a contractor *and* have more time at home with his family. Unfortunately, he had little cash to put down, and when he tried to buy a used truck for $50,000, he was told that, with the mortgage on his recently purchased home, his income was too low to qualify him for a loan. He set aside his plan and resolved to begin saving more for a down payment.

About a year later, in June of 2005, Claudio got a call from a recruiter for Big Red Trucking, one of the largest US carriers. He had had no previous contact with the carrier, but they were offering to sell him a used truck with no money down and provide financing. The truck was a 2003 Freightliner—the same no-frills workhorse I drove for Leviathan. At a little over two years old, it had plenty of good life left in it. The payments would be $416 a week, plus insurance, fuel, taxes, and $225 per week in required contributions to maintenance and "savings" escrow accounts. At the end of three years, Claudio could make a balloon payment of $20,000 and the truck would be his. The recruiter said he could net $1,000 for a twenty-five-hundred-mile week and $1500 for a three-thousand-mile week. At the time, Claudio was making about $800 for a three-thousand-mile week.

The recruiter sent Claudio some glossy brochures advertising Big Red's contractor program. The offer was tempting, and Claudio considered it seriously. But his wife was now pregnant with their fourth child, and he decided it wasn't the right time to make a move this big. The next time the recruiter called, Claudio told her he wasn't ready to take up the offer, but that he might reconsider after the baby was born and things settled down. In fact, Claudio knew this wasn't the best way to become a contractor, and he hoped in a year or two he would get financing to buy a similar truck from a dealership at better terms. Big Red's recruiter continued to call every few weeks to let him know the offer was still on the table.

Then, near the end of August 2005, Claudio returned to work after two days at home and was assigned a load from South Texas to Miami. The route was a regular favorite of his, heading east along I-10 through Louisiana, Mississippi, and the Florida Panhandle and then south along I-75 to Miami. Normally he would "push it a little" and run the load in two days, earning almost $200 per day. But this run wouldn't be normal. During the previous week the massive hurricane Katrina had formed over the Bahamas, hit Florida, and begun strengthening over the Gulf. Claudio had been following the news closely, and he wanted no part of the storm, but shippers were desperate to get loads out before the storm made landfall, so rates for his employer were primo.

> I told the dispatcher, three days ahead, "Don't put me through that" . . . and he said, "Well, we need the loads." [I told him] "Man, are you serious? You expect me to work through that? It is going to go all the way through to New York and North Carolina. It will be all over there!" *They put me there.*

Despite Claudio's pleas, his dispatcher refused to change his load assignment. With a new baby on the way, Claudio was in no position financially to refuse to work or quit his job, so he picked up the load and headed for Miami. He raced the approaching storm, but just above New Orleans he was detoured further north along with evacuees fleeing the city. Outer bands of rain from the storm forced him to stop in southern Mississippi; he was directly in the path of the storm.

> I watched the whole hurricane come through . . . man, it was a hard time I won't forget. I was crying. I was praying, sitting in the truck. The truck got sandblasted on one side. But it didn't break . . . It is not an experience that I would wish anybody to go through and that I don't want to think about . . . people died . . . So I made my delivery in Miami . . . And I came back all the

way to home, tossed the keys on the table of the dispatcher, and I told him, "Next time you want to drive through that, *get your license and drive!*" I was nasty on the [satellite computer too]. Yes, I was nasty. *"This is my life!"* I told him, "No one is going to tell me to risk my life!"

Now, with no job, a new baby on the way, and having just dramatically experienced the worst effects of a lack of control over his work, Claudio decided to take Big Red up on their offer. He wanted to start immediately, but was told it would take about a week to get him into a mandatory orientation, which would last about four and one-half days. The company paid for a bus ticket and promised $300 after he completed the orientation.

Claudio arrived at the orientation hopeful he was taking the first step toward small business ownership. But the high-pressure sales environment he encountered immediately disturbed him. He described the orientation as a "psychological game" of ego stroking: "They make you feel graded. 'You are going to be the best. You are one of the elected.'" It was also a psychological game of fear. It quickly became clear that far more drivers were invited to the orientation than would actually be offered the opportunity to buy trucks. They had all been "prequalified" through applications, but one after another drivers were asked to leave after additional reviews of work history, background checks, drug tests, and interviews. As Claudio described it, the company

[kept] you stressed out, because the investigators are checking on your background and . . . they send you forms to sign in the middle of the orientation. They take you out of the orientation, break your concentration . . . They make it sound like it is a big, big deal checking you out, investigating . . . "You didn't work for two weeks, why you didn't work for two weeks? Explain it to me." "I didn't want to work." "I'll send you a form to sign, you can go back to the orientation" . . . By the time you come to the contract, you never read the contract, you just sign it because you are really psychologically busted . . . They talk about maintenance, taking care of the truck, they talk about safety measures, they take time to do nothing, they just put a bunch of papers in your hands about insurance, they try to go through everything, boom, boom, boom, boom, and they keep you worried about the investigation, "they won't take me, they won't take me" . . . By the time the contract finally comes and everybody is picking up trucks and you are not picking up yours, you worry, "What is going on?"

Claudio signed the contract, which consisted of more than fifty pages of dense legalese.

Claudio had been driving for Big Red for less than three months when I met him. The best loads Big Red gave him were only five-to-six-hundred-mile hauls, and he was waiting long periods for loads to become available. He was still working twelve days on and two off, but now felt lucky to run more than twenty-two hundred miles a week. In his second week as a contractor, which was five working days instead of seven because of a weekend off at home, Claudio's expenses exceeded revenue. After Big Red deducted all his expenses, *he had labored five full days and ended up owing the company $100.* When he complained to his dispatcher about the quality of his loads, which he saw as the source of the problem, he was told his loads would improve if he stayed out longer. So Claudio worked an entire month straight without a day off. Halfway through this work marathon his five-year-old daughter began refusing to go to sleep. His wife would call at bedtime and Claudio would tell his daughter that he would be home before she woke up the next day, even though he had no idea when he would see her next. After telling me this, Claudio locked eyes with me and asked, "Do you know what it is like to lie to your child like that?" Even after these sacrifices, his loads were still bad, and he was taking home less than $600 a week. The month on the road was too much for his family, and Claudio told his dispatcher to return him to a two-week rotation.

By that time Claudio felt Big Red had misled him, but things were about to get worse. Two weeks before I met him he dropped off a trailer less than 150 miles from home and was assigned a new load headed to the Florida Panhandle. Being so close to home, he turned down the load and went home for the night. Claudio had been promised the right to refuse loads without penalty. But after he refused this one, his loads got even worse. He suspected his dispatcher was punishing him, and they began to quarrel. The week before I met him, Claudio's dispatcher gave him the choice of waiting three days for a decent load or hauling a series of very short loads with live loading. He ran the short loads and was then told to deadhead (drive without a load) several hundred miles at a reduced rate to get his next load. As I interviewed him he waited for his dispatcher to call a nearby payphone. Now angry and frustrated, he told me:

> I am going to quit. I got $41.58 in pay last week [a seven day work week].
> That is not going to put food on my family's table. It is not going to pay for
> my home. Every time that I call [Big Red] up they are [too busy to talk].

Twice during our conversation he spoke with people at Big Red, but he
was never connected to his dispatcher.

Employee drivers quit jobs like Claudio's all the time. Some simply
drive to the truckstop closest to their home, park the company's truck, and
walk away. Sometimes they are so angry with the way they have been
treated, they don't even bother to call the company to say they've quit or
where they left the truck. In such cases companies will take wages from
the driver's last paycheck to compensate for the cost of retrieving the
truck. Carriers have a much bigger stick for disciplining drivers like
Claudio. He had entered a "lease-purchase" agreement with Big Red, an
often-abusive contractor arrangement, referred to as "rent-a-truck" by
more experienced contractors. Lease-purchases are now the most common way for employee drivers to become contractors. Before Claudio
picked up his truck at orientation, he had actually signed two separate
contracts. One was to lease his truck from a sister company of Big Red,
little more than a shell corporation meant to give the appearance to courts
and regulators that Big Red could not use the truck lease to control
Claudio financially. The other contract was to haul freight for Big Red.[1]
The lease contract required that Claudio uphold the terms of the hauling
contract. If he breached the hauling contract, the terms of the lease contract would cost him dearly. As we talked more, Claudio told me he wanted
to hire a lawyer to help him get out of these contracts, but could not afford
one. Unfortunately, a lawyer would likely be of little immediate use to
Claudio, as Big Red's contracts were no doubt carefully crafted. Though
challenges to these abusive arrangements are mounting—as I write this,
several class action lawsuits are in court or arbitration—so far none have
been costly enough to deter carriers from these practices.

Though his story has some dramatic details, Claudio's experience of
contracting was not unique. It was determined by legal and financial
constraints that carriers convince truckers to accept voluntarily, which
cause contractors to work harder, have less control, incur greater risk, and
make significantly less money than comparable employee drivers—a

reality that drivers often don't believe could be true until they experience it firsthand.

THE REALITY OF CONTRACTING

Contracting is, for the vast majority of truckers, an extremely bad arrangement. But before we can understand all the ways that it is, we need to understand a little bit more about the two most common arrangements between contractors and carriers.

Rent-a-Truck

Lease-purchases, like Claudio's, are not the only way to become a contractor. But they are the most likely route to contracting for most inexperienced drivers, who typically lack the cash and good credit required to buy a truck directly from a dealership. Though many believe that owning a truck outright gives them a better chance at more money, inexperienced drivers believe that their lack of capital and the competitive nature of freight markets make it critical for them to be associated with a carrier. They see lease-purchases as a bigger investment by companies in that relationship. Many inexperienced drivers see leasing from a large carrier as less risky; another trucker who had just entered a lease-purchase told me when I interviewed him:

> If you [have a lease-purchase with] a company, a big company, there are no true disadvantages because if you break down, the company that you are leased to will front you the money, will give you a loan, so if your credit is screwed up, you don't have a problem, and they will take it out of your check and they will charge you interest. But if you are a true independent and you are working for a broker and your truck goes down, and you ain't got no money and your credit is a mess, you are done.

Drivers like this one believe that the indebtedness of leasing a truck will be a temporary situation, and that they will be able to build enough equity and savings to eliminate the burden of great amounts of debt. Most believe they will soon be able to own a truck outright. Their partnership with large companies will allow them to develop the skills, knowledge, and a financial position to become even more independent and successful, and potentially to own even more than one truck.

Many are told that lease-purchases are "walk-away" leases, as the following driver told me after I asked him if he had considered trying to buy a truck independently:

> Not really, the easiest way to get into a truck is through a company. You can try to get one off the dealer, but you need so much money down, most people want about $30,000 down . . . That is a lot of cash, compared to zero down through a company. If it don't work right, [I will say], "Here are the keys, here is your fuel card" [and give back the truck]. It's a "walk-away" lease, is what they call it.

In reality, these agreements trap drivers in a form of debt peonage. A driver typically cannot leave the carrier with the truck and lease on with another. And contracts often contain incredibly burdensome clauses in case of breach. For instance, in the event of a breach of a purchase contract, it is not uncommon for a contractor to be immediately responsible for *all payments that would have been made over the life of the contract.* In other words, a driver like Claudio, who has just begun a three year contract, might owe $65,000 immediately, but would still not own the truck without a further balloon payment of $20,000. Of course, drivers cannot and would not pay such charges. So companies typically require drivers to set aside thousands of dollars of their pay in company-controlled escrow accounts that can be seized if contracts are violated. For instance, during a period of fewer than three months more than $2,500 of Claudio's pay had been funneled into maintenance and "savings" escrow accounts controlled by Big Red. Big Red requires its contractors to contribute until the balance of each of these accounts reaches $10,000. Not surprisingly, like training contracts for inexperienced employees, these accounts provide a strong financial incentive for workers to not walk away from a bad situation. In Claudio's case he would need to work for three years to fulfill the contract.

In addition to this debt peonage, lease-purchases typically combine inflated truck prices with poor financing, to result in truck payments equivalent to financing a similar truck from a dealership at extremely high interest rates (sometimes equal to an annual interest rate of 70 percent or more according to staff I interviewed at the Owner-Operator Independent Driver Association). In combination with common additional fees and charges for assorted services, such as issuing paychecks, high truck payments leave far less in take-home income than drivers could earn if they bought a truck independently.

To make matters worse, the truck is owned by the leasing company until the final balloon payment is made, and these companies protect their assets by requiring that contractors pay for an expensive schedule of regular maintenance. To ensure compliance, companies often require maintenance to be done at company-owned or approved facilities, which often charge inflated rates. Finally, if drivers try to maximize their use of the truck and drive lots of miles, companies will charge them an additional fee for each mile they drive above a certain limit.

Drivers simply don't understand the full implications of the contracts they sign to lease-purchase a truck. This is not the drivers' fault. I have reviewed contracts like Claudio's with employment lawyers who specialize in them, and we have encountered clauses about important issues that were so dense and so complicated it took a team of us hours to decipher the likely implications. Drivers rarely have a chance to look at the contract in detail before they attend the kind of orientation Claudio experienced. Even drivers who ask for the contract ahead of time so they can review it with a lawyer often cannot get a copy.

Most of the orientation, which normally lasts three or four days, is spent covering the company rules and regulations, how to use the company's communication system, fuel stops and cards, and signing the contract. Several drivers gave me detailed accounts of these orientations, and though carriers portrayed them as something that would prepare drivers for small-business ownership, what they cover was how to reduce fuel consumption (something drivers already largely understand), maintain the truck according to company rules, buy insurance, and how to deal with the change in their employment status. And while this is critical information for new contractors, it is not the kind of information that allows drivers to understand the likely economic outcome of lease-purchasing. According to drivers, companies refused to give a clear sense of the mileage or take-home pay an average driver could expect and avoided talking about the specific costs of company requirements, focusing almost entirely on impossibly rosy scenarios of pay, work routine, and hometime.

Overall, drivers described a common set of intimidation techniques, similar to those Claudio experienced, and reported feeling rushed and insecure as to whether they would ultimately be offered a truck. In hindsight, several drivers expressed a feeling of having been manipulated in these orientations.

The drivers Claudio initially feared becoming, who attended the orientation but were not given the opportunity to buy a truck, were actually the fortunate ones. Still, even these drivers quit jobs and gave up days of work to attend orientations, only to then be told that their work history or some other factor disqualified them from lease-purchasing a truck. As Claudio's story makes clear, these workers end up being props in the orientations. Similarly to the way workers show up at CDL school only to not be hired because a background check turns up something the carrier doesn't like, carriers often invest very little upfront in evaluating would-be contractors, waiting until the orientations to perform work history and other background evaluations. I interviewed one driver who had been invited by a large carrier to become a contractor, quit his job, and traveled by bus for an entire day, only to be told on the fourth day of the orientation that a gap in his driving experience, when he worked for a year in a nondriving job, disqualified him for the program:

> Last year, I went out to try [to buy a truck]. I got all the way out there and stayed there almost four days before they said, "You haven't driven in the last year." "Well, it would've been nice for you to tell me that back home . . ." I took the road course and everything and they said . . . I would have to go through their driver's training [and] out with a trainer for 90 days . . . and I said I don't want to do that, because I was in it to make money, not to make somebody else money. So I had to turn around and . . . rode a Greyhound bus all the way back.

Everything about a lease-purchase is in the company's favor. I did not meet a single driver who had successfully completed the terms of a lease-purchase agreement since deregulation, though I met more than a dozen drivers who had tried and failed, losing the money they had in escrow and damaging their credit. More experienced drivers believed that companies intentionally cause a contractor to fail near the end of a lease-purchase in order to take back the truck and resell it. I met several that claimed it had happened to them, like this one:

> Stay away from [lease-purchases]. All you are doing is maintenance on their truck out of your money. And when you get it about paid for, they don't run you, you get disgusted, and you give it back . . . It's a scam, all of them are . . . Because they are the owner. They can tell you when to breathe or go to the bathroom or anything. It's what you call "rent-a-truck."

As extreme as these claims may sound, even proponents of lease-purchases admit that carriers have intentionally forced drivers to fail—though they claim these problems are in the past. In 2005, the manager of Dart's lease-purchase program, the largest and longest-running in the industry said, "When lease-purchase plans came out, they did get a black eye because companies would terminate drivers before the end of the lease."[2]

Unfortunately, a bad lease-purchase experience does not necessarily cause a worker to not want to be a contractor. Workers who fail at lease-purchases may explain their failure as a problem with lease-purchases, as Claudio did, or with a particular carrier and not with contracting more generally. Some will save up to buy a truck independently even after a failed attempt at lease-purchase.

Betting the Ranch

Experienced contractors believed that if a driver was to have any chance at all of success as a contractor, it was crucial to buy a truck on his own. They believed getting a cheap truck independent of a company, and then running as many miles as possible, were the two factors critical to success. Another Latino driver, this one ten years older than Claudio, captured this belief in his advice to me:

> Becoming a [contractor]? Go outside and get your own truck on your own credit and do everything like you used to do, *only double*. And you are going to be successful. Don't take anything for granted. Just keep on doing it the way you know how to do it.

In other words, the key to being a successful contractor is to be the best worker that you can be and keep your costs low. But while contractors who bought a truck independently did have significantly lower fixed costs than lease-purchase contractors, buying a truck outright subjected them to a bigger risk: major breakdowns.

Lease-purchase trucks are typically either new or less than four years old. These trucks require significant expensive routine maintenance. A new set of ten good tractor tires alone can cost around $4,500. Trucks less than two years old might cost five to seven cents per mile to maintain, or $5,500–$7,700 annually, for a contractor driving 110,000 miles per year. But these expenses, for things like oil changes and tires, can generally be anticipated and don't require days of downtime. Newer trucks also often have warranties on major components. These factors are important for would-be contractors in choosing a lease-purchase.

On the other hand, contractors who buy a truck independently drive relatively older trucks that require significant regular maintenance. Regular maintenance on a truck more than five years old will cost around fifteen cents per mile, or $16,500 for the same mileage. Just as importantly, such older trucks are at a much higher risk of catastrophic breakdowns, due to things like an engine or transmission failure—things that are likely to cost upward of $10,000. These costs and risks are some of the main reasons carriers want to offload older trucks to workers. I interviewed several drivers whose contracting experience was ended by a major breakdown.

As an example of how quickly and devastatingly a breakdown can affect a contractor, take Brian, a thirty-two-year-old white male with about a year of experience in the industry. His brother-in-law, another inexperienced contractor, talked him into trying his hand at contracting right out of driving school. He bought an older used truck and leased on with a carrier. Brian stayed with this first carrier just a few months and then switched to another, hoping for more gross revenue. Although the second carrier initially looked more attractive it, too, was not running him enough. Against his better judgment, Brian stayed with the second carrier while pouring most of his earnings into fuel and maintenance. The day before I met him, his crankshaft broke, and Brian was told by a repair shop that he would need to replace the entire motor at a cost of $12,000.

He could not afford to make the repairs and was hoping to sell the truck for parts.

I met Brian as he was waiting for his brother-in-law to make the four-hour drive from their hometown to pick him up. He was just glad he was close to home when the truck broke down, because he didn't have the cash for a bus ticket, and he had maxed out his only credit card living on the road and maintaining his truck. "I gave it my all . . . I knew the repairs would be big, but I thought that I would get two years out of the truck without major repairs." He told me he was going to return to his previous line of work as a mechanic.

As bad as a lease-purchase can be, when an illness, accident, or other misfortune befalls a contractor who buys a truck independently, the consequences can be even worse. Drivers often mortgage their house or empty a retirement account from a previous job to get a down payment and start-up cash. Since they have equity in the truck, even if they cannot work or are losing money some contractors will continue to make payments. This can rapidly eat through any savings they may have left, and force them to take money from other areas of their life just to keep working. Here is how one contractor who bought two trucks, a straight truck he drove and a tractor-trailer his son operated, described his situation:

> SV: What are your big concerns looking into the future about the plan that you have [for contracting]? What are the unknowns and challenges in terms of being successful?

> Driver: My own personal position? I bet the ranch. I bet my house. I bet everything on this business. If we have a month . . . like, in November of last year I hit a big buck on the Indiana toll road and it did $13,000 in damage to my truck. My truck was in the shop for six weeks. With only two trucks, that nearly crippled us, six weeks without the revenue. So our near-term focus is to keep working on debt reduction, so that you have a little bit of staying power if something major goes wrong that is not covered in the warranty, especially with the bigger truck because it is more expensive. If that thing went down for six weeks, we would be in *deep poop*.

Here is another contractor describing his concerns for the future:

> The job itself is relatively predictable. It is the truck that is not predictable. That damn thing could break down at any time—*for any reason*. It could be

running fine for weeks and everything seems fine and then, all of a sudden, it will just crap out on you for no reason. You run them so much, and so hard, and so often, that it is only a matter of time before things wear down. [An employee's] truck is not his life, he can quit that company today and go have another job tomorrow. Us, on the other hand, our truck *is* our life.

The most experienced contractor I interviewed bought only new trucks. But all the other contractors I interviewed could not afford to buy new. The drivers who tried to avoid a lease by buying a used truck quickly learned that buying older trucks did not save them any money and increased their risk. Some continued to do it, though, because they believed it gave them more independence than a lease-purchase, even though all of them freely admitted that they could not move from company to company without great risk and costs.

Economic Consequences

Unfortunately, whether they buy a truck through a lease-purchase or on their own, the painful reality most contractors learn within months or a few years is that they make significantly less than comparably experienced employees. I gathered self-reported annual incomes for fifty of the seventy-five drivers I interviewed before the start of the Great Recession (thirty-one company drivers, fifteen contractors, four independents).[3] The company drivers I interviewed averaged $46,200 in pretax income during the previous year. After paying the employee portion of FICA (7.65 percent of earnings), the average company driver would have $42,665 in income before other taxes. Contractors I interviewed averaged $37,267 in pretax income after truck expenses. Once the average contractor paid self-employed FICA taxes (15.3 percent on 92.35 percent of income[4]) their income was $32,001 before other taxes, 25 percent less than the average company driver.[5]

Contractors make significantly less than comparable employees, and this has been the case since the beginning of the modern reincarnation of contractors in the 1990s. After adjusting data from a 1997 University of Michigan survey (described in Appendix A) for payroll taxes, I found that the median contractor not employing another driver earned about 16 percent less than the median company driver. Although significant, these figures do not reflect the effect of experience. On average, contractors have more experience than employees working for large truckload firms.[6] In effect, what contracting does is allow firms to utilize significantly more experienced and potentially valuable labor at compensation levels even lower than what they pay less experienced drivers. Even the data of those who promote contracting support the conclusion that contractors make less than they could as employee drivers.[7]

Exactly how much less workers earn as contractors than they would as employees is impossible to know. But if they stayed within their segment, contractors would probably make at least 15 to 25 percent more as employees. If they left the segment and used their experience to get jobs at private fleets, which paid a median salary of more than $74,000 in 2011, they might double their annual income while working far fewer hours.[8] But they don't; instead they are convinced to stay in the segment and become contractors.

Would-be contractors are systematically misled about the net income they can expect, and have extreme difficulty interrogating industry-provided estimates. Most of their difficulties lie in an inability to estimate or account for the costs of owning the truck. Most understand, of course, that they will have to pay for fuel, a truck payment, maintenance, and insurance. But all inexperienced drivers and many experienced ones dramatically underestimate the costs of these as well as other truck expenses and, just as importantly, fail to recognize many of the tax consequences of ownership.

I asked drivers considering contracting to lay out for me what they figured it would cost them to lease or own and operate a truck. All of them underestimated the likely costs by tens of thousands of dollars. This situation is not simply the result of a lack of preparation or effort on the part of drivers. Drivers are systematically denied access to information, and carriers and other sources misrepresent, or never present, information that is critical for drivers to understand. Critical costs that carriers can—but drivers can't—accurately estimate add up to enormous sums for individual drivers.

For instance, let's say that a driver is considering buying a truck that he is told averages 6.5 miles per gallon, typical fuel economy for a loaded tractor-trailer. He plans to run one hundred twenty thousand miles a year, a typical amount for a new contractor. If fuel costs $2.80 a gallon, as it did before the price spikes of 2007 and 2008, he will burn about 18,460 gallons of fuel per year, at a cost of $51,700. But if it turns out the truck isn't quite as fuel efficient as he was told by the dealership, and the company that he leased onto frequently hauls, say, beer across hilly terrain, he could easily see his fuel economy drop to 5.5 miles per gallon, not a poor rating under those conditions. If that happens, he would burn 21,818 gallons of fuel, at a cost of $61,090 per year. That is a difference of $9,390 a year, all of which he expected as take-home pay. In May 2008 diesel fuel averaged $4.20 per gallon nationally. Our hypothetical drivers' fuel cost is now $91,635 on an annual basis, or almost $40,000 more than he estimated.

Most contractors are paid a fuel surcharge that is meant to offset some of the cost of rising fuel prices. However, when fuel prices spiked in 2008, I met several contractors operating at or near a loss despite receiving such fuel surcharges (as I will discuss in Chapter 6).

There are a number of other, more predictable, costs that I found were also always underestimated by would-be contractors, including health insurance, self-employment taxes, and worker's compensation in certain states. Even existing contractors failed to take all of these additional expenses into account when comparing their pay to that of employees.

Here is a list of other expenses a contractor might be responsible for that a would-be contractor is likely to underestimate, if he considers them at all: truck insurance while under loads and not, state and federal licenses, state and federal permits, accounting, truck washes, telephone, tolls, road taxes, and fuel taxes. For the typical contractor these expenses can easily add up to more than $10,000 per year.

Once they buy a truck, drivers initially embrace the idea of contracting as a means to achieve the American Dream of small-business ownership. This justifies some of the additional expenses as they become aware of them. Contractors view the loss of benefits like unemployment insurance and the burden of self-employment taxes as legitimate costs of greater independence. Paying for their own benefits demonstrates their status as business owners not dependent upon an employer. For instance, contractors never complained about having to pay what would have been the employer's portion of Social Security taxes until they came to believe that the promised benefits of ownership were nothing more than a deception and decided to return to work as employees. Here is a typical response about taxes from a contractor, who has owned his truck for less than a year:

> SV: Do you have a separate bank account for truck expenses, or do you keep it all in one account?
>
> Driver: . . . We have a business account. So like, for taxes, we take part of my pay, my settlement, and we put it in that business account because we are responsible for our own taxes. We are owner-operators. If I want to pay workman's comp, it's got to come out of me . . . The medical insurance that we have, we had to go get on our own . . . that is on us—[as] independent businesspeople. And a lot of people when they get into this say, well, I want to own my own truck. Well, sit down. Pay attention. Here's what you're going to be paying. They don't realize what goes into owning your own truck, owning your own business.
>
> SV: It is worth it to you, though?
>
> Driver: To me it is, being my own businessman.

This sense of pride, and the belief that paying costs like self-employment taxes is an acceptable consequence of their status as small businesspeople, stands in stark contrast to the way contractors viewed companies giving them reimbursements for living expenses on the road, instead of wages, when they were employees. Classifying a portion of compensation for truckers as reimbursement for living expenses is an increasingly common tax strategy for firms to avoid payroll taxes. Here is a new contractor explaining why he left his previous job as an employee:

> Driver: The final reason that I decided to [become a contractor] was because my company cut my pay by 30 percent. They cut my pay from thirty-one cents a mile to nineteen cents a mile and gave me the difference as per diem (i.e., reimbursement for living expenses rather than wages). So essentially that gives me more money right now take-home to spend in my pocket, but I am fifty-five, what that does is cut my Social Security benefits by 33 percent.
>
> SV: So they were paying less in Social Security tax?
>
> Driver: They cut their payroll tax by 30 percent, saying that they were making me more money, but what they're doing is screwing me out of 30 percent of my Social Security . . . If I have the per diem system I have to show receipts

and what I cannot show receipts for that per diem I have to show as income, and I have to pay Social Security and federal tax out of that, which [is not deducted] out of my check. So it is also a tax problem.

This worker did not see paying the self-employment payroll taxes as a problem now that he was a contractor, but quit his former job because his employer reduced payments for his Social Security benefits—affecting both the firm's contribution and potentially his future benefit levels. He then agreed to lease-purchase a truck over a period of four years from a firm that makes *no contribution at all* toward these benefits, worker's compensation, or unemployment insurance. This acceptance of additional taxation indicates how contracting changes the way workers view the class relations of employment.[9]

Giving Up Control

A major part of why inexperienced drivers believe becoming a contractor will mean more income is because they think contracting will give them the ability to regularly choose the most profitable loads. They believe this because the company tells them they will have this right, and that it is *guaranteed by their contract and the law*. Workers being able to decide what kinds of work they do and how to do it are central to legal definitions of contracting, and it is critical that companies convince workers, regulators, and courts that trucking contractors have that kind of control.

Existing contractors will cite the importance of the right to refuse loads, even if they do not exercise it. Here is a typical exchange, with a new contractor (leased to a medium-sized company for almost a year):

Driver: Yeah, [you can make more money as a contractor] because you can pick what you haul.

SV: Have you been able to do that, pick the loads that you want?

Driver: I can turn down a load by the [satellite communication system]. They send you a load offer, they call it a load offer, you can refuse it or you can take it.

SV: They actually phrase it that way, as a "load offer?"

Driver: A load offer.[10]

SV: And you do turn those down?

Driver: I haven't yet.

My discussions with inexperienced contractors were filled with contradictions like this, between how important the right to refuse loads is and whether or not it was actually exercised. Experienced contractors, on the other hand, understood how useless the terms of their contract were in the day-to-day relationship with their dispatcher. Despite the fact that nearly all of them cited their nominal right to turn down loads as one of the main reasons they wanted to be a contractor in the first place, only a few contractors claimed to have done it even once in the previous year, and those drivers feared retribution from their dispatchers or the company's brokers if they were to turn down loads more often. This is a twenty-seven-year-old white male, who failed at a lease-purchase and had been a contractor with another company using his own truck for four months when I interviewed him:

> SV: Do you ever refuse loads with [your current] company?
>
> Driver: No. They are small . . . that is one of the problems with a small company. They don't have access to a lot of extra loads. Normally, when they find a load, it is something that they need you to run. Normally, it is either a customer that they go to a lot or they are going through a broker, and the last thing that you want to do is piss off one of the better brokers. Because then they are going to give them a whole bunch of these three- and four-hundred-mile loads, which is only going to screw you in the long run.

Here is another contractor explaining how to be successful:

> SV: So [you are saying] you have got to be a little bit more flexible?
> Driver: If you work with the company, the company will work with you. But if you tell the company I ain't going to do that and I can't do this, the company is going to say we ain't got a load for you. We don't need you. And that is the bottom line.

In theory, the right to choose loads would allow you to choose loads that were lighter, longer, or kept you in areas where your next load was likely to be good. But any sort of strategy like this that would actually result in significantly more net revenue would require regularly selecting loads. In fact, the pressure to accept bad loads was at least as great for contractors as company drivers, because they were responsible for paying significant fixed expenses. A day or two of sitting would really hurt them. But inexperienced contractors did not see this vulnerability and lack of control as evidence of a problematic relationship with their carrier. They viewed these problems as part of running their own business. Here is a typical exchange on this point:

> SV: What are the keys to being successful as a contractor? I mean I hear a lot of guys don't make it.
>
> Driver: Like I said, there's times that you have got to do stuff that you really don't want to do, but you got to do it. Because somebody has got to do it. It's gotta get done . . . If you are going to pay your bills, you got to work, so that is the big thing right there. Some guys say, well I am not going to do that or I'm not going to go there. While you sit there you ain't making no money. So, a lot of people just pick and choose and put themselves out.
>
> SV: So being too picky about loads is a problem?
>
> Driver: It is a business. If you want your business to thrive, any business, I don't care what business you go into, there are various things that you have got to do whether you like it or not, you have got to do it. Somebody has got to do it. If you are sitting there waiting for some special load to come up and everybody else is out there running, and you ain't, you ain't going to pay your bills.

Like these drivers, nearly all contractors quickly learn that turning down loads will only hurt them financially, and so contractors end up accepting almost all loads assigned to them, just as company drivers do.

Additional Work and Effects at Home

Many drivers are surprised by the amount and type of additional work they have to perform as contractors. Here is one driver describing the extra work he didn't expect:

> Driver: Well as a company driver, you don't have to worry about paying the bills for the truck, maintenance, fuel, any of that. There is a lot more to running your own business than I thought. It has been a learning experience every day. Everything from the taxes, fuel, maintenance, whatever. Trying to

keep everything straight, you have got to be able to maintain it. My wife was a schoolteacher so she helps out a lot. But it is a lot more work than I actually thought. And I don't think a lot of people actually realize how much work is involved in owning your own truck.

The worst part for many contractors is how contracting negatively affects their personal lives. Long-haul driving is hard on anyone who has a family, whether they own a truck or not, but contracting makes it even harder. Even the simplest things can cause problems at home. For instance, one of the problems many contractors face is that they do not use a separate bank account to keep truck expenses apart from the rest of the family budget. As a result, they never have a true accounting of what the truck and life on the road are costing them, compared with what their partners and children are earning and spending at home. Many described arguments with spouses over spending at home when truck expenses increased. While this can be extremely stressful, sacrifices at home are understood as part of being a small businessperson and the cost of maintaining independence. Here is a contractor who has owned for three years.

> It is a little bit different running a trucking company, even a one-truck trucking company . . . I mean, I don't, I don't make as much *personal* money, I don't think, as I would if I was driving somebody else's truck . . . You gotta watch your pennies. Even your expenses at home, you have got to watch them, too. Because you have got to take money out of the business to pay yourself . . . I mean don't go buy you a brand new Cadillac and don't go buy you a $150,000 house . . . It is a lot more stressful [being a contractor], but it is worth it to me. [very long pause] I've thought about getting rid of the truck. I called [the dealership that financed it] three weeks ago and told them to come get it. "Well, it will hurt your credit." And I said, "I don't care, I'll file bankruptcy. Come get it." I was *sick of it*. "Come get it." My wife looked at me and said, "You're not doing that, I've seen you when you are a company driver, you are no one that you want to deal with when you have to listen somebody else." She said, "Keep the truck." I said, "*Okay*, we are [going to have to] stretch things a little bit, we're going to have pinch here and pinch there" . . . [I am thirty-three years old], I feel like I am about sixty, though.

As one might imagine, the need to make economic sacrifices like this at home because of contracting often puts great strain on personal relationships. Several former contractors told me they believed that contracting had ruined their marriages.

More generally, problems arise from the fact that working while at home becomes a critical part of a contractor's job; often spouses and children help contractors work this extra margin. Here is a description of arriving home given by a sixty-year-old white male, who was downsized from his last job and became a contractor in the expedited freight business about a year and half before I met him:

> In the expedited business, you don't know when the call is coming. So you get home and you are going to be home until next Wednesday or you might be going out on the road again tomorrow. And I learned this the very first week. Never again. When I get home, if I get home during the daylight hours, I empty the truck, the wife starts my laundry. I mean immediately. Right now. If it is during daylight hours, I put the truck at the end of the driveway and wash it. And then she prepares the food. Because I carry a little refrigerator and it is very expensive eating on the road all the time. I get that truck ready to go, so if that phone rings unexpectedly I can be on the highway in fifteen minutes. You have to do that. You can't not have your truck ready. Because I did it once. And I wasn't late, but I drove a lot faster than I should've been driving to be there on time. It was an awful scramble. And I just told my wife, we've been married for forty years, this will not happen again. First order of duty—if I've been gone two weeks it doesn't matter—say hello, give a kiss, deal with an emergency, but thirty minutes later, I am cleaning the truck and she is cleaning the clothes. And you don't want to do that. You roll into your house and the adrenaline just drains from your body. You don't want to keep pushing.

Maintenance, or lack of it, is an additional margin that contractors can try to work. Most contractors don't have the skills to do more maintenance than I did as a company employee, such as changing a blown light bulb or replacing a broken hose clamp. Still, if their contract permits it, contractors try to save money by performing maintenance themselves or delaying needed maintenance. The former, such as oil changes and basic repairs, can consume a good portion of what little time contractors have at home, and the latter can place an owner at risk for tickets, breakdowns, or worse. Contractors who performed their own maintenance described coming home from work on the road only to spend their nondriving time shopping for and working on their truck. As one former contractor told me, there is always something to fix or adjust. The most financially successful contractors were those who performed as much maintenance as they could on their own trucks and, as a result, spent years sacrificing what would have been their home time to perform additional work.

The amount of time contractors spend on the road and working at home often overwhelms the rest of their lives. The more experienced drivers I spoke with who were or who had been contractors described great personal sacrifice in order to "successfully" own. Contrary to what would-be contractors believe, contractors often take less time off than employees (which is significant, given how few days off employee drivers take). The drivers I spoke to described a sense of needing to be on the road as much as possible in order to be successful. I did meet two contractors who took as much time off as comparable employee drivers with good jobs. But they were by far the lowest-paid truckers I interviewed, and were very aware of the direct trade-off that they made between income and time at home. These drivers had owned their own trucks for at least ten years, and had sacrificed to get to the point where they could afford truck payments while taking off every other weekend and a week or two for vacation each year. Newer contractors, however, often forced themselves to stay out on the road for longer periods of time than they did as employees, as Claudio did. They saw this extra time, like other sacrifices required of them, as an investment that would pay off sometime in the future. But all drivers eventually get tired of living constantly on the road. As one very experienced and successful contractor sarcastically suggested when I asked him what advice he would give to an employee driver considering becoming a contractor:

> I would tell them, *you like driving a truck?* Go for it! You'll like it whether you are making money or not. It is the lifestyle. And if you are not married, you probably never will get married. So you better have your ducks in a row before you start driving a damn truck. Because it would be hard to keep a girl, or have a girlfriend, I think. At least you will have a shot at it. If you are one that is out there four thousand miles a week, you aren't going to have a girlfriend. You are going to have a boat, and a car, and a house, and that is about it—*you aren't going to have anything else.* A boat you won't use. A car you won't drive. I had a pickup truck for seventeen years, I put *seven thousand* miles on it.

This sense of having given up the rest of their lives in order to pursue the dream of contracting was universal among "successful" contractors.

Intensifying the Game

As the quote above suggests, contractors often work longer hours and drive more miles than they did as employees in the hope of succeeding as small business owners. They were far more likely than company drivers to say they wanted to work more hours and feel pressure to work illegally in order to increase their take-home pay. Often the costs of truck payments, insurance, fuel, etc., meant contractors who had taken time off, or who were dispatched on poor-quality loads, would be working for no take-home pay or for less than minimum wage for a week or more at a time. As a result, they are forced to produce more through self-sweating or illegal driving in order to achieve the same or even less pay than employees with comparable skills and experience.[11]

Self-sweating can come in many forms, including literally sweating to save fuel. Here is a driver, who failed at a lease-purchase, describing what he was taught in his orientation about increasing fuel efficiency:

> [They basically focused on] fuel. Trying to keep your fuel costs down. But see, they are sitting there saying, "Well, you don't need to run your truck at night." Well, that is true if it's nice, like now, but if it is 90° outside at night when you're sitting in Arizona, you are not going to be able to sleep in your truck . . . if it is 90° *out there,* it is a 100° *in the truck* and you're going to sit there and sweat and then get up and drive the next day? I don't think that is even possible.

Some contractors attempt to cut other corners that expose them to the risk of tickets and worse. Here is a contractor explaining that he chose to lease with his current carrier because it is known for being more "flexible" with enforcing regulations:

> Driver (visibly hesitating): The drivers that I have talked to [told me the company runs] a little bit, I guess you would say, outlaw. But they are trying to improve their safety. They basically put us in control, let us run our own hours, we have to follow what the DOT says obviously, but they're not on top of us every five minutes, a little more flexible. They say, "I need you to pick

up here and drop it here, how you get there is your problem." And you're supposed to be a professional driver and they treat us like that.

There is no "flexibility" in the DOT rules, only in enforcement by carriers and compliance by drivers. This driver, like most employee or contractor drivers, is winking and nodding at the idea that he follows the DOT rules. Contractors like this can self-sweat to a degree that is extreme even for trucking. When I asked this contractor if he likes his current company, he responded:

Driver: They keep you running. Very rarely do I take [time off] like this, but I needed it. I am just kind of recovering from pushing my last load. Because I know that when I get a load tomorrow I'll probably be going to California. And I know that as soon as I get to California I'm going to turn right around and head back to the East Coast and that is where they keep it running. I'm usually averaging thirty-eight hundred to forty-five hundred a week.

SV: That is a lot of miles.

Driver: That is a pretty nice paycheck, but that is the only way that you can (pauses) . . . it is the only way that you can make it profitable.

SV: You are not pushing the seventy-hour rule [the total number of hours a driver can work over eight days]?

Driver: (laughing) Oh, *yeah*.

SV: Are you taking a restart [a thirty-four-hour break that resets the seventy-hour rule]?

Driver: You take time off and try to keep nine or nine and one-half hours a day.

SV: On the book [i.e. recorded in his logbook].

Driver: On the book, because that way you are always picking up hours. I kind of pushed it with this load. But I know that I've got ten or twelve hours that I'm going [to wait for the next load]. So as long as I [underreport the hours I spend waiting for loads and driving I will] keep dropping farther away from that seventy. And if you can keep it like that, you will always be able to run. But the thing is just to keep running profitable.

What this driver is describing is a common strategy that drivers, both contractors and employees, use to falsify their logbook, so they never appear to violate the seventy-hour rule. To put how much this driver is working in perspective, even with the best loads I had to work more than ninety hours a week to drive over three thousand miles. Needless to say, even if they have all "miracle" loads that give them long runs from coast to coast, the risks for drivers like this are great. Violating Hours of Service (HOS) regulations can put their license at risk and result in fines of thousands of dollars. HOS violations have far greater consequences for a contractor with his own truck and insurance than for an employee. Most importantly, drivers like this, who push themselves to (or past) the point of exhaustion, put themselves at greater risk of an accident. Any experienced driver will tell you that this sort of self-sweating is not sustainable. Sooner or later fatigue will collide with the wrong circumstances, and a trucker could lose his truck and future prospects of a better trucking job, if not his life.

Many drivers reported experiencing greater fatigue as a result of the increased self-sweating while owning their own truck, and believed it had negative consequences for their health. One former contractor, who now worked as an employee, told me:

> I used to believe that you couldn't make a good living unless you did run two log books [to always have one current to show law enforcement]. You couldn't make a living if you run legal. No way. But I don't believe that any more. It's not true. And if a man has to pop pills and do everything else to make a living (voice trailing off and shaking his head) . . . No, I had never run legal before . . . I used to run auto parts [when I was a contractor]. I ran so hard [my dispatcher] thought I was running team [i.e., had a partner sharing the driving]. He said, "You are not running team?" I said, "No, no. I'm just nuts." But anyways, all that did was make an old man out of me. I'm worn out. I'd retire yesterday if I could.

Nearly all the experienced drivers I spoke to who had been contractors mentioned the huge toll that the stress and self-sweating required by contracting took on them. For most the efforts were impossible to sustain.

CONCLUSION

In the end, the harsh reality for nearly all drivers who try their hand at independent contracting is that they work harder than they did as employees and make far less than they hoped. Some will quickly, perhaps in a matter of a few months, realize that they have made a mistake. Others will continue to sacrifice for years, partly because the promise of more control and financial reward is so powerful for workers hoping to make a career out of trucking. After listening to current and former contractors, I began to sincerely wish that independent contracting did offer that kind of opportunity for them. Regardless of the outcome, most behaved as if more control and more money were within reach, and the amount of work and risk they would take on to achieve them was often stunning. Again, it is exactly these kinds of efforts our economy is supposed to reward. But sustaining such efforts without a return was no mean task. Of course, it is in a carrier's interest to keep workers working as independent contractors as long as they can. As the next chapter suggests, over time carriers have paid increasing attention to developing ways to sustain the efforts of independent contractors when they begin to realize the rewards are not coming.

5 Someone to Turn To

MANAGING CONTRACTORS FROM
AN ARM'S LENGTH AWAY

Like Claudio, contractors often quickly realize they aren't enjoying the benefits they expected. While truckload contractors have lower rates of turnover than inexperienced employees—half as much, according to some carriers—their turnover rates are still high. Exactly how high and what happens to these workers when they leave is unclear, partly because many truckers leave the industry entirely when they fail at contracting. In a recent presentation, trucking insurance consultants reviewed the reasons contractors they insured voluntarily left their employer. Twenty percent could not be reached for an interview; 1 percent left because they "didn't like" their dispatcher; 8 percent left due to truck breakdown; 31 percent left because they were not getting enough miles or their pay rate was too low. The remaining 40 percent of contractors left the industry entirely.[1]

Like new employees, if contractors become disgruntled and quit companies too quickly, the cost of that turnover can exceed the benefits contractors provide to carriers. Carriers are well aware of the problems discussed in the last chapter and use various means to try to retain contractors as long as possible. Some of these methods are little more than simple financial and legal coercions, like lease-purchase contracts and escrow accounts. Others are far less visible to drivers, and like recruitment of

contractors, constitute a new set of labor market institutions that influence how workers behave by influencing what they think. Inexperienced
contractors view much of what carriers do in this regard as an attempt to
help them as business partners. But in reality, what carriers are doing is
outsourcing the management of workers. Partly they do this because it is
illegal for carriers to manage independent contractors. Managing workers—telling them how to work—would mean that the workers were not
self-employed, and this would make carriers employers, with all the costs
and responsibilities that entails. So carriers use third parties to influence
contractors' behavior, while protecting themselves from worker misclassification charges and the legal and financial responsibility of employers.
The use of third parties has other benefits as well, including allowing carriers to coordinate their labor market strategies with each other, develop
and legitimize new labor market norms, and avoid competing with one
another for contractors—which ultimately keeps down the cost of labor.

There are ways carriers can directly assist contractors in taking home
more income, including setting up discount and group purchasing plans
for tires, fuel, and services like insurance. But other than these, carriers
can only advise a contractor on how to take home more money by giving
tax advice or suggesting they work differently. This advice is often done
through the use of "business" classes, company advisors, and outside consultants, most often trucking accountants. But the "business skills" that
firms teach contractors have nothing to do with things like maximizing
the price they get for their services, and everything to do with being a better worker, having a better attitude toward management, and learning to
survive on less income.

An article in the trade press argued that for carriers to be successful
employing contractors it was important to ensure that workers can keep
enough of their gross revenue to continue in the position. It offered this
advice to carriers:

> Take steps to ensure your new owner-operators are successful. Prime, for
> instance, which leases trucks to its drivers and makes them independent
> contractors, requires them to go through a two-day seminar. The four-year-
> old "ACE 2" (Associate Career Enhancement) course, which Prime pays
> them to attend, has resulted in bottom-line profits for owner-operators that
> are 15 percent better, and 50 percent lower turnover for the company.[2]

As discussed in Chapter 3, the contracting discourse suggests contractors are business savvy and that carriers know this and must treat them with respect. But in the trade press and their treatment of contractors, it is clear that carriers believe many drivers lack the basic skills needed to survive as a contractor. Here is an excerpt from another article describing carrier-provided training programs for new contractors:

> Smart carriers that lease on owner-operators are finding ways to help their owner-operators with ... business skills. For instance, O&S Trucking in Springfield, Mo., has developed a six-module training system that uses board games and other methods to teach owner-operators business skills. The idea is to get new—or even not-so-new—single truck owners to think like businesspeople. Many come to the job with almost no business skills, despite a six-figure investment in their equipment. Charlotte Eckley, chief development officer, says many don't even possess a calculator. But turnover at the all-owner-operator fleet has dropped 60 percent as drivers begin to understand there's more to being an owner-operator than shining the truck on the weekends.[3]

After such initial attempts at education and developing "business skills," larger carriers will provide regular support using company personnel. Here is a Schneider National manager explaining how his company has employees dedicated to helping contractors manage their costs on a regular basis:

> "We feel that addressing the cost side of the owner-operator's business is helping us attract and retain [contractors]," says Norder. When signing on a prospective independent, according to Norder, Schneider looks for safe driving and financial stability. Once onboard with Schneider, owner-operators receive advice and direction on a daily basis from the fleet's independent carrier advisors (ICAs). "Our ICAs have the business and financial acumen to help ensure our independents succeed," explains Norder. "We also bring outside professionals into our facilities to provide direction to independents on business topics such as taxes."[4]

THE POWER OF COLLUSION: ATBS, ITS CLIENTS, AND STRATEGIC PARTNERS

Some of Schneider's outside professionals, like those of many other major carriers, will likely come from American Trucking Business Services

(ATBS). ATBS was started after its owner, Todd Amen, converted all the employees at his family's four-hundred-truck firm into contractors. When Amen presents ATBS to contractors and would-be contractors, as he regularly does at seminars at truck shows and on the radio, he says something like this (an excerpt from a video on the company's website): "ATBS was developed with owner-operators in mind in 1998 . . . to help them be more successful. [We take the burden of taxes and accounting, and provide businesses services] to allow them to do what they do best, which is drive the truck."[5]

ATBS advertises its accounting and business consulting services directly to contractors and states, "Owner-Operators who work with ATBS can make over 40 percent more profit and save thousands in taxes over the life of their business."[6] For $86.67 a month, a contractor can get "unlimited business consulting" and send in all of their receipts to ATBS, which then provides them with a monthly profit-and-loss statement and a year-end statement to use for tax purposes. It provides them with a benchmarking comparison of their costs relative to other contractors, to show them where their expenses are above or below the average.

Though ATBS claims its main business is providing services to contractors, its more important customers are one hundred or so "strategic partners," such as major manufacturers like Freightliner and nearly all of the largest carriers that employ contractors, which have included FedEx, Swift, Schneider, Landstar, J. B. Hunt, Dart, Greatwide, and many others. Many of these carriers provide ATBS services either for free or at a subsidized rate for their drivers. Some carriers have required that their contractors use ATBS. As a result of these relationships, ATBS has grown dramatically and is now the largest company of its type, handling accounting for more than forty thousand contractors.

Just like trucking media, this "accounting and tax professional" and "professional business consultant" is actually in the business of recruiting and managing labor for carriers in a number of different ways. ATBS has its own radio show, hosts seminars for trucking executives, and partners frequently with *Overdrive*.[7] Along with *Overdrive*, Schneider, and Freightliner, ATBS runs Partners in Business (PIB), which they describe as the leading business training program for owner-operators.[8] This joint venture conducts seminars at trucking shows, online webinars, and publishes *Partners in Business: A Business Manual for Owner-Operators*, an annually updated business manual for contractors that costs about thirty dollars. The manual provides basic information on accounting and the legal requirements of being a contractor.

ATBS's messages to contractors contain all of the contracting discourse, which is represented as the advice of a business consultant. For instance, in the opening section of the PIB manual it states, "Owner-operator income has averaged 20 percent to 30 percent higher than company driver income in recent years."[9] Though ATBS has exact numbers for forty thousand contractors, it does not present information on how much these truckers make in the manual. Instead, throughout the manual there are hypothetical scenarios of cost and revenue figures that consistently suggest that contractors earn $50,000 to $60,000 a year after expenses. On the all-important decision of lease-purchasing a truck, discussed in the last two chapters, PIB weighs in with this assessment: "Some carriers have been suspected of using these programs primarily as profit centers, but most such plans are fair."[10]

While ATBS recruits contractors similarly to, and some times in partnership with, Randall-Reilly and carriers, ATBS plays important roles in structuring the relationship of carriers to contractors, helping carriers to retain contractors, and coordinating the labor market behavior of carriers as a group.

For instance, it now offers its own truck leasing program for carriers. Here is ATBS's description of the value of this enterprise:

> Owner-operators are the ultimate capacity development tool allowing you to reduce capital expenditure and have a safer and more reliable driver while delivering higher quality service. A partnership with ATBS Leasing can help you build a leasing program to attract and keep drivers who want to become owner-operators, saving you time and resources while maintaining an arm's length business relationship with your operators. We ensure that the owner-operator has the means, experience and capability to be successful as an owner-operator and our turnover tracks at least 50% lower than average turnover. We own the trucks and manage the owner-operator truck lease [we provide business services and education]. What you get is a qualified owner-operator in a reliable truck that has the knowledge and support to run their business efficiently.[11]

ATBS also offers a Fleet Conversion Program, a service that helps carriers convert existing company fleets into contractor fleets. Here is how ATBS describes that program:

> Owner-operators can [allow] you to expand your fleet quickly with little outlay of capital. However, costs for recruiting can be high and competition is fierce. ATBS Fleet Conversion Programs provide a more cost-effective solution to an owner-operator fleet, helping you with the logistics of converting your fleet, and providing products, services and truck leasing options developed to assist owner-operators with every aspect of their business.[12]

ATBS offers a "Triage program [that] has helped finance companies and fleets save millions by avoiding repos and reducing turnover." When contractors are threatening to break a lease agreement or may go bankrupt, ATBS's triage consultants will intervene for the carrier or note holder, do "a thorough evaluation of business and personal issues," develop "an action plan" and conduct "ongoing consulting" to help "at risk owner-operators turn their businesses around."[13]

Finally, ATBS provides benchmarking services, which it describes as "a key strategic management tool that allows you to evaluate how your owner-operator program compares to others running similar operations. Provided for ATBS Partner Carriers, [benchmarking] can help you understand your competition, manage your recruiting efforts and identify areas that may need improvement."[14] In other words, what this "accounting and business consulting" company does is keep track of contractors' income and expenses and then provides that information to their existing and potential employers, who use it to gain an advantage in the labor market. ATBS's strategic partners know exactly the income of their contractors' "businesses" and the average costs and income of the contractors their competitors employ. Companies can thus set compensation plans using far more accurate data than could possibly be available to an individual carrier, let alone to contractors. This allows carriers to avoid unnecessarily bidding up the price of labor.

Carriers can also use ATBS as a way to learn from one another in developing new kinds of compensation plans. For instance, here's an excerpt from an article about how ATBS was helping carriers during the Great

Recession to develop new compensation schemes that shifted risk to workers:

> "Carriers went to percentage pay because freight that's marginal has weak margins. Carriers and owner-operators have been sharing in a weak freight market." Percentage-pay programs offered in earlier years confused some owner-operators, who were accustomed to simple per-mile plans, says Todd Amen, president of owner-operator business services provider ATBS. The confusion hampered recruiting efforts, and some fleets reverted to mileage pay. Despite these missteps, at least five "significant carriers have asked us who does it and how it works," Amen says. "They're thinking long-term. They want it (percentage pay) now because their rates from shippers have dropped and they're still having to pay drivers the same amount (per mile), which has hurt their margin. They'd rather have everything variable, so the driver made less." Other carriers, however, have been forced to cut pay as business slowed. Amen says he's hearing of carriers "tweaking their packages—maybe taking a penny or two away from base-mile pay. They're going from a 5.5 mpg fuel surcharge average to 6.5 mpg, or they're not paying for base plates and licenses like they used to. These are things that add up to probably 1 to 3 cents a mile, things the driver may not notice as blatantly as a huge pay change."[15]

As carriers began exploring percentage pay systems, *Overdrive* ran a number of articles about how percentage pay was increasingly popular among the most successful owner-operators. These articles quoted ATBS staff and positively portrayed ATBS's partner carriers' percentage pay programs. At the same time, the PIB manual added additional discussion of the benefits of percentage systems for contractors.

ATBS serves to coordinate the labor market behavior of employers by providing the benchmarking data companies need to set compensation rates that reduce competition for labor and driver turnover. Benchmarking data allows firms to set pay rates that are comparable to similar firms, allowing them to keep pay as low as possible and capture more profit. But in presenting the issue of pay to drivers, they suggest that companies are powerless to set pay rates. Here for instance, is one of the "myths" dispelled in PIB's business manual:

> "Myth 5"—Your company can control how much they pay you. Your company does not have much influence on the rates they charge shippers because it is their consideration of the marketplace that dictates the rates.[16]

In fact, firms have complete control over what to pay drivers and are constantly deciding what to pay both contractors and employees in order to optimize the trade-off between low pay and turnover in the most profitable way.

ATBS also publishes a newsletter for the contractors that use its services. In this newsletter, and presumably in its one-on-one advising with contractors, ATBS acts as a labor manager and suggests things that carriers could never argue to their employees. One critical area that ATBS focuses on is control over time. Much of their advice suggests that contractors make themselves available in exactly the ways that drivers want to avoid. It suggests that they make sacrifices at home as a business investment. For instance, the period right before holidays is often a difficult time for carriers to keep their trucks moving, since both contractors and employee drivers want additional time off just as freight markets are busiest. In one newsletter, for the sake of building up their business, ATBS argued:

> No one should miss a holiday with their family, but it is important to protect your business. What can you do? Work until right before each holiday. The days before a holiday can be the best times to generate revenue. Other drivers have gone home and shippers are often desperate to get freight moved . . . Make up missed holiday time in January: Even though you may miss one of the holidays with your family by working as much as possible, you can take extra time off in January and make it up to them [when freight is slower] . . . For additional tips, for support or even for a cheery Happy Holidays, call your Business Consultant.[17]

Whether the issue is working through the holidays or new systems of pay, ATBS will be there to advise contractors on how they should understand it and respond. Most of the advice in its newsletters deals with cutting costs for truck operation and expenses at home. They advise contractors to do things like cut credit card debt, establish a family budget, and spend less on entertainment. One such newsletter on how to cut expenses at home began by saying, "If your revenue is good and you're not making it there is only one conclusion: You're spending too much" and ended with, "*It simply comes down to your choices* [emphasis in original]."[18] In other words, ATBS is encouraging workers to integrate their business management with their personal spending to ensure that the compensation they receive is sufficient to continue working as a contractor.

Beyond cutting fuel costs, no specific theme is addressed more clearly and more often by ATBS than the cost of switching carriers. Here is how a 2010 newsletter discussed the issue of switching carriers for higher rates:

> [The economic recovery and a shortage of supply will raise the pay carriers offer to contractors] This will rekindle the temptation for owner-operators to switch carriers. The upside to switching seems obvious—more revenue. However that doesn't always work out financially. If you've been an ATBS client for a while, you already know that it's not just about more revenue. There is a high cost to switching that usually exceeds $10,000 . . . We can help you out or do your own math and see why it costs so much to make the change. Many owner-operators have lost their business after the process of changing carriers and often have no idea why it happened . . . You made it through some terrible economic times because you figured it out and then you did a lot of things right. One of those things you've done right was that you picked a good carrier and counted on them in the tough times. That was smart then and it should be smart now. Recruiting ads, sign-on bonuses, and new compensation packages will make it tempting to switch but make sure the picture becomes clear before risking your business.[19]

One of ATBS's strongest selling points to carriers is reducing turnover among contractors. In this case ATBS is trying to convince workers not to leave for offers of higher revenue—it is hard to believe any "math" ATBS does for contractors will favor doing otherwise.

In effect, ATBS is a labor management firm for carriers that would otherwise compete with one another for contractors. Their management activities seek to influence the behavior of contractors relative to their employer in the workplace *and* in the labor market. When the industry's major players are trying to rework labor market institutions, such as changing pay from a per mile to a percentage system, ATBS can help them figure out how to do this, and then convince workers it's a good thing for them, too. ATBS establishes its legitimacy to achieve these ends by presenting itself to drivers as an expert accounting and business consulting firm working in their interest. They are so successful in this regard that tens of thousands of truckers voluntarily pay for their services.

I met several drivers who use ATBS because their company recommended it and/or subsidized the cost, and I have read dozens of discussions among drivers about the company on internet forums. While negative comments about the quality of the accounting services ATBS provides are routine, it does not appear that contractors question the ultimate nature of this company's business or its relationship to the carriers that employ them. They appear to see ATBS as a company that provides business services to contractors and nothing more. For instance, in one online discussion, prompted by a question from a contractor who wanted to know if anyone had used ATBS, several dozen contractors responded. Many reported being dissatisfied with the company's service or prices. At the end was a reply from the originator of the thread along with a final comment:

> Reply: Thanks for all the helpful information. It doesn't seem like anyone has had a good experience with them. If that's the case, how did they get so big?

> Final comment: They have a good sell tactic and many companies actually recommend them to drivers or even pay the fees. That is how we ended up using them. It is still amazing to me they are as big as they are.[20]

DEFENDING THE USE OF CONTRACTORS

There is one final hurdle for carriers using contractors that has created a role for third parties like ATBS: avoiding tax and legal challenges to their use. Most importantly, carriers must ensure that their relationship with contractors meets the legal requirements that govern the use of independent contractors. The most immediate cost advantages of using contractors result from tax avoidance. Carriers avoid paying FICA payroll taxes (Social Security and Medicare), worker's compensation, and federal and state unemployment insurance. Contractors are also not covered by most labor laws. As a result, there are a host of state and federal agencies that are interested in ensuring that employers are not just classifying workers as contractors to avoid taxes and labor regulation including the IRS, Social Security Administration, state and federal Departments of Labor, and the National Labor Relations Board.

Unfortunately for carriers, the definitions of independent contractors used by these agencies are complicated, and the consequences of not ensuring that contracting arrangements meet these definitions can be severe. Class action lawsuits claiming misclassification by trucking carriers are increasingly common, as are aggressive audits at both the state and federal levels. For instance, in a 2015 settlement of a lawsuit filed in 2010, FedEx Ground agreed to pay $225 million dollars for misclassifying just a portion of its contractors. A case against UPS, tentatively settled in January of 2010, awarded 660 of its contractors $12.8 million, more than $19,000 per worker.[21] While these profitable industry giants can absorb the costs of such settlements, less profitable truckload carriers could be bankrupted by a misclassification suit.

As a result, large and small carriers often consult with specialized legal firms to structure their employment relationships to avoid having independent contractors reclassified as employees. I interviewed two company owners who had converted their fleets from company drivers to contractors. Both did so to save on capital and labor costs. Both told me that they had been considering switching to contractor labor for several years, but were reluctant to do so because of the legal challenges involved. When these owners finally felt that they had no choice but to employ contractors to remain competitive, they sought out the help of legal specialists and third-party leasing companies.

There are two key issues in trucking that tend to be determinative in misclassification lawsuits and audits: 1) the degree of control over work; and 2) the degree of financial control. Issues of financial control typically center on the potential for profit and loss, and investment in equipment, which in the case of trucking comes down to owning the truck.

In order to avoid appearing to have financial control over their contractors, lawyers recommend that carriers lease trucks to contractors through a third party, either a shell corporation or something like ATBS's leasing service. The Truckload Carriers Association, one of the largest industry associations, published an article by a leasing specialist entitled "Owner-Operator Finance Programs Boost Profitability" that described this role:

> With the high turnover rate among company drivers and the growing cost of seating new drivers, trucking companies with an owner-operator equipment

leasing program can be more successful at attracting and retaining experienced, reliable owner-operators . . . Implementing a lease option to attract owner-operators allows the carrier to eliminate or reduce many of the costs associated with the employer-employee relationship, such as paid time off, health insurance and other benefits . . . [Additional benefits] are reduced balance sheet leverage, improved cash flow, reduced maintenance expenses, increased gain on sale from equipment dispositions, reduced training expense, increased driver loyalty and more . . . Partnering with an experienced leasing company to develop a financing program can transfer the uncertainties of extending terms to drivers to the leasing company . . . Put simply, by working with a third party, your company will receive many benefits with nominal risk.[22]

As the quote illustrates, such specialists not only assist companies by creating legal distance between them and the leasing process, they promote contracting to carriers. They serve as a source of information about new models and the behavior of competitors. For instance, in light of increased enforcement and legislative scrutiny of independent contracting, law firms that specialize in structuring employment relations are now encouraging their clients to further "refine" their contracts and explore the use of other legal arrangements. In a recent presentation to trucking firms on the legal status of contractors, sponsored by PIB, a tax lawyer stressed the need to carefully review the risks of various features of the employment relationship, but concluded that the current multiple definitions and enforcing agencies made hard and fast rules for defensible contracts impossible:

> [Structuring contracts] is more of an art form than a science at this point. It is important that you . . . think out your method of operation for this whole control issue . . . It's not what you do, it is often times, *how you do it*.[23]

This lawyer also reviewed two of the most promising potential strategies for minimizing the risk of having contractors reclassified as employees. These strategies were using labor-leasing companies, who would assume the responsibility of an employer, or getting contractors to formally incorporate as limited liability corporations (LLCs). Here is how he described the benefits of getting contractors to form an LLC:

> The alternative model would be one in which a motor carrier would encourage owner-operators to obtain their own authority [to haul freight as a

motor carrier] and then provide dedicated service to the larger carrier's bro-
ker fleet and provide leased equipment to that carrier . . . [recently several
larger carriers I work with] were looking at the alternative model to hedge
their bets . . . I advise [companies to get their owner-operators to incorporate as LLCs]. I am not saying that it is outcome determinative, but certainly it gives you a basis for saying, "we encouraged this guy to incorporate,
to form an LLC, we treated him as if he was more than just an individual,
that he was a business and we required that" . . . I have suggested that to
clients, and they say, "well, it is a hassle" . . . Obviously if you are going to tell
an owner-operator that you want him to incorporate, you are going to want
to make that as easy for him [as possible].[24]

This quote illustrates the role legal specialists play in defending the use of
contractors and in diffusing new models of employment relations from company to company. It clearly indicates that at least some employers currently
using contractors will not simply return to traditional models of employment if changes to tax and employment law or enforcement of existing law
make contractors less attractive. The incentives are simply too great to walk
away from without exploring alternatives, which some employers are already
doing.[25] Most importantly, the quote illustrates the tremendous differences
in resources between firms and their potential contractors, and the conscious
recognition by firms and their advisors of their power to shape alternative
employment arrangements and convince workers to accept them.

This web of third parties serves to coordinate the action of employers
in the labor market and to directly intervene on employers' behalf in
recruiting, training, and managing workers. It also serves as means for
employers to collectively monitor specific sets of practices, experiment
and improve upon them and, when necessary, defend them against challenges from the state. Such arrangements have thus taken on many of the
historical responsibilities of worker organizations and unions relative to
workplace and labor market institutions, now that those labor-dominated
institutions are gone.

AN UNTENABLE SITUATION

Contracting arrangements are a means to retain and exploit the hardest-
working truckers by making them feel like they have *more* control over

their work and are *less* economically exploited. But, without fail, those who have done it end up summing up the experience of being a contractor and the self-sweating it leads to as "working for the truck." All of the management and retention strategies that carriers and their third-party partners employ will only prolong the inevitable departure of the nearly all contractors.

Some drivers stay in contracting for years, working hard and hoping things will get better, before they are convinced that they should return to being employees or find a new line of work. Here is a driver who has been a contractor for several years, reflecting on his current situation:

> We put in a lot of hours and we're not compensated, nobody ever really is. There have been days that I've been paying somebody else to work. I was so far in the negative I was sitting there thinking, what the hell am I doing this for? There are *times* as a company driver that you are actually working for nothing. But as an owner-operator there a lot of *days* like that. Because of the cost of fuel—one breakdown will set you back two months or better or put you out of business . . . I got into the truck with no money down, I didn't have any maintenance money, so I had to do it on my own. And they would take the money directly out of my paychecks and advances. So there was weeks just to keep the truck on the road and try to make a living I didn't get any money to the house, so I have got behind on those bills.

For many drivers, admitting that contracting isn't what they hoped for feels like a failure, and going back to work as an employee would pour salt in that wound. But after a few years of being subjected to the harsh realities of contracting, contractors' beliefs change. First, they begin to believe that the promised economic benefits of contracting cannot be realized without sacrificing the rest of their life.

At this point they also begin to see firms as a necessary evil rather than as a valued partner. Contractors like this express a strong sense of injustice and talk about how companies lie and abuse drivers. But they still see being an employee as a worse position. They accept that they do not exercise more control over load assignments and are often forced to work more than they would like, but some still say they feel more independent because they *could* exercise control if they wanted to, whatever it might cost them. They generally see themselves as better truckers than employees, because of the additional risk and responsibility that they take on and the greater amount of work that they perform. These contractors don't try to hide the fact that they have to work harder than employees; they are proud of it, particularly the number of miles they run. Being a successful contractor is, as these contractors see it, the ultimate test of one's ability to work hard. Others do not necessarily take pride in contracting, they simply want a measure of dignity they feel is unavailable to employees. Such drivers would often bitterly refer to their gross revenue as they reflect on the additional costs of contracting, potential risks, and the slim margins available to pay themselves.

Like less experienced contractors, these moderately experienced contractors define themselves in contradictory ways that reveal their subjugation to firms. They claim to be independent, risk-taking, small business owners, and yet frequently speak as if they are employees. Some talk about the possibility that their companies might give them a "raise" in their new contract, rather than speaking of renegotiating rates for their services. Others complain about being responsible for all of the costs of operation and being subjected to market conditions. Here is the kind of reflection the interviews prompted from such drivers:

SV: What are the biggest problems for contractors?

Driver: Well the high price of the fuel. *The costs.* Owner-operators shouldn't have costs. They have got a company that they are working for, it should pay them costs.

SV: If you were going to [switch companies] . . . what would you want if you were going to lease on with somebody else?

Driver: I would want them guys to absorb the costs involved. Make sure that I get paid, pay enough to cover the costs, that are created by that job. Instead of my company [i.e., the driver] absorbing it—all of the expenses that are incurred. Instead of them taking the profits and me taking the losses. And that exactly is pretty much what it is . . . I'm kind of thinking, while I'm talking to you, what the fuck am I doing in this business, anyways? Like I said . . . it is paying for itself, I guess. But barely.

More frequently than they blamed the companies they were leased to, struggling contractors blamed their difficulties on government restrictions over their work, tax burdens, or exploitative customers. These drivers understand some of the constraints on their opportunities as structural in nature. In particular, they recognize the importance of economies of scale. But these drivers do not criticize the economics behind their relationship to larger carriers. Overall, these drivers believe in free market principles. They do not see the disadvantages they face as the result of class power, but as the outcome of natural processes of competition. They don't begrudge those who have been successful and built the large companies that now dominate freight markets. They see these people's rise to success as the result of smarts and hard work, though they believe that once companies get "too big" they can be influenced by the government, which some believe wants an oligopolistic market in order to control HOS and taxation.

Some dissatisfied general freight contractors (where most start out) will move on to other segments, particularly the flatbed and refrigerated segments, where they try, most often in vain, to find higher incomes. A very small portion of contractors, recognizing the importance of price setting and access to more profitable niche markets, will try their hand at the even riskier game of becoming independents. But most contractors felt that they didn't have the resources or knowledge to operate without leasing on with a carrier. It was risky and involved the additional work of finding freight, negotiating rates, and getting brokers to pay. For example, when I asked one driver if he had considered becoming an independent, he told me:

> To operate under your own authority takes a lot. Because you are responsible for everything, base plates, all of it. I would be the first one to tell you I'm not ready for it. Understanding the laws. Understanding what goes into it. Understanding how to properly operate. The failure rate is like 90 percent.

Others contractors, who have cheap, reliable trucks, will continue to be contractors to preserve a sense of autonomy and status, or "dignity." These drivers were committed to staying in the industry but did not want to return to being an employee. Here is one driver describing why he wants to remain a contractor:

> SV: So do you figure you have made any more money [then you did as a company driver]?
>
> Driver: Not really.

SV: [If you are making less than you want to], why do you stay a [contractor]?

Driver: Mainly you are your own boss. You take a little less money for the independence of it. More the freedom than anything else. When you work for a company and you drive their truck, you have got to live by their rules.

Sooner or later, though, contractors begin to feel exploited.

Driver: You don't get paid for what you really work . . . If you take my time, if you consider my time, that ain't going to be worth it. Owner-operators don't get paid a true picture of the costs involved in doing the freight. That is why the companies [hire contractors], to eliminate some of them costs.

Seasoned workers know what contractors like this are experiencing, and they know what they should do about it. But new contractors often don't know these workers or interact in any way that would allow them to learn from their experience.

IF ONLY THEY HAD KNOWN

Inexperienced and would-be contractors have an almost romantic sense of how they can achieve the American Dream through hard work and sacrifice. The more I talked to them about contracting, the more I wanted the trucking industry to be a place where they could succeed as one-truck small-business operators. But other than very small niche markets, it isn't. And, in time, workers come to understand that. One driver who failed as a contractor summarized for me what he had learned from the experience this way:

Driver: I think [contracting] is 70 percent to 90 percent a scam. If this company is going to be making all this money with the truck, why would they want to give a truck to you? If they are out here, "Okay this truck is netting me $20,000 clear a year," they are not going to give *you* a truck. They're going to [put an employee in that truck and say], "Here's my $20,000 I make over the expenses, over driver's wages" . . . If it wasn't good for them, they wouldn't be doing it.

SV: So if you were you going to give advice to a driver thinking about [becoming a contractor], what would you tell them?

Driver: I would tell them, no, don't do it.

SV: Do you regret doing it?

Driver: Yeah. There is just not the money . . . the picture that they draw you, for leasing the truck, just does not match with what you are making out here.

SV: So you think that the companies are making more money off contractors than they are off of the company drivers?

Driver: Oh, *absolutely!* That is why they want [contractors], *they are making a pile of money.*

For experienced drivers there is no way contracting can benefit both drivers and carriers economically—to them it's a scam in a zero-sum economic game. They also reject the idea that contractors have more freedom than employees. Here is an employee driver reflecting on the experience of his friends and family and how the economics of contracting results in greater self-disciplining and risk:

There ain't no money in [contracting]. By the time you pay your truck payment, buy your insurance, buy your fuel, buy your maintenance for the truck, it is all out the door. You ain't made nothing . . . I have got several friends that were owner-operators and ain't owner-operators anymore. They lost their trucks because they couldn't pay for them . . . All of them are company drivers now . . . I had two uncles that owned their own trucks. They are both driving for somebody else now . . . They thought they would be in charge, that they could do what they wanted to do and stuff. You still can't do that. They want to go out and run the speed that they want to run. Well, you can run that for about a year and then you won't have any license anymore because you got too many tickets. And you burn more fuel . . . so it costs you more. Plus spending all that money on maintenance . . . all that money goes to the truck. None of it goes to you . . . I was a mechanic before I was a driver for eight years, I know how much it costs to work on those trucks and keep them running . . . Them companies like Select and all them, man, that is all that they do. They are ripping the drivers off . . . Doesn't make any sense to me. You are working for them still, why not drive a truck for somebody else? . . . You are still going to have to [drive miles] . . . [In fact,] you are going to have to [drive a lot more miles] when you own your own, because you have got to keep making money. There ain't no money in it . . . If you do make any profits, the next month you're going to have a blowout or whatever. And it's going to cost seven hundred bucks to get a tire put on out on the road somewhere. And there went all your profit.

Experienced drivers believe companies dupe drivers into contracting—draw them "a picture" of contracting, as the driver above puts it—that makes it seem like they will make lots of money, because inexperienced drivers do not understand the value of their labor. To experienced truckers, contracting is a job, not a business. It would only be a business if drivers could invest in and manage an asset that can return something beyond *the value of their labor as a driver.* For experienced drivers there must be significant profit, defined in this way, to justify the extra work and risk of owning a truck. For them, contracting obscures the value of drivers' labor and thus keeps it low. For instance, when I asked a white fifty-year-old employee from Arizona, who had previously worked as a contractor for ten years, how he would advise a driver considering becoming a contractor, he said,

> About 75 percent of the drivers that [become contractors] are beginners. You are out here on a job making six or seven dollars an hour. You get your paycheck, come home, "look at me, $300 cash!" They get you [to buy a] truck, next time that first paycheck comes you've made $600–$700. It's a lot of money, especially when they send them through school [and] six months later they are an owner-operator . . . Like I say, you make at least an initial investment, you have got to figure—*and they don't figure*—you have got to make something over and above what you are going to make as a company driver. Like I said, as a driver I made $54,000–$55,000, this year closer to $60,000 . . . in order for [contractors] to make that, [they] have got to gross $200,000. Now people might say, "Oh, well I made $130,000 last year with this truck." *Yeah, you did. Yeah, you did.* You made about $30,000 is what you made! Because I have been down that road too many times . . . I have [owned trucks three times] . . . If anybody asked me anything about it, the first thing I would say would be, "No, don't do it."

Like many inexperienced drivers, the reader may wonder why a few drivers have remained contractors for many years if it's not better than being an employee. Carriers argue that these drivers are a testament to the benefits of contracting. But the most experienced contractors I met disagree. For instance, take Bill, a sixty-two-year-old white male who had more than thirty-four years of driving experience, including more than a decade working as a contractor. He now works as an employee for one of the few large TL companies that pays well. He made about $55,000 in the previous year and gets home to Ohio every weekend. Here is how Bill explained why he became and remained a contractor for so long, even though the money and freedom he was looking for continually eluded him:

> Bill: If you are looking at the gross amount of money you are going to make with your own truck, it looks good. Until you go looking down the line and you actually go to put the pennies together, what it is going to cost you additionally to operate that truck, the unseen dollars, that you don't think about . . .
>
> SV: So why didn't you figure that out the first couple of leases?
>
> Bill: It always looked better . . . it looks like you can make it . . . [You think,] "if I had bought a better truck, if I had less breakdowns, had less down time, things would have been great" . . . It just got to the point where, if the work was going to be there, it had to be there every day, every week, a consistent thing. It is not like, "Oh, I am an owner-operator, I don't have to go here, I don't have to go there," once you get tied up with all of the expenses coming out, all of the payments, if you miss a week or two, *you are done* . . . The myth is freedom. If your truck breaks down, you go home and you work on your truck that weekend . . . And I don't care how new it is, there is something that needs to be fixed on that truck . . . you are working on the lights, you are inspecting the thing, if you're not working on the brakes, you are adjusting this and there is something new every weekend on that truck. [Contractors] think they got more freedom to go when and where they want. *They can't!*

Larry, by far the most experienced and successful contractor I met, is another example. He is a white male, fifty-five years old. Unlike many drivers, Larry has avoided the weight gain of those who make a long career of trucking. He is married and his children are grown. He began working as a contractor before deregulation, when he believes terms with companies were more favorable to contractors. If the contractor dream exists, Larry was living it. He always buys a Peterbilt and trades them in before they need serious maintenance. Larry likes to fish and takes a month off every summer to do so. For eight years he has had a very good lease with a liquid-tanker carrier that hauls chemicals for a major pharmaceutical company. He makes it home to Attica, Indiana, every weekend. The year before I interviewed him Larry made $66,000—about as much as the highest-paid company driver I interviewed. Still he believes that companies hire contractors because they are cheaper. He said his income was that high only because he didn't have a truck payment that year. When he has a truck payment he makes about $45,000 a year, far less than a comparably skilled employee with his kind of job. He attributes his overall success to "getting lucky" in terms of maintenance with his first few trucks, sacrificing his family life for more than two decades, and then falling into a lease in a niche market that served shippers who paid a premium to ensure reliability and safety. Now he was rewarded with equity in his truck, four weeks of vacation a year, and what he described as an "old-man's job."

Larry made it as a contractor, but it was clear that he regrets the costs:

> People kept telling me that I would never pay for [my first truck]. Bullshit! I paid for one . . . It was like four years later and I paid for it. Another two or three years later I bought a Pete [Peterbilt]. And then I bought another Pete . . . Like I said, the "weekend" at home was get home on Saturday and leave out on Sunday. But that is what I was doing as an owner-operator . . . And I did it for a lot of years. Raise the kids? The wife had to raise the kids almost on her own. And I would show up, *maybe* once a week. And usually you get home mad. It usually takes you several hours to unwind. It does. All of that shit, it takes you a while to unwind. And then the kids are gone . . . [Larry pauses, looks out the window, takes a deep breath and exhales audibly] . . . well, it just got easier then.

Here is the response of the next-most-experienced contractor I interviewed, when I asked him if he would become a contractor if he had to do his career over again:

> No. It is just not profitable. It is a dog-eat-dog world. It is hard. It is harder now than it was years ago and it gets worse because there are people coming [into contracting and] working for nothing. And they'll haul freight for *nothing*. I don't see how they do it . . . Man hauling that [cheap] freight . . . his pencil is sharper than mine. I don't see where he is coming out [ahead].

CONCLUSION

This chapter has illustrated the great contrast between the way that employers and labor learn about and shape trucking's labor market.

Employers work together through a network of third parties to avoid competing with each other and to gain the upper hand with regard to workers and regulators. Truckers, on the other hand, face a confusing set of conflicting opinions and an avalanche of misinformation as they make critical decisions. Better sources of information are largely limited to experienced workers and the Owner-Operator Independent Drivers Association (OOIDA). OOIDA is a large advocacy organization that has battled against many of the worst abuses in the industry, and tries to steer inexperienced drivers away from abusive arrangements. OOIDA, through a popular radio show and a magazine, provides some of the only high-quality and accurate information available to drivers. Unfortunately, the inexperienced drivers who need this information most are often so new to the industry that they don't know about the organization and are unlikely to be members. And though it provides some of the most important challenges to the worst abuses (aside from recent class-action lawsuits), in the end OOIDA is a voluntary membership organization that defends contracting and owner-operating. So when push comes to shove, as it did during the Great Recession, OOIDA refuses to advocate for drivers acting collectively and doing things like withholding their labor power from employers.

6 "No More Jimmy Hoffas"

DESPERATE DRIVERS AND DIVIDED LABOR

On a cold, rainy day in March 2008, I rode in a convoy protesting high fuel prices with Dean, a contractor who hauled general freight in the Northeast. In early 2007, Dean had been in a near-fatal truck crash that left him unable to work for a year. During that time he had a religious awakening and came to believe that he was meant to spread the gospel to truckers by CB radio. A few months before our trip, Dean had used a cash settlement from his accident to put a down payment on a 1998 International Eagle. The tractor had been a fine machine in its day, but now it was in need of lots of expensive maintenance. Still, the black exterior of the truck gleamed even on a cloudy day. It was tricked out with chrome from the front bumper to the rear splashguards—that's trucker for mud flaps. In fact, it looked exactly like a favorite Matchbox tractor I had as a child, a classic owner-operator rig.

Dean's pride was obvious not only in the way he maintained the tractor, but in the way he talked about it. It was the physical embodiment of his rebirth. On the side of the sleeper cab was a white cross and cherry red letters reading "Truckers for Christ, CB Channel 7."[1] Slightly farther back was more lettering: "Owner/Operator Dean Smith." This lettering was smaller but matched the color and style of the lettering over the driver's door advertising the name of the carrier Dean was leased to and its Motor Carrier authority and DOT numbers.

Other than the personalized lettering, the only upgrade Dean had made to the tractor was a top-of-the-line CB radio. For several months, he had been counseling truckers on their marital, personal, and financial problems, and spreading the gospel via CB while he worked. As we moved along with the convoy, Dean told me how satisfying this work was for him. But he confessed that lately his mind had been preoccupied with his own financial problems. With the recent spike in fuel prices, he was losing money on most loads. The fuel surcharges he was receiving from his carrier weren't even close to covering the additional cost of fuel. To add to the problem, freight volumes were dropping, and Dean was having trouble getting loads at all. For weeks now he had been hauling every load he could get his hands on, just to make his truck payment, his insurance bill, and meet other overhead costs. He was now using part of his wife's income to buy fuel. Though Dean believed his faith was being tested, he didn't believe God had created his financial problems to do so. Dean blamed the oil industry.

The convoy of several hundred contractors was headed to the Pennsylvania state capital, Harrisburg. The trucks circled the Capitol building as speakers on the steps addressed a crowd of several hundred supporters, mostly families of the protesting contractors. They demanded that the state reduce its tax on diesel fuel. They emphasized the effect of high fuel prices on the cost of goods and services to working families, and they railed against the manipulation of oil markets by Wall Street speculators. They demanded an investigation. But no speaker suggested that the carriers determining the contractors' compensation, and their fuel surcharge, might have a role in producing their hardships.

In a meeting I attended after the convoy, the organizers deemed the protest a success and vowed that this was just the beginning of a national movement of truckers.

That evening I drove out to Pittsburgh, where a group of steel-hauling contractors had invited me to witness the multiday work stoppage they were carrying out—they called it a "strike," even though they were all contractors without a legal employer to refuse to work for. Along the way, I checked in at a major truck stop. There, sitting in their parked rigs, contractors pleaded over the CB for employee drivers to stop driving. The best argument they could muster—that employee drivers would suffer because the high cost of fuel would be passed on to them as consumers—failed to persuade them to stop working. The employees frequently expressed sympathy but saw no relevance of high fuel prices to themselves as employees—they didn't pay for fuel.

In the end, scattered actions by contractors in a few places across the US had no noticeable impact on freight movement, and within hours or days the contractors were back driving. Other efforts in the coming weeks and months across the United States met similar ends. The Owner-Operator Independent Drivers Association, the only organization other than perhaps the Teamsters that might have endorsed a work stoppage by contractors, refused to advocate for one. Jim Johnston, the longtime leader of OOIDA, admitted that many of the organization's members were clamoring for a strike, but he steadfastly refused to endorse one. He called the situation a "trucking nightmare," but pointed out that while some truckers were "at the end of their ropes," others were getting increased fuel surcharges. OOIDA, he said, could not call for a strike, because it was a trade, not a labor, association and could be subject to fines and lawsuits for violating antitrust laws. Truckers who stopped working, Johnston argued, would suffer from it and gain nothing, because many truckers would not participate. He concluded that calling for a strike would only reveal how weak and divided drivers were.[2]

SHIFTING RISK IN THE GREAT RECESSION

After I finished my first set of interviews in spring 2007, it seemed obvious to me that a constant stream of new workers and contractors had fractured trucking's labor force, leaving workers vulnerable and incapable of undertaking collective action to protect themselves. What Dean and more than two hundred thousand contractors like him experienced soon thereafter painfully and dramatically supported these conclusions, and showed just how much carriers had changed things in their own favor. In late 2007 diesel fuel prices across the United States skyrocketed, and they remained high through much of 2008. At the same time, freight volumes and rates began to drop as the economy nosedived into recession. Industry experts suggested that these were the worst market conditions trucking firms had experienced since deregulation. Carriers were quick to act, and they weathered the storm incredibly well: within two years some of the largest firms were making good profits again. They did this by rapidly reducing the size of the industry's labor force and by shifting many of their costs onto workers. The first to feel the pain were contractors.

When fuel prices rise rapidly, carriers add fuel surcharges to their customers' bills (or increase existing ones) to help defray the additional cost of fuel, but these surcharges often do not keep pace with rising prices. Carriers shifted most of the difference to contractors.[3] To make the problem even worse for contractors, carriers often don't pay for fuel use not associated with loaded miles (e.g., empty miles or fuel burned while idling). The higher cost of that fuel could easily cost a contractor hundreds of dollars per week. At the same time, freight volumes were low, so contractors were driving more empty miles to get to available freight. As a result, the news media were filled with stories of contractors who had made $40,000 in 2007 but were on pace to make just $10,000 in 2008.[4]

During the Great Recession, the trucking industry experienced one of the worst shakeouts in its history, but it was different from past downturns. Estimates suggest that 20 percent of independent contractor capacity, representing about fifty-five thousand trucks, was removed from long-haul trucking between 2006 and 2010.[5] Thousands of very small trucking firms also went out of business, and 20 percent of truckload capacity was removed overall.[6] But large companies appeared almost immune to the most severe effects of the downturn. Whereas previous shakeouts had typically sent dozens of large companies into bankruptcy, this time only a few large, highly leveraged firms suffered that fate.

Large firms managed an impressive downsizing of their fleets beginning in 2007. They stopped replacing their company trucks and had contractors shoulder an increasing share of the costs and risks of truck ownership. Some shifted to using contractor labor by selling their used trucks, now devalued on a flooded market, to their employees in order to shed the liability of the assets. As companies stopped hiring employees, turnover dropped to its lowest levels since deregulation, and carriers soon began cutting employee driver pay significantly. Several major carriers stopped training new drivers and closed their CDL schools. The ability of major carriers to weather the` downturn by adjusting their labor supply and shifting risk to contractors was already clear in 2008, and the value of publicly traded carrier stocks began rising. In 2008 thousands of small firms and tens of thousands of contractors like Dean were wiped out, but despite the worst conditions since deregulation, only two out of one hundred of the largest trucking firms stopped operating.[7] In 2009 the industry faced a precipitous decline in demand, though the largest carriers reported profits, while the elimination of small companies and contractors continued, and wages declined for employees. By 2010, large carriers were enjoying record profits. In short, it appears that the largest trucking companies have done what was historically impossible without the help of economic regulation or strong labor partners: they have insulated themselves from the risk of trucking's notorious volatility. They did so by relying on an especially flexible and compliant labor supply, and on shifting enormous costs to contractors.

Some carriers' survival and success actually resulted in part from the spiking of fuel prices during the crisis. Just as fuel surcharges paid by customers don't keep pace with rapidly rising fuel prices, they don't keep pace with rapidly falling prices either. When fuel prices dropped from around four dollars per gallon in mid-September 2008 to around $2.30 per gallon at the end of the year, carriers did not pass all of the excess they were collecting from shippers on to contractors. Instead they cashed in.[8] Controlling fuel surcharge payments gives carriers a lot of flexibility to shift the consequences of changing freight and fuel markets to their advantage: contractors take the losses, carriers take the profits.

In a similar way, collaborating to control the recruitment and training of new employee drivers, and to reduce competition for them by standardizing pay across the industry, allows firms to shift the risk of downturns to workers and the benefit of good markets to themselves. Unfortunately, at present there is next to nothing that workers can do about this, either individually or collectively.

NO MORE JIMMY HOFFAS

Truckers have serious grievances. At the top of the list are low wages, huge amounts of unpaid work, and lots of time spent away from home.

Employees and contractors virtually all believe that these problems are so severe that truckers should engage in collective action to address them.

When I asked drivers what they should do about their problems, the vast majority suggested that they should strike, and believed that a successful strike would have dramatic consequences. Most drivers said things like this:

> [If truckers went on strike] it would shut this country down. Trucks move this country, and at that point somebody would have to pay attention to the needs of the trucker. Truckers have to get better working conditions and more money.

Every trucker I talked to had a similar perspective on drivers' critical position in the economy, and on the potential power that gave truckers to engage in collective action that would disrupt the economy.

Unfortunately, high turnover among employees, and the prevalence of contracting, are circumstances that fracture the industry's labor force and prevent drivers from organizing themselves. Truckers I spoke to believed that the chance of drivers successfully striking was slim at best, because drivers could not agree on what the goals of a strike should be. They could not speak with one voice:

> It is like the old joke, "How many drivers does it take to screw in a light bulb? Nobody knows because they can't stop *arguing about it!*" The worst thing that has happened in the trucking industry is drivers themselves. We are our own worst enemy. We don't have the organization. Even if everyone could get together and say, "Okay, we are going to shut down for one week," not everybody can agree on what they want out of that shutdown. Do they want lower fuel prices? Less regulation? Do they want to change the HOS? Do they want higher rates?

Drivers were probably right in their assessment that they would not be able to come to agreement easily, even if they had an organization or some other forum allowing them to have a sustained conversation. While all agreed that the ultimate goals should be raising incomes and reducing work hours and time on the road, contractors and employees had fundamentally different understandings of who should engage in collective action, who their opponents and allies would be, and what the demands of strikers should be.

Inexperienced contractors were most likely to suggest that the key goals should be getting the government to reduce fuel costs and/or minimize the regulation of hours and safety. They saw these as the key to raising incomes for truckers, including employees:

> I think the government needs to step in because if the government brought the cost of fuel down, then right off the bat your owner-operators are going to make money. And your companies are going to save money because they are not putting it in the fuel tank, so, in turn, they could throw a little bit of that back to their company drivers.

In line with their understanding of themselves as managers of small businesses, inexperienced contractors often saw collective action as something that should be engaged in *with* carriers and against shipping customers and government. They commonly suggested that the most, if not the only, effective strategy would be to get carriers to organize a shutdown.

> [Truckers] sit around and talk about [striking], but there is actually nobody that actually gets it all together. You would have to have somebody go to all the big companies and say, "Hey, shut down."

Some inexperienced contractors believed that contractors could not organize themselves primarily because they value their independence. The very idea of collective action through an organization is antithetical to what attracted them to trucking and contracting. According to these drivers, truckers don't have unions because truckers don't want unions:

> [We should have] a convoy, stop on the highway and shut down the highway and all of that stuff that they talk about. A strike. It would never work. Everybody won't stick together, that is why we don't have unions. Everybody is independent. Freedom of speech, freedom of drivers.

Another said:

> [Not working together] is not an attitude *problem*, it is an independent spirit that you have as a truck driver . . . Drivers are truly independent people. That is one of the things that gets drivers to stay in the business: they are truly independent.

Some inexperienced drivers believed contractors could take action without companies but feared employees would undermine such an effort:

> You will get owner-operators to talk about it all day long and we will all agree that we should [strike]. But how are you going to get a company driver to stop? He is not paying for the fuel. He is not paying for the truck. He is just out there running the miles. Making the money, that is all that he cares about . . . And to us, yes, the cost of freight makes a difference, to us the cost of fuel makes a difference, to them it don't matter. The company pays for everything; they can burn as much fuel as they want.

Because they need a means to organize, enforce discipline, and receive financial support during a strike, some inexperienced contractors believed that "something like a union" is required. But others rejected this idea because they saw even "something like a union" as taking away individual freedom and as being self-serving. Some inexperienced contractors specifically said that union drivers would be an obstacle to a successful strike:

> You got too many company drivers that won't [strike]. You've got too many union drivers that, I know, won't do it . . . They ain't going to lose that dollar.

On the other hand, experienced contractors saw the economic vulnerability of less-experienced contractors as the crucial problem:

> You tell an owner-operator, "Okay, we are going to strike on April 30." The first words out of a guy's mouth are, "I can't afford to shut down for two or three days" . . . If you can't shut down for two or three days or a week, then you need to get out of the business. But that is the first words out of an owner-operator's mouth.

The most experienced employees and contractors focused directly on wages and hours, and saw companies and the structure of the industry as the fundamental problems. They saw controlling the labor market as the key to raising wages, and unions—even if some said they didn't like admitting it—as the only effective means for doing this. Here is an employee driver:

> We should make a union—a real union. You know how many members we are going to have? We are going to be the most powerful union in the

country. It is the only way. We have got to take our fate in our hands, because if you never been behind the wheel in a truck, you don't know what it is.

Very experienced drivers were adamant that a union is the only thing that can help truckers. Such drivers knew that the Teamsters had greatly benefited drivers, even those who weren't union members. Here is an experienced contractor who worked as a contractor before deregulation but was never a Teamster himself:

> When the Teamsters union was in charge, I made okay [money]. Jimmy Hoffa was a crooked man, everybody in the world knows this, but he did more for this industry than anybody has ever done. He made the wages fair. Before that the truck driver was damn near starving to death. He could damn near just barely feed his family. [Hoffa] got a truck driver a livable wage, if not a little better than average, because we sacrifice virtually our lives to do the job and he came in and changed all of that . . . I think that the majority of the drivers out here would support the Teamsters Union to come back into power like they used to be.

Other experienced drivers also recognized and bitterly lamented the absence of Teamster power and influence today:

> I used to belong to the Teamsters Union in Detroit—Jimmy Hoffa's [Local] 299. Back then it was a union, now it is just a name. It is not like it used to be. Before, the union stood up for you. Companies respected the union. Now [companies] just laugh in the face of the union . . . [Union drivers] may get more benefits and a little bit better retirement, but it is not like it used to be. I feel that if a man is not in the union, . . . [an employer's] not going to pay him X amount of dollars because he likes him. He will pay dirt wages if he can get away with it.

Unfortunately, experienced truckers were among the most pessimistic about the chances of unionizing long-haul drivers, especially given companies' resistance:

> There is a union, the Teamsters Union. The problem is the companies absolutely will not allow the union to come in.

Even employees who desperately wanted a union believed the lack of worker power across the industry makes the challenges to unionization nearly insurmountable:

[Unions] are not worth going into. Not anymore. You have no union support, you don't have enough drivers in your union to be strong enough to control anything. You control your own local wages to a certain extent, your own working conditions. [But] you have got to have a stronger union than what they got. Once you strike, the company can bring in anybody they want.

While some managers and industry analysts do seem to relish carriers' victory over the Teamsters, most wouldn't laugh at the Teamsters, as some drivers suggested. Though the Teamsters have not mounted a serious organizing effort aimed at long-haul truckload carriers since deregulation, they do maintain a significant presence at less-than-truckload carriers and the parcel carrier UPS. Most importantly, the Teamsters have been involved in extensive organizing activities among truckers at several major ports in the US in recent years. Some of these efforts have resulted in public criticisms and even legal challenges of independent contracting practices.[9] Large truckload companies fear the organization of their firms by the Teamsters, and they guard vigilantly against it. New drivers are given substantial antiunion training, and the ATA lobbies vigorously against efforts to make union organizing easier and in defense of contracting, which firms see as a critical hedge against unionization.[10]

In contrast to inexperienced contractors, who saw values and different perspectives among drivers themselves as the key impediment to class action, experienced drivers believed that companies deliberately play contractors and employees against each other and keep drivers separate to prevent collective action:

There is not a hell of a lot [drivers] can do because they . . . are kept too stirred up, too disassociated with one another. They don't even let us—even company drivers—they don't like a lot of us sitting around in the same terminal or the same truck stop. *They don't want us together.* Because when you get together, it could cause dissension in the ranks. If you keep them apart and keep them stirred up—treat a few of them better—they can figure out who is going to cause the problems real quick.

Experienced truckers cited the high turnover of drivers in the industry and the constant stream of new drivers as the biggest obstacle to overcoming employer resistance to unionization. Most important, experienced truckers believed that companies are "mass producing" new drivers in "CDL mills" that allow companies to control the labor market and easily replace drivers who attempted to unionize:

> [A union] wouldn't happen because the companies know drivers are a dime a dozen. They will get you out and put another one of these students behind the wheel.

Finally, experienced drivers argued that even if drivers were able to organize particular companies, what drivers would gain would be limited, because nonunion firms with cheap, flexible workforces would quickly drive unionized companies out of business:

> If you fight for too much, there is always somebody who [will haul the freight] cheaper—*always*.

In the end, experienced drivers saw unionization as a catch-22 situation, given the way the industry is organized. Truckers need leadership and connections to one another to control the labor market and build a successful union, but they can't achieve those things without a union—or at least something that could do those things—especially given the challenges of how truckers work today compared to under regulation.

> The first thing that it will take will be strong leadership. You would have to have somebody . . . that could convince the drivers to stand behind them. There are no more Jimmy Hoffas. That is the big stopper, I believe. If some person were to come along, . . . stand up, and people would listen and say, "Well, I am going to stand by him regardless of whether it's right or wrong." [But] where would you get this guy from? [Before deregulation] you probably knew half of [your fellow drivers], because you made short runs and you saw them every other day or so. And that way you could communicate with each other. [Today] you meet a driver here picking up a load . . . You may never see him again—you'll *probably* never see him again, *even if you're in the same company*. I rarely ever see one of our drivers after I have loaded with them. We will run loaded from the same dock, and I'll never see him again. So that is the problem right there. "I won't stand by this guy, I only met him one time."

All experienced truckers felt that the isolation of drivers from one another, sometimes the result of deliberate efforts by employers, was the first obstacle they would need to overcome if any effort to improve wages and conditions was to be successful.

WHAT'S A DRIVER TO DO?

As should be apparent, experienced drivers have a nuanced, structural, and highly critical assessment of the industry, but that doesn't mean that they have rejected employer dominance or that they can avoid it. In fact, their views reveal a more complete submission, a relinquishing of control in the labor process that ensures greater compliance. This is not about drivers being deluded, this is about making strategic choices to further their own economic interests. But these drivers don't see themselves as being in an alliance or partnership with the carriers the way inexperienced contractors do. They see their own outlook as the best way to maintain economic power in a relationship defined by antagonistic interests. Here is an experienced driver describing how younger drivers should approach their careers:

> Don't be in a hurry. Believe half of what [companies] tell you and shop around. There are a lot of good jobs out there that pay well. Can't take the first or second or third one that comes along . . . Your driving record is the most important thing you got. If you have a good driving record, you can go to work for anybody, and if you want to leave somewhere, you go somewhere else, you can also demand, tell them what you want to be paid. Because *good drivers* are hard to find—I mean somebody that is conscientious, careful, doesn't tear up the equipment . . . That is what the [good] employers want, someone who is going to take care of their equipment and get the freight off in a timely manner, that is all that they want. And somebody who isn't going to get tickets. Because when you get tickets, whether the company pays for it or you pay for it, their insurance is going up.

While inexperienced and would-be contractors were likely to use concepts like trust, partnership, honesty, and even love to describe the relationship they wanted with firms, experienced drivers did not identify with or have an interest in a personal relationship with their employers. They typically didn't see the common problems in the workplace as resulting from the personal characteristics or morals of owners or managers. They saw employer-employee and manager-employee relationships in strictly economic terms. Here is an experienced driver describing working for a large company:

> We're not gonna go out to church together. We're not going to go out here and have drinks after work or whatever. With the people that I work for, the work is based exactly on what I want. I work for you, you furnish me with work, I work for you. The bottom line is my paycheck. That is what everybody is in it for. No, I don't want to go on a picnic with you and your family.

The only differences among companies and industry segments that mattered for these workers were the working conditions and the pay. While they acknowledged that there are better and worse employers, they scoffed at the implication that a company's values could lead it to treat drivers better. They saw companies blurring the lines between firms and workers as a means to manipulate drivers. Here is one driver reflecting on the advertising of his employer:

> They say you are part of a family. How can you be part of a fourteen-thousand-employee family? Don't expect any hugs from the dispatcher.

These workers believed that the value of their labor is determined by the segment of the industry in which they work and the scarcity of capable drivers willing and able to work in those segments. They saw their relationship with carriers as antagonistic in terms of economic interests, but believed that good companies have to treat skilled drivers with clean records well in order to retain them. They thought that the primary cause of workers' problems is the fact that in industry segments that can use cheap labor the employment relationship is skewed in favor of carriers. These drivers were likely to cite the existence of destructive competition or hypercompetitiveness in particular segments of the industry as the source of variation in labor-capital relations across the industry.

Here is one driver's assessment of the value of his labor:

> They don't want to pay you high wages . . . The only reason a lot of us my age have jobs is because they can't get anybody else into it, so they are keeping us around . . . They have to make profits themselves to pay all of their people. Plus the majority of these companies are publicly owned. They are on

the stock market, and their stockholders come first. And the only way that they can get the money and show a profit to these stockholders is to keep the drivers' wages and benefits low. That is the bottom line. *Economics.* Economics: they want to put all of the money in their pocket and make themselves rich.

CONCLUSION: THE CLASS RELATIONS OF TRUCKING

The history of trucking can be understood as a struggle between drivers and carriers for control over working conditions and pay. The strength of each side, the strategies available to them, and the benefits of those strategies have largely been determined by the economics of trucking and by state regulation. During the years of regulation, when less-than-truckload carriers dominated the industry, carriers and the IBT actually cooperated to ensure working conditions and employment relations that were mutually beneficial. After deregulation, the profitability of carriers declined, long-haul truckload carriers emerged and flourished, and the most powerful union in American history was eviscerated. At first the truckload carriers were marginally profitable and buffeted by the volatile swings of market demand. But over the last few decades, larger carriers have developed increasingly successful business models that have allowed them to achieve healthy profits and insulate themselves from risk by shifting it to an astonishingly vulnerable labor supply.

This remarkable transformation resulted from sustained class action of employers vis-à-vis labor. Carriers have intentionally transformed the contractor model in order to lower costs, shift risk, retain drivers, and prevent unionization. Individually and collectively they disseminate a carefully crafted discourse to their employees, from the moment they are recruited and trained, that encourages them to become contractors. In the absence of effective counterefforts on the part of truckers, for most inexperienced truckers the discourse promoting contracting is opposed only by truck-stop talk. Despite a clear history of industry practices that harm contractors, the harsh lessons learned are not transmitted from driver to driver effectively. It is as if carriers continually wipe labor's memory clean. For several decades now the abusive practices of carriers have gone essentially unchallenged by workers, their advocates, and regulators. In contrast, carriers have a network of collaborators, including specialized lawyers, accountants, media outlets, and benchmarking companies, to coordinate their efforts and advance their interests as a class relative to labor.

This coordinated class action, or class project, has fractured and degraded labor through superior coordination and information. It does not simply dominate labor; it leads it. It has changed the very identity of truckers at certain career stages, so they believe they are small business owners and not workers. As a result, contractors identify their interests with the interests of the carriers rather than employee truckers, even those working for the same firm. Using a universalizing discourse, this class project transforms the way workers see economic relations, so they deny the potential for antagonistic class-based interests in the industry. Doing so obscures the sources and consequences of unequal class power in the industry, while it diminishes the potential for workers' to exercise power on their own behalf.

The contracting discourse expands the central symbolic category of capitalism—that of owner—and applies it to contractors. Ownership by definition confers the right to control production and appropriate profits. But when contractors try to exercise those rights, carriers can easily use coercive legal and financial means to ensure their own dominance, sometimes without the contractors abandoning their self-identification as owners.

Viewed historically, the trucking industry has experienced a continual process of changes in class relations that can be understood as a series of class projects. After an initial struggle between carriers and the Teamsters immediately before and after World War II, there were several decades in which regulated carriers and the union established an alliance that offered significant returns to both capital and labor. This alliance rested on two key bases: the power of labor to prevent the development of other kinds of labor relationships (such as increased use of owner-operators), and the protected marketplace that benefited employers by limiting the number of operating authorities. The Teamsters galvanized workers in support of their leadership. Carriers, in turn, limited competition among themselves through collective rate setting that ensured healthy profits, and through an owners' association that negotiated with the Teamsters to establish the National Master Freight Agreement (NMFA), which set the standard for wages and working conditions throughout the industry. Though there was continual give and take between labor and carriers during the decades of regulation, both sides remained invested in and committed to these collective efforts. Most crucially, both sides understood the great importance of defending against deregulation. Until the late 1970s the two fended off multiple attempts to alter the rules underpinning their successful collaboration.

Deregulation was brought about by a competing class project that allied emergent segments of the trucking industry, mostly private and contract carriers, with a range of outside interests that stood to benefit from deregulation, most importantly large shippers. This effort destabilized the dominant class relationship in trucking by chipping away at regulated trucking's market share, and then removing the regulatory framework on which its capital-labor partnership ultimately rested. With the market in chaos, a new alliance emerged that brought together deunionized carriers with existing contractors and cheap nonunion employee labor. This alliance crushed the previously regulated carriers as well as the Teamsters union. But sustaining the new alliance has required a near-constant stream of alterations to address the central problem of reproducing its labor supply.

Just as the employer's association that negotiated the NMFA was a collective response to the strength of the Teamsters, the development of the modern contracting system is a collective response to competition and a churning labor supply. For this solution to their labor problems, carriers rely on third parties, such as Randall-Reilly and ATBS, and on contractors, however temporary their consent to the arrangement might be. Maintenance of this system, as of the previous one, also requires the political support of employers and workers, especially to defend against legal and regulatory challenges to the use of independent contractors.[11]

The alliances between the regulated carriers and the Teamsters, and now between the nonunion carriers and their contractors, have both been dependent on a particular legal and normative structure and on collective action by potentially antagonistic interest groups. This collective action has been generated by political and economic alliances that have required a collective understanding that defines the interests of the various partners. In each period the dominant alliance has faced significant challengers, who undertook competing efforts and sought to organize the industry in alternative ways.

However, there is a notable difference between those efforts before and after deregulation. Unlike the dominant alliance of the regulated period, the dominant alliance today is severely unbalanced in terms of class power. It favors capital to such an extent that it cannot reproduce its labor partner without tremendous costs—many of which it externalizes— and, as a result, the industry has once again drawn the attention of outside critics, who argue that it should be reregulated to reduce negative externalities, such as highway accidents, traffic congestion, decreased tax revenue, and pollution. Perhaps these critics will become convinced that the industry should be regulated to protect the interests of workers as well.

In trucking, industrywide, employer-dominated labor market institutions produce consent and reproduce labor power. Such a process is not inconsistent with theories about how employment relations are marketized (see Cappelli 1999). The mechanisms by which workers come to make the choices they do are rooted in very specific contexts that we cannot understand by looking at one or even a few workplaces in isolation. In this case, and perhaps in many others, the industry may be the essential level of analysis, where the larger phenomenon of changing employment relations, as well its unequal effect on different kinds of independent contractors, can best be understood.

The story of how the trucking industry has used contracting to create cheaper, harder-working drivers who shoulder the burden of risk that used to belong to the carriers is far from unique. Employment relations are being marketized for millions of low-skilled workers in dozens of occupations. Employers are transforming the meaning of the American Dream for real estate agents, home healthcare workers, even janitorial workers. A trucker's American Dream in the 1960s was to earn a good income, own a home, and have dignity at work. This dream was shaped and achieved through collaboration between the Teamsters and regulated firms. Today, a trucker's American Dream centers on the myth of economic self-reliance as an individual producer, and the chance to strike it rich by owning a trucking company.

The opportunities facing truckers, like millions of workers in other industries that encourage independent contracting, differ radically from those that would have been available to them even a generation ago. A class project has transformed trucking from an industry with some of the best-paid workers and one of the strongest unions in American history into one in which unions play almost no role, and workers live for weeks at a time out of the machine they operate, often earn less than minimum wage, and work hours equivalent to two full-time jobs, sometimes more.

And contracting does more than this. It sets workers outside the legal and regulatory framework and the class compromise that built the middle class in the United States—a compromise that steadily reduced economic inequality for decades. The foundation of that more equitable American economy is being eroded by processes like the ones described in this book. This erosion is justified by the promise of an ownership society in which individual economic freedom reigns, and each of us is able to create and live out our own American Dream. But if trucking is any indication, what this erosion really represents is a path toward an increasingly brutal set of conditions that limit opportunity and exacerbate inequality.

APPENDIX A: Data and Methods

This book relies on a variety of data, from participant observation and interviews to written, video, and audio materials produced by the industry, technical and government reports, news articles, and various webpages and blogs.

ANONYMITY OF STUDY PARTICIPANTS AND
COMPANIES

All names of drivers and companies that I interviewed or observed myself are pseudonyms, with the exception of a few individuals who specifically asked that they be identified. I have changed minor details in descriptions of drivers and firms and particular work scenarios (e.g., customer locations) to prevent readers familiar with the industry from identifying workers or firms.

THE PARTICIPANT OBSERVATION

When I began this project I knew I needed a detailed sense of what truckers do. Given the fact that truckers were forced to maximize their productivity under strict regulations that I knew were likely negotiated on a regular basis, having firsthand experience was essential. I soon found out that you can't really understand what it is like to spend nineteen days on the road, working night and day in all kinds of driving conditions from Florida to Maine, Wisconsin to Texas, unless you have done it. In many ways I was just like most workers who enter into the industry: I had a few vague notions of what the job would be like, but I had no idea how difficult it was to actually be a long-haul trucker day after day.

I admit that once I decided on the project design, I was deeply ambivalent about becoming a trucker. I was excited about the challenge of driving a "big truck," as eighteen-wheelers are referred to by truckers. But I knew that it wouldn't be easy, and I seriously doubted my ability to be successful as a trucker. Two previous experiences had taught me enough to be aware that the work was more about long hours, difficult working conditions, and too much time away from family and friends than about sightseeing trips around the country. In college I had worked a summer job moving military families into and out of their homes for a major moving company franchise. The work required riding with crews of men, many of them ex-convicts or drug addicts, in tractor-trailers from a central warehouse to military bases up to three hours away. The job was technically local and we were home every night, but the work was difficult and the hours were extremely long. At the peak months of July and August we often worked sixteen-hour shifts loading and unloading furniture. This was quite a bit different from my work as a long-haul trucker, but it taught me valuable lessons about bad jobs and industries that chewed people up, and a little about trucking. Among other things, we found out later the company was illegally denying us overtime pay—we had been told, and I accepted, that we were seasonal workers and thus not entitled to it. This was also my first personal introduction to truckers, who had chosen these jobs because they found it better than OTR driving. Working in tight-knit crews for long hours I became friends with several drivers, and listening to them took the luster off the more romantic portrayals of trucking in popular culture.

My only other information about truckers came from my father, who had for my entire life operated a truck gate and scale at one of the largest copper rolling mills in the world. I had worked at that plant during college. My father dealt directly with truckers all day, handling their paperwork, weighing their trucks, and directing them in and out of the plant. He always had a funny story to tell about one trucker or another. And despite the way their behavior and demeanor occasionally vexed him, he developed long-standing, positive workplace relationships with many truckers. I think his appreciation and empathy for the difficulties involved in their line of work had an impact on me.

Because of this background I didn't go into my fieldwork thinking it would be fun or exciting traveling around and seeing the country by truck. Beyond that, I knew what everyone knows about trucks and truckers, and what I picked up from the few academic books published on the subject. From this rather limited base of knowledge, I wanted to form an in-depth understanding of the work, and to systematically study variations in how it was organized. I also wanted to examine how workers understood the organization of the industry, and how their understandings influenced the work and employment decisions they made. There were very few options to do this. Trucking doesn't lend itself to more traditional kinds of ethnographic observation. Truckers work primarily in public spaces, but most of the work is completed alone.

Riding along with drivers had several disadvantages that made it an undesirable choice. First, I would be a burden on the driver. Second, if I went to a large company and asked to be placed with a driver, the driver might be pressured to allow me to ride along. Third, and finally, it was possible that my presence would cause the driver to act differently than he otherwise would have, particularly with regard to laws and company policies.

As it turns out, riding along would not have been a good choice. The job is filled with long and uneventful days of driving that would have told me little as a passenger, but taught me much through the experience of working through them consistently over weeks and months. These were punctuated by frequent but randomly scheduled hours of frustrating unpaid work, where one is largely dependent on the efforts of other workers, and very infrequently by important interactions with supervisors. For me the latter typically consisted of a text message or two per day and a five-minute phone call every two weeks.

Driving instead of riding along also demonstrated to me that an initial concern about not being able to witness truckers breaking the law was more than justified. Truckers regularly engage in behavior that is illegal. In most cases these behaviors constitute only minor violations of the technical provisions of the law and company rules. However, most truckers commit significant violations of the basic rules routinely. If I hadn't driven and committed the same illegal acts, I would not have understood how they are the product of the labor process and not simply a disregard for the law or safety, and I certainly would not have been able to discuss them so easily with my interviewees.

Getting a Trucking Job

Fortunately it is not hard to get a trucking job. Or, I should say, it is not hard to begin to get a trucking job. Prior to the Great Recession the industry had extremely high turnover. At the time, the largest companies advertised throughout the US and were interested in workers with all kinds of backgrounds. The largest also provided training to those with no experience, and emphasized that they could have someone like me driving a truck across the country in a matter of a few months.

I decided I should work for one of the companies typical of the new leading organizations in the industry. That meant working for one of the bigger, quickly growing firms. Dozens of medium-sized and large companies were hiring in my area. I saw a Leviathan ad in the local paper and researched the company on the internet. It is among the largest, and at the time had training facilities and operating centers across the US. From what I read on trucker blogs, it wasn't the worst of the big companies to work for, and it probably wasn't the best. They had several divisions, but concentrated on general freight. Like the other major players, it was growing rapidly, expanding its independent contractor fleet, and it offered a lease-purchase program. Leviathan also had GPS satellite-based tracking systems in its tractors. In all of these important respects it was a typical leading firm in the industry, and would provide an excellent baseline for understanding variation in trucking practices.

The actual training to become a truck driver is quite difficult. In hindsight, it seems deliberately designed to test whether or not you will be a good trucker by subjecting you to weeks of poorly paid hours, near constant frustration, and inadequate explanation of the rules governing the process (as discussed in Chapter 1). But I had what it took to be a good trucker. I have always loved to drive. I don't mind being alone. I had worked several different manual labor jobs in the past, so I knew how to follow directions and work safely when physically fatigued. And, most importantly, I was able to work twelve to sixteen hours a days for twelve to nineteen days at a time, checking in by phone only once a week or less, which is what really makes a trucking supervisor happy. I did mind being away from family and friends, but the rest of the lifestyle—sleeping in the truck and reeking of diesel fumes—was acceptable for a short period.

In fact, the job went well. I had read secondary sources about trucking and the basic organization of the work, so I knew what veteran truckers did to increase their pay. As a result, within a few weeks I had it down pat. I was planning and executing my loads efficiently.

After a couple of months driving I was my home terminal's nominee for Leviathan's Rookie of the Month award. That felt pretty good, because our terminal had more than a hundred rookie drivers. Unfortunately, I did not stay with the company long enough to find out if I would win. The company probably had several thousand rookies at the time, but I might have had a shot at winning it, since I now know that I had reached the productivity level of the average driver with two years of experience within two months.

Despite the fact that I was a natural at the job and only doing it temporarily, I could not avoid some of the most important problems faced by truckers. In particular, home time was a big problem for me. I had a friend's wedding and a party for my grandmother, who was turning ninety, that had to be scheduled in my first month of solo driving. But before either of them, there was a family medical emergency. And, oh yeah, my wife and I were trying to conceive our first child. Needless to say, the routines of truck driving can have a serious impact on your personal life.

My blue-collar upbringing and experience in bad jobs, along with auto-mechanic classes in high school, likely made me more comfortable with the work than most new truckers, who together are a remarkably diverse group. While diversity might initially seem like a disadvantage, it was in fact a tremendous advantage for me as an ethnographer. The diversity of the labor force and the anonymity of life on the road allowed me to easily fit into the workforce. While there may be a stereotypical trucker in the public mind, there is no typical trucker in reality (aside from the fact that they are much more likely to be male). At the same time the organization of the industry creates tremendous uniformity of experiences and views among truckers, as I hope the book makes clear.

Having been originally trained in field methods in undergraduate and graduate anthropology programs, I initially set out to undertake a full year of driving. A year is considered a minimum standard for cultural anthropology programs, because researchers traditionally studied nonindustrial societies whose routines vary tremendously from season to season. I initially applied the same sort of logic to trucking, believing that since the job occurred in a setting largely out of the control of the driver, influenced heavily by weather conditions and seasonal freight volumes, it would be useful to experience driving at different points throughout the year. Inadvertently I managed to attain this varied driving experience within my first few months. I experienced everything from the heavy snows, slippery conditions, and freezing bunk sheets of winter in Maine during March to the sweltering heat of an un-air-conditioned truck cab during July on the Gulf Coast.

While I planned to spend a year training and driving, I stopped after six months, because I reached what ethnographers call saturation, the point where your data gathering is no longer providing new empirical insights. At first it surprised me that I reached saturation so quickly, but upon reflection it really shouldn't have. With turnover in Leviathan's segment of the industry at well over 100 percent in a typical year, it is absolutely essential that companies be able to integrate new drivers into their system and give those drivers the tools needed to produce profits in a relatively short period of time. While my experience was certainly not typical, it was not that far from what most drivers experience. In fact, the biggest difference, as my cousin's husband, who had worked as a trucker, pointed out, was that I had the good fortune to know that my time as trucker was only temporary. Despite this, it didn't take long for me to look forward to the day that I would have the rest of my life back.

My experience working as a driver proved invaluable. In the course of training and driving I met and talked with several hundred drivers as a fellow trainee or trucker. I drove tens of thousands of miles across twenty-eight states and hauled everything from steel coils to beer for customers ranging from Wal-Mart to mom-and-pop shops. And I spent more nights in truck stops and rest areas than anyone ever should. The work not only provided a mountain of basic information about the industry, the work, and the lifestyle, but it also plainly and sometimes painfully illustrated in personal terms the points of conflict in the production process.

Finally, while working as a trucker, I got to experience some of the most important variations in the long-haul segment. I had the opportunity to drive for a week for Wal-Mart as one of their regular drivers, hauling between distribution centers and stores. Leviathan, as well as several other large companies, essentially rents out its drivers to Wal-Mart during busy periods and the summer, when many of Wal-Mart's regular drivers take vacation. This experience was especially enlightening, as Wal-Mart, the largest private truck fleet in the world, pays its workers a salary (I was paid by the day while I worked for them) and not by the mile, has no independent contractors, and hauls only its own freight (i.e., it does not compete in the general freight market). These differences result in a fundamentally different organization of the work (one that paid better and was much less stressful, which I detail in Chapter 2), and the attitudes and behaviors of drivers vary accordingly.

I also worked for several weeks hauling freight on a dedicated account. Dedicated account drivers haul freight for one primary customer, in my case for a major consumer products manufacturer. These drivers often get fewer miles than the typical general freight driver, but tend to have much more regular schedules in terms of load types and frequent particular locations. Again, this experience allowed me to understand the important variations in the work potentially available to long-haul drivers.

Training and working as a trucker provided many benefits. In terms of understanding the work, it allowed me to assess in a detailed fashion the differences between the prescribed and actual behavior of drivers, and allowed me to encounter the points of conflict between managers and workers, and among workers themselves from the perspective of a worker. It was this detailed sense of the job as it was actually performed that allowed me to create a research design for the interview phase of the project focused on the issues that most affected drivers, and to incorporate reasonable data collection strategies. My work experience also provided me with very practical knowledge about the job, and the way it was described by truckers, that allowed me to ask appropriately phrased questions. Finally, driving allowed me to understand in a very personal way the emotions that drivers experience, and to be able to successfully empathize with their experiences.

THE INTERVIEWS

My original plan had been to conduct interviews while driving. I thought I could start my work routine early in the day, work a full day, and then conduct an interview each night. I quickly discovered how naïve that idea was. The job was far too demanding to allow for this, and I was tired—dead tired—by the end of the day. I rarely had a spare hour or two, and when I did it was devoted to writing in a personal journal, finding a decent meal, showering, or trying to get in twenty minutes of exercise. Interviews while driving were out of the question.

But data from driving alone was certainly not enough. I brought my own ideas, experience, and background to the job, but the goals of the research were to understand how workers vary in their understanding of the job: how their different backgrounds and experiences affect their perspectives and the decisions that they make, and how companies shape these things. Also, the job I had with Leviathan, while the most common, was only one kind of trucking job, I needed to understand how, if at all, different jobs varied, and how workers saw them. In order to do all of this I needed to talk with drivers systematically and at length.

The Initial Interview Sample

I conducted seventy-five formal in-depth interviews in 2005–2007. Sixty of these were conducted over a single several-month period in the fall of 2005 and spring of 2006. The remaining fifteen were conducted in the fall of 2007, during a period of rapidly rising fuel prices. All of the interviews were with drivers on break at a truck stop in the Midwest during the normal performance of their jobs. The truck stop is located near the junction of several major interstates. Most importantly, the site of the interviews had two amenities I was interested in: a TV lounge and a set of booths with internet access and phones. These amenities were key, because they were a draw for truckers taking their mandatory DOT break, or waiting for load information or a repair on their truck. In both periods I conducted anywhere from one to five interviews in a single day. Most days I conducted two or three interviews. The interviews ranged from approximately half an hour in length to more than two hours and averaged about fifty minutes. The length of the interview usually corresponded directly to the driver's time in the industry.

I had very little trouble getting truckers to participate in the study. Truckers will often sit in truckstops during their off hours and discuss their companies, weather, traffic conditions, and equipment. If drivers were in the lounge, chances were they were in the mood to talk, a fact demonstrated by the extremely high participation rate I received. I had only four refusals out of seventy-nine people asked, and one of these refused because he did not speak English. Nearly all of my participants seemed eager to tell me their stories and share with me their thoughts on the industry. A few initially assumed I was looking for some sort of "correct" answer that only an experienced driver could give me, and felt they were not experienced enough to participate. I had to reassure these drivers that I was indeed interested in their experiences.

A typical interview would begin with me approaching a potential participant, who was either in the TV lounge or sitting at the booths. I would begin by asking whether the individual was a "driver," which is how truckers refer to each other, and if he was on break. If the answer to both questions was yes, then I offered a brief description of the project and asked if the driver would be willing to participate by submitting to a set of interview questions that would take at least thirty minutes to answer. At first I found the ease of getting interviews to be quite surprising. But on reflection I realize I should have expected that drivers would be willing participants. During my own driving experience I found drivers to be extremely helpful and outgoing, despite the fact that a significant proportion claim to enjoy being alone. While some drivers are in the truck stop because they need to take care of routine tasks such as showering, eating, or making phone calls, many are there to socialize and/or relax. For someone who has not worked a job like trucking, it is hard to describe the effect of being alone in a truck for twenty or more hours a day for weeks at a time. You begin to crave interaction with other people—even if it's just their immediate presence—to alleviate the loneliness of the lifestyle. As a result, truckstops are places where truckers expect to interact with strangers, and it is very common for people to strike up a conversation by simply turning to the person nearest to them and speaking. The lounge itself is usually kept clear of any solicitation by hitchhikers, prostitutes, and salespeople, so one is largely free of the concern that someone striking up a conversation has an objective beyond socializing or harmless information gathering. Occasionally, the truck stop staff would circulate through the lounges, checking to make sure everyone had a commercial driver's license. Only once did I see someone asked to leave.

Once a driver had agreed to an interview, I would ask them to walk with me to the booths. These booths were normally used for eating, talking, filling out paperwork, using laptop computers, and making phone calls. After listening to recordings of several early interviews I quickly learned the importance of sitting as far from the louder arcade games as possible, as they made transcription much more time consuming. The interview process normally did not draw attention to the driver and me, though on occasion nearby drivers would spontaneously begin participating in the conversation or volunteer to be interviewed next. Several times group discussions initiated by responses of eavesdropping drivers to an interviewee's statements began after an interview was complete. Through these conversations, which typically lasted several hours and ended only when I had to leave for night, I discussed the central issues of the interviews with dozens more drivers not counted in my totals.

The Interviewees

Truck drivers truly come in all shapes, sizes, colors, and backgrounds. I interviewed workers of every race and ethnicity, immigrant and native, old and young. My respondents had educations that ranged from less than high school to graduate degrees. They hailed from small towns and inner cities across the US and spanned the entire range of the American working class. They were nearly all men. There were two main reasons for this. First, only a small proportion of long-haul drivers are estimated to be women (see Table A. 1), though it appears that they may be entering, if not

Table A.1 Comparison of Interview Sample to National Long-Haul Driver Population in 2014

Driver Characteristic	Interviewees	Driver Population
N	75	–
Percent Male	97	94
Percent White	80	74
Percent Black	12	17
Percent Hispanic	5	9
Percent Asian	3	–
Other/Multiple/Unknown	–	10
Percent Immigrated in Last Ten Years	7	–
Average Age (Median)	45 (46)	42
% Owner-Operator	43	35
Average Years Driving (Median)	13 (10)	16.4
Average Months with Carrier (Median)	33 (12)	–
Average Company Size (Median)	2865 (400)	–
Percent Union Member (Number)	(1)	3
Percent Former Union Member in Trucking	14	–

remaining in, the workforce at increasing rates. Female drivers are far more likely to team drive with a family member or romantic partner than males, and as a result are less likely to spend much time in truck stops, as team drivers are not required to park their truck in order to take the mandatory DOT rest period (instead, one often sleeps while the other drives). Despite the low number of women I encountered during the interview phase (two of the seventy-five were women), I trained with five women over the first two phases of training and interviewed three who were no longer driving at all. I discuss the tremendous challenges female solo drivers face at the end of Chapter 2.

I am confident that my sample is largely representative of truck drivers as a whole, with three exceptions. All over-the-road truckers use truck stops, and the truck stop that I chose was at a major crossroads traveled by truckers. However, my sample includes only one team driver. This is probably not a serious problem for my ability to generalize, as teams represent very few drivers and typically last no more than a few months unless they are couples. I was able to interview several former team drivers. Team driving can potentially change the economics of owning, but I can't say much with certainty about the views of team independent contractors. Former team drivers I interviewed did not appear to differ significantly from solo drivers.

The second selection problem may be that I have underrepresented the number of drivers from large companies because of the prevalence of company-owned facilities. For instance, in the city where I conducted my interviews there was a Leviathan facility and, as a result, I did not encounter a single Leviathan driver during the formal interview phase. However, if there is an effect of this sample bias, it is most likely that I have understated the influence of these larger carriers on inexperienced workers.

Third, my sample has less Latino drivers than more recent surveys suggest exist. I believe this can be attributed to two factors. First, my initial interview sample was taken in the Midwest, where fewer drivers are likely to be Latino. Second, all indications are that Latinos represent an increasing share of truck drivers, likely due to larger demographic shifts in the US workforce and increased recruitment of the population by the industry, but these trends may have just begun affecting the industry when I began my interview phase, leading to fewer Latino drivers in my sample.

My strategy to avoid bias in my sample involved two steps. First, I would approach the nearest driver to me in the TV lounge or booth area. In other words, I did not go looking for drivers by moving around the stop. When presented with several drivers in the same area, I initially attempted to overrepresent groups that were unlike myself. That is, I deliberately sought out nonwhite drivers, older drivers, drivers who appeared to be from areas outside the northeastern US, or who appeared to be owner-operators. Aside from physical characteristics, I used clothing (e.g., style, logos), speech (e.g., accents), and activities (e.g., negotiating a truck repair by phone) to identify drivers who appeared different from myself. I initially sampled in this way on the assumption that my natural tendency would be to avoid interviewees that forced me to deal with the potential social distance due to race, ethnicity, immigrant status, cultural differences, and age. I used this strategy for most of the collection process, though often the strategy was not necessary, because there was only one person available to interview. As I neared the end of the first seventy-five interviews I concentrated on interviewing younger white males, because they were lacking in my sample. Again, this is likely because they tend to work for large companies that had facilities nearby. The exception to these rules was female drivers, whom I interviewed whenever they were present. As it turned out, my concern with representation regarding background characteristics proved to be unimportant. I found nuances but no serious differences related to gender, race, immigrant status, and age in terms of independent contracting (though as I suggest in various places, there were important differences in how the industry attempts to recruit from different populations, the likelihood that these workers enter the industry at all, and what their experiences are as workers more generally). Whether someone was from a rural background had some influence on work histories. But only whether they were or had been an independent contractor, and how long and in what segments of the trucking industry individuals, their family or close friends had worked, seemed in any way related to the way they viewed independent contracting.

General Format of the Initial Interviews

Interview questions began with a series of survey-style background questions about personal and work life (e.g., how old are you?, how long have you been driving?, are you married?). These questions, particularly those about work history, were effective rapport builders, allowing drivers who might have felt a bit uncomfortable with me, the interview process, or their own ability to answer questions to relax and begin talking freely. Once these background questions were answered, I used a series of open-ended questions about drivers' likes and dislikes about their current and, if applicable, former employers to get them talking in detail about monitoring, compensation, operational efficiency, government regulation, and other topics relative to their work. I would immediately follow up, asking them to explain, with specific examples, what they liked or disliked. If they were independent contractors, I would ask similar opening questions about what they liked or disliked about the company they were leased to.

The next step in the interview process was to explore drivers' thoughts on potential changes in their work arrangement. Had they considered changing companies? What would they want to see in a new company?

Was buying a truck a possibility? If so, would they lease to a company long-term or go independent?

Next I would ask a series of what I framed as "opinion" questions, which were deliberately intended to free the interviewees from any sense of needing to speak narrowly from their work experiences and specific career plans. I would ask what they thought the biggest challenges facing drivers were. Was there anything that drivers could do about these problems? I also asked questions that concerned the fairness of compensation and work arrangements.

Because the topic areas of the study concerned worldviews, there were times in the latter sections of each interview that I deliberately forced participants to answer the kind of "why" questions ethnographers typically avoid. I did this in an attempt to understand the kinds of relationships that truckers took for granted in economic situations. I wanted them to articulate the assumed economic relationships that they might not otherwise discuss. Ultimately I believe these types of questions, while unorthodox, proved very useful. Becker (1970) describes this type of approach as a way to cross-check data and test conclusions, to ensure that what has been produced is not biased unnecessarily by the structure of the interview process. I used these unconventional questions for this purpose and also to understand what concepts taken for granted might be justifying interviewees' stated beliefs. With regard to the latter goal, my approach is similar to that of Lamont (1992). In nearly all cases, these questions at least illuminated the conceptual building blocks that drivers used when forced to articulate the nature of economic relations within the industry. Only in a few cases, all of them very inexperienced workers, did these questions produce the kind of blank stares interviewers are warned to expect. Furthermore, these questions produced remarkably consistent responses that aligned with other features of the worldviews discussed in the book.

Rapport

In order to establish rapport, I adopted a particular style of dress and language. I wore the same kinds of work clothes that I wore while working as a trucker. I also deliberately used informal speech, and phrased questions to reflect native terms. Overall my goal, which I believe I largely achieved, was to make the interview sound and feel no different than a conversation the interviewee might have with a fellow trucker. While this was obviously impossible and undesirable to achieve completely, I had enough success in this regard that eavesdropping drivers nearby would sometimes jump into the interview as if it were just another truck stop conversation. One of the most successful techniques I employed was to ask drivers to explain their experience to me as if I were an inexperienced driver seeking advice.

My own experience of driving was sometimes critical to establishing rapport. Drivers believe that driving a tractor-trailer, and the lifestyle that is required of over-the-road drivers, are relatively unique experiences, which you can't understand fully without actually doing it. Some initially voiced skepticism about the value of an academic study. But once such drivers knew that I had driven, they usually responded enthusiastically. Nearly all clearly respected the fact that I had experienced the work firsthand before I started the interviews. However, at the beginning of the interview I would not tell most drivers that I had driven. I would usually wait to tell them until just before we covered issues surrounding either cutting corners around company routines or logging hours for the Department of Transportation. The reason for not telling drivers I had experience as a trucker was to get them to talk about the taken-for-granted aspects of the job, and to get a sense of how they might present the job to an outsider.

The most immediate challenge for conducting the interviews surrounded issues of breaking company policies and laws governing the behavior of drivers. I was very concerned from the start with issues of rapport in this regard, because drivers are required to self-report on their driving behavior to companies and in logbooks, and more often than not they provide inaccurate information. Fortunately I was aware of this from my own experience, and I structured interviews in such a way as to make drivers comfortable divulging sensitive information. For the most part this was achieved by establishing good personal rapport, assuring anonymity, careful question development, and, when necessary, by letting them know that I understood that the job essentially required falsifying information in order to make a living. Occasionally I was forced to tell a driver about my experience if he brought up illegal activities immediately and I realized that he was reluctant to come clean to me. Normally those interviewees hesitant about discussing illegal behavior would signal this to me by saying things like, "I am not sure if I should tell you this." At this point I would repeat the guarantee of anonymity that was in my initial project description and the overall academic nature of the project to reassure them that this project was not part of any company-sponsored spying or government enforcement program. Then I would let them know that I understood that illegal behavior was essentially the norm for drivers, and that I had committed the same offenses that they had. This always set workers at ease, and as a result I am confident that drivers did not hold back general information regarding illegal activities. In fact, nearly all voluntarily admitted to cheating on their logs without my asking about it or having to make such declarations, and only a few claimed to work completely by the book. Those who claimed they drove legally had incomes, work hours, and average miles that corresponded with reduced productivity or were paid by the hour.

Emotional Content

The next major challenge was dealing with the emotional nature of many of the interview topics. Some interviewees were in a difficult financial situation and/or felt a company was or had exploited or misled them. Many drivers vividly described bad experiences with former employers or failed attempts at ownership. My interviews also brought up very personal or sensitive issues about a driver's background, work history, or family life. Most commonly, drivers would describe the problems that their jobs caused for them as a parent or spouse. More than a few believed that trucking had destroyed important relationships in their lives. In interviews such as these it was difficult but necessary to let drivers speak their minds, while still staying on topic. And though my own driving experience was much less trying than most, I encountered enough problems to allow me to empathize to some degree with the difficulties drivers reported.

In several cases the drivers that I interviewed were in the truck stop because of its proximity to a service shop. In two cases, my interviewees were waiting for rides home after they decided that their truck was beyond repair. In both cases these drivers had just been financially wiped out. While these were the most extreme cases, aside from two recently unemployed and homeless drivers I interviewed, it was not uncommon for many inexperienced truckers to discuss at length and quite intensely their financial troubles.

Over the course of the interview phase it did not get easier for me to remain focused on the task of interviewing while a driver discussed at length, for instance, how his failure to make contracting a financial success was destroying his marriage. The following is a fieldnote I wrote during the interview phase:

> I also thought today, I hope that I'm not too much of a downer in these guy's lives. Some of them seem to really enjoy [the interview] and they all seem really interested in talking once they get going and discussing the issues . . . But a few of them definitelyv leave sad, and I think reflecting on what they are doing and on the options that they have taken advantage or haven't taken advantage of, can be challenging for them personally and emotionally. Like this one guy today, he said, by the end, he was really like, "now that I talk about it, I just really don't want to be in this job. I want to change careers. I think I want to see if I can go back to school, and become a police officer."

Status and Self-Representation

Experienced drivers consistently suggested to me that the inexperienced contractors misrepresented how much money they actually took home by focusing on the gross revenue of the truck rather than net income. Not surprisingly, success or failure as an independent contractor are often deeply tied to identity and status for truckers. There was significant potential that the interviews might not penetrate the deliberate self-representation of drivers that might fool me, fellow drivers and, perhaps, the drivers themselves. The rapport I was able to build, in combination with the detailed information I gathered from my own experience and research on the economics of independent contracting, allowed me to effectively create an atmosphere in which drivers revealed to me the economic difficulties and their very personal frustration with contracting, rather than some more romantic posturing. The data described in the preceding chapters makes this quite clear, as only a handful of drivers have very positive views of independent contracting, and these were all inexperienced drivers.

Salience of Contracting

I was initially concerned that contracting and other central issues of interest to me might not be salient for drivers. There might be several causes of this problem. Perhaps drivers did not consider these issues important or did not consider them at all. Or I might analytically construct and express the issues in ways that drivers would not recognize as meaningful. The consistency of the data produced convinces me that I had no problem in this regard. In only one area were the topics of interest to me not salient to drivers: deregulation of the industry. Only drivers with more than twenty years of experience had anything to say on this topic. On the issues such as ownership and working conditions, drivers had much to say and needed little more than basic prompts to begin speaking at length.

Politics, Religion, Sex—The Challenge of Associated Topics

Finally, some of the topics covered in the interviews, such as regulation by government, were inherently political in nature. While most drivers would probably not describe themselves as particularly political, a few are deeply so. And while most of these more political drivers fall into what we might consider standard definitions of liberal and conservative, there was the occasional outlier, such as the deeply committed evangelical who gave an interview on the condition that I give him the opportunity to save my soul. There was also a self-identified sexual deviant, a racist, a militia member, a 9–11 conspiracy theorist, and an ideologically driven tax evader. I don't believe I had difficulty appearing professional in the face of any personal objections I might have had to their views. The greater challenge was to not allow what appeared to me in the moment confusing or illogical patterns of thought to disrupt a systematic discussion of the issues. If, for instance, a driver cited the need for prayer in response to unjust treatment of drivers by companies, I believed that it was critically important to not dismiss this as simply unrelated to my questions, but to understand how this driver believed God, prayer, and/or religion might influence the out-come of class struggle. To those who study social movements these may not seem an entirely strange set of ideas, but for truckers these were indeed outliers—most simply didn't see God's influence in the industry—and such moments definitely required me to think on my feet and off the interview schedule as it was originally conceived. I managed to mitigate the effects of such apparently off-topic issues to the point that I am not concerned about their effect on the validity of the data gathered in the interview phase. I believe that the richness and consistency of the inter-views supports this conclusion.

Strike Driver Interviews

Just as I was in the middle of writing a first draft of my dissertation in the spring of 2008, owner-operators around the United States began the most significant attempts at collective action in the last several decades. It was simply good fortune that two of the most prominent actions, a rally to protest fuel prices at the state capital of Harrisburg, Pennsylvania, and a shutdown of leased and independent owner-operators (mostly steelhaul-ers) near Pittsburgh, were within reasonable driving distance for me. I was able to make contact with the drivers organizing these efforts, which were not associated with one another, and was welcomed with open arms by both groups. I was able to attend planning meetings, ride along with owner-operators during convoys, and spend several days with protesting and striking workers, conducting more traditional fieldwork and in-depth interviews. In a way these events served as natural experiments that con-firmed several of my key hypotheses.

I conducted in-depth interviews with twenty-five drivers during this portion of the research, and I collected most of the same basic information about these drivers as with the main group. These drivers consisted mostly of owner-operators, both independent and leased, and a few company drivers. From primary data I collected on organizing efforts, such as mem-bership lists and websites, I believe these drivers are fairly representative of others participating in collective action during the fuel crisis of 2008 throughout the US. In addition, press reports from the time suggested that drivers participating in events such as these in other areas of the country were similar to the independent contractors I interviewed. Because of their relevance to my questions about class action, interviews with these drivers differed significantly from the initial seventy-five interviews. Although these interviews contained brief work histories, they focused more heavily on the rapid rise in diesel prices in 2008, the experience of truck ownership during the crisis, and drivers' attempts to address the situation through collective action. These interviews were generally short, typically just fifteen to twenty minutes long. None of these interviews were used as sources of quotes except where explicitly stated, because of the unique context in which they took place.

Processing of the Interviews and Field Notes

The interviews constituted the core data for my analysis of truckers' worldviews and decisions regarding independent contracting. I transcribed all of the interviews word for word myself. After they were transcribed I used qualitative software to organize and code them. Each interview was coded twice over the course of about six months. The coding process involved identifying sections of the interviews according to the topic covered and/or its relevance to the hypotheses I began with and those I developed over the course of the analysis. In all I used more than one hundred different codes in my analysis. These varied from highly specific and descriptive to very abstract constructions derived from my working hypotheses. For instance, one highly descriptive code was "speeding," which was applied to any instance where the driver mentioned speeding as behavior, its control through monitoring, its effect on safety, insurance, driving record, sanctioning, etc. This example illustrates an important point about my codes. Some of the codes were native categories used by the drivers themselves to make sense of their work. Other examples of these, which were more abstract, were trust, freedom, etc. These differed from codes that were derived from my own analysis, such as "games" or "hegemony," which would have been unrecognizable to drivers and often represented my own synthesis of several overlapping or crosscutting native categories.

Because the transcribed interviews represented nearly one thousand pages of text, the more common nodes (all of those sections sharing the same code) would often contain fifty or more pages of text. Analyzing the data in light of new hypotheses was thus often extremely time consuming and cumbersome, despite the advantages of qualitative software (NVivo7). In order to combat this problem I created summaries of drivers that allowed me to model relationships by treating each driver as a unit. Each summary gave a basic description of the background characteristics of the driver, his/her work history, and attitudes toward the various critical issues covered in later chapters, such as the social relations of production, class action, etc. These summaries ranged from roughly two hundred fifty to six hundred words. All told, I estimate that I spent an average of around six hours transcribing, coding, summarizing, and analyzing each of the initial seventy-five interviews.

In addition to the formal individual interviews, over the time I worked as a driver and collected interviews I spent hundreds of hours in and around truck stops, company facilities, rest areas, warehouses and drop lots, observing and interacting with truckers in the process of doing their jobs and in their off time. During this time I talked with dozens of drivers about their experiences, and participated in many group conversations about the problems drivers faced. This observation produced more than one hundred pages of field notes, which were also coded.

Nondriver Interviews

In order to understand the differences between the company that I worked for and the other employment opportunities available to truckers, I interviewed owners and/or managers at seven trucking companies, for a total of twenty additional interviews. One of these companies was a large one similar to Leviathan with multiple divisions. Two represented the kinds of companies that my drivers referred to as "good," one of which was a union furniture hauling company and the other a nonunion specialized freight company. I also interviewed staff and/or owners at two companies that consisted entirely of independent contractors, one loan brokerage house, and one port hauling company. In total these seven represent the range of companies that my respondents hauled for. These interviews allowed me to understand how ownership and management adopted business and management models to shape the behavior of drivers.

Other Interviews

I conducted more than a dozen interviews with experts, activists, and others associated with the trucking industry as well. These included an organizer for the Teamsters union, activists working on worker misclassification, staff and leadership of the Owner-Operator Independent Drivers Association, staff at industry lobbying and consulting groups, a business advisor at American Trucking Business Services, and an executive at a company that sells equipment to the trucking industry, among others. Each of these interviewees helped to provide specific information on particular operational or market-related issues in long-haul trucking or the politics of the industry.

Interviewees Compared to the National Driver Population

My interviewees ended up looking much like what surveys suggest the driver population overall looks like. Above is a table listing characteristics of my interviewees alongside weighted estimates for the national long-haul driver population based on a survey conducted at twenty truck stops along key freight corridors across the US in 2014.[1]

Other Sources of Note

I collected many primary written materials published by the industry or read by truck drivers, which were useful for understanding recruitment, labor market participation, and framing of industry-wide issues by employers and drivers. I also followed all of the major trade journals aimed at both company managers and drivers. In addition, for several years, I read discussions on trucker blogs, corporate filings with the SEC, trucking websites, etc. In 2010, I began tracing the connections between various business interests in the trucking industry, using SEC filings, business journals, and other sources. At this time, I began researching the history of unionization, regulation, and independent contracting in trucking, using a wide range of primary and secondary sources.

My initial research design was guided in part by findings reported in a 1997 survey conducted by the University of Michigan Trucking Industry

Program (UMTIP) which included 505 long-haul drivers.[2] The population this survey sampled was almost identical to the population that I sampled for my interviews (though it was conducted nine years earlier). The UMTIP survey was conducted at truck stops in midwestern states, including the state in which I conducted my interviews and the states in which I did my training and much of my driving. This data set was made available to the public. It proved to be an excellent resource for me to develop and test hypotheses.

Notes

1. Author's audio journal entries. Notes edited for clarity.

2. Federal Highway Administration 2014.

3. In contrast, less-than-truckload (LTL) carriers, who move shipments of less than ten thousand pounds, and parcel carriers, like UPS, often use smaller trucks or vans for local pickup and then consolidate shipments at terminals into truckload-size shipments based on their destination. These consolidated loads are then sent over long distances to another terminal, where they are broken down and delivered to their final destination.

4. See Burks et al. 2010.

5. Corsi 2005.

6. Burks et al. 2007.

7. Ibid.

8. Ibid.

9. For a recent overview of the issue of driver turnover in the industry and the extensive literature on the subject see Harrison and Pierce 2009.

10. SCDigest 2012.

11. While the industry often portrays turnover as a crisis and suggests that the industry has a shortage of workers, truckers and a number of academics have questioned if firms view the constant churn of the truckload segment's labor

market as a serious problem at all. Some suggest it is simply a stable secondary job market that pays and treats its workers badly because of competitive pressures (see Burks et al. 2007). One study reviewing the extensive literature on turnover in the industry concluded that little has been done to address turnover and asked: "So—is there a turnover and retention problem in the trucking industry or is it a turnover and retention condition in the trucking industry where the problem is tolerated as a part of the business environment that is too costly or too much trouble to solve? Thirty years without a general solution suggests that the latter situation may be the case" (Harrison and Pierce 2009).

12. Nearly all analyses of the industry imply or conclude that regulation made union strategies far more successful, but it is also clear that prior to regulation affecting the industry, the IBT was already making tremendous strides in organizing intercity trucking on a large scale, with significant effects on the structure and economics of the industry (see Dobbs 1973, and Garnel 1972).

13. Belzer 2000.

14. Leiter 1957, 266.

15. Perry 1986, 46–8.

16. Sloane 1965, 28.

17. James and James 1965, 177.

18. Sloane 1991, 199.

19. Ibid., 205.

20. Ibid., 200.

21. James and James 1965, 147.

22. Ibid., 175.

23. Ibid., 98.

24. Sloane 1991, 407–8.

25. According to one investment analysis conducted at the time, as Hoffa carried out his most ambitious efforts, trucking revenues and profits improved substantially and far outpaced those of other modes of freight transport. Operating ratios of the 540 largest carriers declined from an average of 96.3 percent in 1954–1957 to an average of 95.5 percent in 1961–1964 (they averaged just 94.97 percent in 1964). Pretax net profit increased 50 percent from 1957 to 1964, and return on investment was almost three times that of railroads. The analysis concluded that the industry would enjoy "superior stock performance" and "promising prospects" (Debe 1965, 77).

26. Sloane 1991, 244.

27. James and James 1965, 377.

28. Sloane 1991, 318.

29. Ibid., 319.

30. Belzer 2000.

31. Russell 2001, 225.

32. Belzer 2000, 28.

33. Ibid., 124–25.

34. Perry 1986, 59–60; Belzer 2000, 107.

35. Perry 1986, 53–54.

36. Hamilton 2008.

37. For instance, in 1967 the Ford Foundation gave the Brookings Institution $1.8 million for a research program on economic regulation that supported the production of twenty-two books, sixty-five journal articles, and thirty-eight dissertations (Madar 2000, 39).

38. Rich 2005, 149.

39. Ibid., 214.

40. Belzer 2000, 121.

41. Robyn 1987, 17.

42. Hayden, 134.

43. Robyn 1987, 16–17.

44. Ibid., 78.

45. Crain 2006–7, 446.

46. Nader later came to believe that trucking deregulation was a mistake.

47. Robyn 1987.

48. Quoted in ibid., 95.

49. Ibid.

50. Ibid.

51. Robertson 1998, 39

52. Robyn 1987, 42.

53. Derthick and Quirk 1985, 108.

54. Ibid., 238.

55. Office of the Federal Register 1980, 1265.

56. Madar 2000, 53.

57. Ibid., 53.

58. Ibid., 54.

59. Zingales 1998, 917.

60. Belzer 2000.

61. Peoples 2005. Belzer (2000) disputes the existence of true productivity gains, suggesting that increased working hours, which are not accurately reflected in Bureau of Labor Statistics data, likely explain much of the increased output.

62. Corsi 2005.

63. Belzer 2000.

64. Hirsch 1993.

65. Belman, Monaco, and Brooks 2005; Belzer 2000.

66. Corsi and Stowers 1991.

67. Peoples and Peteraf 1999; Hirsch and MacPherson 1997.

68. Belzer 2000.

69. Ibid.

70. ICF Consulting 2002.

71. Wright 2000

72. Ibid.

73. See Kalleberg 2011, 32–33, for an overview.

74. Ibid.

75. See Cappelli 1999; Smith 2001.

76. The subject of independent contracting from workers' perspectives is woefully understudied relative to its prevalence and importance, particularly for less-skilled workers. For studies of more-skilled workers, see Barley and Kunda 2004. Also see Osnowitz 2010.

77. Smith 2003.

78. Smith and Neuwirth 2008.

79. Ibid.

1. THE CDL MILL: TRAINING THE PROFESSIONAL STEERING-WHEEL HOLDER

1. For basic demographics of the driver population see Table A.1 in the appendix.

2. Federal Highway Administration 1998, 145.

3. Knipling et al. 2011.

4. Social Security Administration 2008.

5. Private CDL schools obviously have an interest in recruiting students, and also provide misleading income figures. For instance, Sage Truck Driving School, which controls one of the largest networks of CDL schools, offers to train drivers and provide job placement assistance. In its advertising it states: "Newly trained drivers typically earn $37,000–$41,000 per year, according to industry data such as the U.S. Department of Labor and the American Trucking Associations. Drivers can earn up to $44,000 their first year out of school. The average experienced driver earns over $50,000 plus benefits, according to ATA industry estimates. Motivated drivers with some experience can earn well over that amount. Owner-operators, teams, and specialized equipment drivers can earn over $100,000 per year, although that is not typical" (Sage, www.sageschools.com /sage-employment.htm).

6. American Trucking Associations 2009.

7. American Trucking Associations 2012.

8. Heine and Klemp 2011.

9. For additional demographics of these drivers see Hoffman and Burks 2013.

10. ATA 2012.

11. McClanahan 2012

12. Commercial Vehicle Training Association 2015.

13. ATA 2012

14. Burks et. al. 2008, 61

15. Hoffman and Burks 2013.

16. Cleaves and Tackes 2002, 4.

17. Truckinginfo.com 2009.

18. Recruiting Media n.d.

19. United States Department of Transportation 2014.

2. CHEAP FREIGHT, CHEAP DRIVERS: WORK AS A LONG-HAUL TRUCKER

1. Burawoy 1979.

2. Burks et. al. 2007.

3. This included $2,333.64 for 8,317 paid miles, thirty dollars as bonus for two loads with extra stops, and forty dollars for an extended loading time.

4. Sloane 1991, 238.

5. Corsi and Grimm 1989.

6. ATA 2012.

7. These terminals are not like the terminal systems used during regulation, as discussed in Chapter 2. No work is done to freight at these facilities to break down loads for local delivery or combine them for long distance transport. Drivers can and do regularly bypass terminals entirely. For these reasons, terminals are not likely to be sites of union efforts as pre-deregulation terminals were to Teamster efforts.

8. Belzer 2000.

9. Truckload Carriers Association 1999.

10. See for example Oullett 1994 and Upton 2015.

11. See for example Klein 2014.

12. See Upton 2015 for more on fatherhood, masculinity, and trucking.

13. There are some aspects of certain driving jobs that do require well-above-average strength. For instance, flatbed drivers are often required to chain down and cover loads with tarps. Truck tarps can weight close to one hundred pounds and need to be lifted to the top of the load before being spread out.

14. See Williams 1989, Williams 1995, and Denissen and Saguy 2014. For aspects of this in trucking in particular, see Ouellet 1994.

3. THE BIG RIG: RUNNING THE CONTRACTOR CONFIDENCE GAME

1. Corsi and Grimm 1987; Peoples and Peteraf 1995.

2. Corsi and Grimm 1987.

3. Nickerson and Silverman 2003.

4. Corsi and Grimm 1987.

5. Corsi and Grimm 1989, 285.

6. Ibid., 290.

7. Corsi and Stowers 1991.

8. Cullen 1998.

9. Wyckoff 1979.

10. Agar 1986.

11. Belman, Monaco, and Brooks 2005.

12. Ibid.

13. Wyckoff 1979; Agar 1986.

14. Maister 1980.

15. Kvidera 2010a.

16. According to the US Department of Transportation, in 2003 of the 1,408 firms defined as general freight TL carriers with more than $1 million dollars in revenue, 69 percent used contractors (Hans, Corsi, and Grimm 2008). Of the one hundred largest for-hire trucking companies in 2008, 80 percent employed contractors. The 20 percent that did not were all either LTL carriers, vehicle haulers, or hauled highly specialized freight (e.g., hazardous chemicals). According to the leading industry trade journal, of the ninety-eight largest for-hire companies reporting the number of company trucks and owner-operator trucks in 2008, forty-seven hauled primarily TL freight and did not provide warehousing services or haul highly specialized freight. All of these firms employed contractors and twenty-two employed more contractors than company drivers. In total these forty-seven firms employed approximately 150,000 tractor-trailer drivers, 44 percent of which were contractors. If we remove the four largest companies (which tend to train and employ the most inexperienced drivers and attract relatively few contractors) the remaining forty-three companies employed 102,000 tractor-trailer drivers, 59 percent of which were contractors (Transport Topics 2009).

17. Malloy 2004.

18. Short 2009.

19. Kvidera 2010b.

20. Roehl Transport 2010, 3.

21. Ibid., 2.

22. Ibid., 3.

23. Cullen 1998.

24. Swain 2007.

25. Macklin 2006.

26. The most notable exceptions in this regard are media, including a magazine and radio show, produced by the Owner-Operator Independent Driver Association (OOIDA).

27. Hamilton 2008.

28. Ibid.

29. Overdrive Staff 2008b.

30. 3.9 percent of the drivers in the UMTIP study had a two-year college degree.

31. The exception to this is a radio show and magazine produced by the Owner-Operator Independent Driver Association.

32. Randall-Reilly 2010.

33. Ibid., 12.

34. Randall-Reilly 2010.

35. Dills Todd 2009.

36. Overdrive Staff 2008a.

37. Ibid.

38. Ibid.

39. Randall-Reilly 2010.

40. Ibid.

41. Ibid.

42. *Folio* Staff, January 29, 2008.

43. Kinsman 2006.

44. For instance, all drivers in the UMTIP driver survey were asked to report how much they "earned in 1996 from their work as a truck driver." Contractors were later asked to report gross and net earnings after truck expenses. I compared contractors' answers and found that only about 20 percent of them reported their net earnings, or something close, for the first income question. The remaining 80 percent or so reported their gross revenue or something close to that. And because inexperienced drivers cannot accurately estimate the costs they will incur as contractors, as I explain in the next chapter, they incorrectly believe the high gross revenues they hear about from existing contractors translate into substantially higher net incomes.

45. ATA 2012.

4. WORKING FOR THE TRUCK: THE HARSH REALITY OF CONTRACTING

1. Purchase contracts with sister companies are used in part to convince government auditors and courts that contractors are not "financially controlled" by the carrier directing their work, a key requirement in defending classification of a worker as a contractor rather than an employee.

2. Bearth 2005.

3. Five contractors claimed to be unable to provide me with their income after truck expenses. The rest were excluded because they had not worked a full year,

or had switched from being a company driver to being a contractor, or vice versa. While the number of drivers I excluded may seem high, it is consistent with the fact that the UMTIP survey found that 25 percent of all long-haul drivers had quit their company in the previous year, and about 38 percent of general freight contractors had owned for one year or less.

4. Independent contractors may deduct a portion of self-employment taxes from their gross adjusted income for federal income tax, resulting in some benefit. Most, however, are likely to pay little in federal income tax; they do not make their self-employment tax payments on the mandated quarterly basis and can pay penalties of up to 10 percent plus interest.

5. Academic studies have found relatively little difference in compensation between owner-operators and employees. Belman et. al. 2005, using data from the UMTIP survey, reported OTR owner-operators earning 1 percent less per mile driven than nonunion employees. The largest reported difference one will find between employees and owner-operator compensation is 8 percent less total earnings for owner-operators (Peoples and Peteraf 1999). In light of such findings, economists have largely agreed it is reasonable to conclude that owner-operators are making an informed tradeoff between take-home income and control over their work schedules. The dramatic difference between my findings and those of other studies results primarily from two factors: 1) adjusting income for self-employment taxes; 2) differentiating between contractors who employ others and those who do not. In my own analysis of the data from the UMTIP that Belman et. al.'s 2005 figures come from, I took into account the effects of additional FICA payments. If we do that, the median owner-operator earns about 8.6 percent (rather than 1 percent) less per mile than the median company drivers. But this owner-operator group includes contractors who reported employing another driver (about 21 percent of all OTR contractors in 1997) and their earnings likely reflect income generated from this arrangement, since drivers were asked to report "net earnings after truck expenses." When these drivers are removed, the median contractor then earns 16 percent less per mile than the median employee driver.

6. The sample is limited to nonunion drivers with three or more years experience, because it can take up to two years of experience for drivers to reach full productivity and be able work for better paying companies (see Burks, Carpenter, Gotte, Monaco, Porter, and Rustichini 2007). Drivers with more than thirty days unemployment in the previous year were excluded. The sample excludes contractors with one year of experience as an owner-operator, because the UMTIP data set coded all drivers with less than two years experience with a 1. Thus it is not possible to know whether their income represents a full year of earnings from that arrangement.

7. ATBS, a major promoter of contractors discussed in the next chapter, reported average net income for 2011 for dry van contractors of $44,868. Once

these contractors pay self-employment payroll taxes their income would be $38,529. According to the ATA 2011 benchmarking survey, on average employee drivers in this segment made about $48,000, or $44,328 after employee payroll taxes (ATA 2012). But dry van employee drivers tend to be the least experienced; the average contractor would likely be close to the top average pay rates if they were an employee. Still, even if they earned the average, dry van contractors would take home 15 percent more if they were employees. This estimate is probably very conservative because ATBS admits it "cleans" its data to remove very low incomes, which likely means removing new contractors without a full year of experience, those who quit or have disruptions in their work due to major breakdowns, accidents, or illnesses. Dr. Michael Belzer conducted a benchmarking survey in 2003–4 of OOIDA members that included net income figures for owner-operators who made no money or showed a loss for the year. When those drivers were included, the median owner-operator with one truck netted just under $18,000 (Belzer, personal communication).

8. Heine and Klemp 2011.

9. This self-identification is also important with regard to misclassification audits. The IRS, for instance, considers the parties' understanding of the nature of the relationship in determining whether the worker is an employee or self-employed. Thus, if a worker does not think of himself or herself as an employee, the IRS is more likely to determine that he or she is not one for tax purposes.

10. Note the specific language used. The information regarding the load he is sent is not called an "assignment" as it would be for an employee, it is an "offer." Legal specialists encourage companies to tailor every part of the labor process to indicate to auditors, courts, and contractors themselves that contractors have control over their work.

11. Michael Belzer 2000 also argued that trucking contractors experienced tremendous pressure to self-sweat for the reasons I have outlined.

5. SOMEONE TO TURN TO: MANAGING CONTRACTORS FROM AN ARM'S LENGTH AWAY

1. Feary and Smith 2009.

2. Lockridge 2001, 34.

3. Park 2010.

4. Cullen 2004.

5. American Truck Business Services 2010a.

6. Ibid.

7. *Overdrive* articles on contractors typically cite ATBS as an expert and portray at least one of ATBS's forty strategic carrier partners in a positive light.

8. Partners in Business 2010.

9. Ibid., 5.

10. Ibid.

11. ATBS 2010a.

12. Ibid.

13. Ibid.

14. Ibid.

15. Kvidera 2010a.

16. Partners in Business 2010.

17. ATBS 2012.

18. ATBS 2008.

19. ATBS 2010b.

20. www.cdlofit.com, accessed July 21, 2010.

21. CNN Money 2007.

22. Erwin 2006.

23. Partners in Business 2009b.

24. Ibid.

25. FedEx now requires its contractors to formally incorporate as firms. ATBS has developed a special program to handle this process for FedEx contractors.

6. NO MORE JIMMY HOFFAS: DESPERATE DRIVERS AND DIVIDED LABOR

1. There is a significant Christian trucker subculture in long-haul trucking with which Dean identified. For more on this population see Upton (2015).

2. Johnston 2008.

3. For instance, during the week of June 18, 2008, diesel fuel on the central Atlantic coast averaged $4.87 per gallon at the pump. According to the National Transportation Institute, that week shippers paid medium and large carriers an average of 53.8 cents per mile (cpm) in fuel surcharges for dry van shipments in that region. The carriers, in turn, paid contractors an average fuel surcharge of 54.5 cpm—or .7 cpm more than they were charging shippers. But the break-even point at which the fuel surcharge would meet the actual cost of fuel was 59.3 cpm—or 4.8 cpm more than the carriers were paying the contractors. Thus while carriers were absorbing .7 cpm of the cost of increased fuel prices, contractors were absorbing 4.8 cpm—nearly seven times the burden of their better-financed counterparts in this wildly unbalanced partnership. For a typical contractor running 110,000 paid miles per year, this would come out to roughly $5,280 on an annual basis, about 15 percent of the average take-home pay of the contractors I interviewed.

4. Uchitelle 2008.

5. Truckload Carriers Association 2013.

6. Ross 2012.

7. Watson 2009.

8. This practice can be quite beneficial for carriers. In the week of June 23, 2010, the break-even point for fuel surcharges in the Central Atlantic states for dry vans was 29.4 cpm. Carriers in NTI's survey collected an average of 41.5 cpm in fuel surcharges from shippers, but paid contractors only 27 cpm. If carriers had passed on the 14.5 cpm difference, it would have meant an average $350 increase in weekly pay for the contractors.

9. For a similar perspective on the effects of deregulation and independent contracting in the context of port driving, see Bensman 2009. Also see Smith, Bensman, and Marvy 2010.

10. The industry maintains that antitrust regulations forbid contractors, who are legally self-employed, from forming a union.

11. For instance, employers have created a lobby group called the Coalition for Independent Contractor Freedom that is attempting to organize independent contractors to oppose attempts to restrict their use.

APPENDIX A: DATA AND METHODS

1. Seiber 2014.

2. See Belman, Monaco, and Brooks (2005) for a general description of this dataset and its methodology.

Glossary

ATA	American Trucking Associations
ATBS	American Trucking Business Services
BMV	Bureau of Motor Vehicles
CDL	Commercial Driver's License
CVTA	Commercial Vehicle Training Association
FMCSA	Federal Motor Carrier Safety Administration
ICC	Interstate Commerce Commission
IBT	International Brotherhood of Teamsters
GAO	Government Accountability Office
LTL	Less than Truckload
OOIDA	Owner-Operator Independent Drivers Association
OTR	Over-the-road
NTI	National Transportation Institute
NMFA	National Master Freight Agreement
PIB	Partners in Business
TCA	Truckload Carrier Association
TL	Truckload
UMTIP	University of Michigan Trucking Industry Program
USDOT	United States Department of Transportation

Bibliography

Agar, Michael. *Independents Declared: The Dilemmas of Independent Trucking.* Washington, DC: Smithsonian Institution Press, 1986.

American Truck Business Services. 2010a, http://www.atbsshow.com /transportation.htm (accessed July 2, 2010).

———. "It's Not How Much You Make, It's How Much You Can Keep!" *Owner-Operator Newsletter*, 2008.

———. *Owner-Operator Newsletter*, November 2012.

———. "Quality Shortage I." *Owner-Operator Newsletter*, 2010b.

American Trucking Associations. *Benchmarking Guide for Driver Recruitment and Retention.* American Trucking Associations: Arlington, VA, 2012.

———. "Driver Turnover Rate Rises." *Transport Topics*, June 25, 2007, 1.

———. 2009, www.gettrucking.com (accessed April 3, 2009).

Ashford, S. J., E. George, and R. Blatt. "Old Assumptions, New Work: The Opportunities and Challenges of Research on Nonstandard Employment." *Academy of Management Annals* 1 (2007): 65–117.

Barley, S. R., and G. Kunda, G. *Gurus, Hired Guns and Warm Bodies.* Princeton: Princeton University Press, 2004.

Bearth, D. P. "Buyers' Leverage: Go with the Group." *Transport Topics*, March 28, 2005, 11.

Becker, H. S. 1970. "Problems of Inference and Proof in Participant Observation. In *Sociological Work: Method and Substance.* Chicago: Aldine, 1970.

Belman, D., and M. Belzer. "The Regulation of Labor Markets: Balancing Benefits and Costs of Competition." In *Government Regulation of the Employment Relationship*, edited by B. E. Kaufman, 179–220. Ithaca: Industrial Relations Research Association, 1997.

Belman, D., and E. E. Kossek. "Truck Owner-Operators: Entrepreneur or Galvanized Employees?" In *Research on Entrepreneurship*, edited by R. Heneman and J. Tanksy. Greenwich, CT: JAI Press, 2006.

Belman, Dale L., Francine Lafontaine, and Kristen A. Monaco. "Truck Drivers in the Age of Information: Transformation without Gain." In *Trucking in the Information Age*, edited by Dale Belman and Chelsea White III, 183–211. Burlington, VT: Ashgate, 2005.

Belman, Dale L., and Kristen A. Monaco. "The Effects of Deregulation, Deunionization, Technology, and Human Capital on the Work and Work Lives of Truck Drivers." *Industrial and Labor Relations Review* 54, no. 2A (2001): 502–24.

Belman, Dale L., Kristen A. Monaco, and Taggert J. Brooks. *Sailors on the Concrete Sea: A Portrait of Truck Drivers' Work and Lives.* East Lansing: Michigan State University Press, 2005.

Belzer, Michael. *Sweatshops on Wheels: Winners and Losers in Trucking Deregulation.* New York: Oxford University Press, 2000.

Bensman, David. *Port Trucking Down the Low Road: A Sad Story of Deregulation.* Demos: New York, 2009.

Burks, S. V., M. Belzer, Q. Kwan, S. Pratt, S. Shackelford. *Trucking 101: An Industry Primer.* Washington, DC: Transportation Research Board, 2010.

Burks, S. V., J. Carpenter, L. Gotte, K. Monaco, K. Porter, and A. Rustichini. "Using Behavioral Economic Experiments at a Large Motor Carrier: The Context and Design of the Truckers and Turnover Project." IZA Discussion Paper No. 2789 (May). Bonn, Germany: IZA, 2007.

Burks, S. V., K. Monaco, and J. Myers-Kuykindall, J. "How Many Trucks, How Many Miles? Trends in the Use of Heavy Freight Vehicles in the U.S., from 1977 to 1997." Working Paper, Trucking Industry Program, Georgia Institute of Technology, Atlanta, GA, February 15, 2004.

Burawoy, Michael. *Manufacturing Consent: Changes in the Labor Process under Monopoly Capitalism.* Chicago: University of Chicago Press, 1979.

Cappelli, Peter. *The New Deal at Work: Managing the Market-Driven Work Force.* Cambridge: Harvard Business Review Press, 1999.

Cato Institute. "Trucking Deregulation—A Long Haul." *Regulation* 5 (1979): 3–13.

Cleaves, E., and G. Tackes. "Show Me the Money and Keep My Career Options Open." *Commercial Carrier Journal* 157, no. 5 (2000): 89–93.

CNN Money, December 21, 2007, http://money.cnn.com/2007/12/21/news /companies/fedex/index.htm?section=money_mostpopular (accessed 3/27/2015).

Commercial Vehicle Training Association. "Fact Sheet," 2015, https://cvta.org
/about/fact-sheet.html (accessed November 18, 2015).

Corsi, Thomas M. "The Impact of Multiple-Unit Fleet Owners in the Owner-
Operator Segment on Regulatory Reform." *Transportation Journal* 19
(1979): 47–71.

———. "The Truckload Carrier Industry Segment." In *Trucking in the Age of
Information,* edited by Dale Belman and Chelsea White III, 21–42. Burlington, VT: Ashgate, 2005.

Corsi, Thomas M., and Curtis M. Grimm. "ATLFs: Driving Owner-Operators into
the Sunset." *Journal of Transportation Research Forum* 29 (1989): 285–90.

———. "Changes in Owner-Operator Use, 1977–1985: Implications for Management Strategy." *Transportation Journal* 26, no. 3 (Spring 1987): 4–16.

Corsi, Thomas M., and Joseph R. Stowers. "Effects of a Deregulated Environment on Motor Carriers: A Systematic Multi-Segment Analysis." *Transportation Journal* (1991) 30: 4–28.

Crain, Andrew D. "Ford, Carter, and Deregulation in the 1970s." *Journal on
Telecommunications and High Technology Law* 5 (2006-7).

Crisper, Jason. "Buyer's Paradise." *Landline,* March, 2000.

Cullen, D. "Owner-Operators: A Measure of Success." *Fleet Owner,* June 1, 1998,
36.

———. "Rebirth of the Owner-Operator." *Fleet Owner,* August 1, 2004, http://
fleetowner.com/management/feature/fleet_rebirth_owneroperator
(accessed March 3, 2015).

Debe. J. A. "Investment Aspects of the Trucking Industry." *Financial Analysts
Journal* 21, no. 4 (July/August 1965): 72–77.

Denissen, Amy M. and Abigail C. Saguy. 2014. "Gendered Homophobia and the
Contradictions of Workplace Discrimination for Women in the Building
Trades." *Gender and Society* 28, no. 3 (2014): 381–403.

Derthick, M., and P. J. Quirk. *The Politics of Deregulation.* Washington:
Brookings Institution, 1985.

Dills, T. "Hard Financial Choices." *Overdrive,* September 1, 2009, http://www
.overdriveonline.com/hard-financial-choices/ (accessed March 27, 2015).

Dobbs, Farrell. *Teamster Power.* New York: Pathfinder, 1973.

Dudley, S. E. "Alfred Kahn 1917–2010." *Regulation* 34, no. 1–2: 8–12.

Eisenach, J. A. *The Role of Independent Contractors in the U.S. Economy.*
Washington, DC: Navigant Economics, 2010, http://www.aei.org
/wp-content/uploads/2012/08/-the-role-of-independent-contractors-in-
the-us-economy_123302207143.pdf (accessed November 20, 2015).

Erwin, P. C. "Owner-Operator Finance Programs Boost Profitability, Owner-
Operator Relations," February 6 , 2006, http://www.kefonline.com
/Downloads/PDF/KEF_02062006.pdf (accessed August 22, 2010).

Feary, G., and J. Smith. "Independent Contractor Fleets in North American

Trucking." Annual Global Conference, Council of Supply Chain Management Professionals, Chicago, 2009.

Federal Highway Administration. "Freight Facts and Figures 2013." Washington, DC: USDOT, January, 2014.

———. "OECD TRILOG Plenary Symposium: Public Policy Issues in Global Freight Logistics, Conference Proceedings." Washington, DC: USDOT, December 17–18, 1998.

Folio Staff. "Why Randall-Reilly Sold to Investcorp," January 29, 2008, http://www.foliomag.com/2008/breaking-randall-reilly-acquired-investcorp (accessed July 2, 2010).

Garnel, Donald. *Rise of Teamster Power in the West.* Berkeley: University of California Press, 1972.

Government Accountability Office. "Employment Arrangements: Improved Outreach Could Help Ensure Proper Worker Classification." Report to the Ranking Minority Member, Committee on Health, Education, Labor, and Pensions, U.S. Senate. Washington, DC: GAO, 2006.

Gramsci, A. *Selections from the Prison Notebooks.* Trans. Q. H. Smith. New York: International, 1971.

Hamilton, S. *Trucking Country: The Road to America's Wal-Mart Economy.* Princeton: Princeton University Press, 2008.

Harrison H. D. and J. Pierce. "Examining Driver Turnover and Retention in the Trucking Industry." Center for Intermodal Freight Transportation Studies: Memphis and Nashville, March 2009.

Hayden, James F. "Teamsters, Truckers, and the ICC: A Political and Economic Analysis of Motor Carrier Deregulation." *Harvard Journal of Legislation* 17, no. 1: 123–55.

Heine, Max. "Panelists Forecast Increased Driver Demand," May 23, 2003, www.etrucker.com.

Heine, Max, and Gordon Klemp. "Keeping Up with Driver Pay Changes." Trucker Webinar Series, August 15, 2011, www.truckerwebinars.com (accessed September 5, 2012).

Hirsch, B. T. "Trucking Deregulation and Labor Earnings: Is the Union Premium a Compensating Differential?" *Journal of Labor Economics* 11, no. 2 (1993): 270–301.

———. "Wage Gaps Large and Small." Discussion Paper Series. Bonn: Institute for the Study of Labor, 2008.

Hirsch, Barry T., and David A. MacPherson. "Earnings and Employment in Trucking: Deregulating a Naturally Competitive Industry." In *Regulatory Reform and Labor Markets,* edited by James Peoples, 61–112. Norwell, MA: Kluwer Academic Publishers, 1997.

Hoffman, Matthew, and Stephen Burks. "Training Contracts, Worker Overconfidence, and the Provision of Firm-Sponsored General Training," May 31, 2013, http://ssrn.com/abstract=2220043.

ICF Consulting. *Economic Effects of Transportation: The Freight Story.* Washington, DC: Federal Highway Administration, 2002.

James, Ralph C., and Estelle Dinerstein James. *Hoffa and the Teamsters.* Princeton: Van Nostrand, 1965.

Johnston, Jim. "Why Doesn't OOIDA Call for a Strike?," March 14, 2008, http://landlinemedia.blogspot.com/2008/03/why-doesnt-ooida-call-for-strike.html (accessed June 8, 2015).

Kalleberg, A. L., B. F. Reskin, and K. Hudson. "Bad Jobs in America: Standard and Nonstandard Employment Relations in the United States." *American Sociological Review* 65, no. 2 (2000): 256–78.

Kalleberg, Arne. *Good Jobs, Bad Jobs: The Rise of Polarized Employment Systems in the United States, 1970s to 2000s.* New York: Russell Sage Foundation, 2011.

Kinsman, M. "Randall Rising." *Folio,* January 4, 2006, http://www.foliomag.com/2006/randall-rising (accessed July 9, 2010).

Klein, Debbie. "Feeling the Driver Shortage? Recruit Women Truck Drivers," September 11, 2014, http://www.hni.com/blog/bid/91738/Feeling-the-Driver-Shortage-Recruit-Women-Truck-Drivers (accessed June 11, 2015).

Knipling, Ronald R., Stephen V. Burks, Kristen M. Starner, Christopher P. Thorne, Michael R. Barnes. *Driver Selection Tests and Safety Practice: A Synthesis of Safety Practice.* Washington, DC: Transportation Research Board, 2011.

Kunda, G., S. R. Barley, and J. Evans. "Why Do Contractors Contract? The Experience of Highly Skilled Technical Professionals in a Contingent Labor Market." *Industrial and Labor Relations Review* 55, no. 2 (2002): 234–61.

Kvidera, M. "Custom Pay." *Overdrive.* February 1, 2010a, http://www.overdriveonline.com/custom-pay/ (accessed March 27, 2015).

———. "How to Become an O/O: To Lease or Not to Lease." *Overdrive,* February 1, 2010b, http://www.overdriveonline.com/how-to-become-an-oo-to-lease-or-not-to-lease/ (accessed March 27, 2015).

Lamont, Michèle. *Money, Morals, and Manners.* Chicago: University of Chicago Press, 1992.

Leiter, R. D. *The Teamsters Union: A Study of Its Economic Impact.* New York: Bookman Associates, 1957.

Lockridge, D. "Recruiting Drivers in a Recession." *Heavy Duty Trucking* 80, no. 12 (2001): 34.

Macklin, G. "Owner-Operators Supply Greatwide's Capacity." *Refrigerated Transporter,* September 1, 2006.

Madar, Daniel. *Heavy Traffic: Deregulation, Trade, and Transformation in*

North American Trucking. East Lansing: Michigan State University Press, 2000.

Maister, David H. *Management of Owner-Operator Fleets*. Lexington, MA: Lexington, 1980.

McClanahan, Robert. "Driving School 2012 Survey Shows Lower Enrollment." National Association of Publicly Funded Truck Driving Schools, 2012, www.napftds.org (accessed March 12, 2013).

Moore, G. "The Beneficiaries of Trucking Regulation." *The Journal of Law and Economics* 21 (1978): 327–43.

Nickerson, Jack A., and Brian B. Silverman. "Why Aren't All Truck Drivers Owner-Operators? Asset Ownership and the Employment Relation in Interstate For-Hire Trucking." *Journal of Economics and Management Strategy* 12, no. 1 (Spring 2003): 91–118.

———."Why Firms Want to Organize Efficiently and What Keeps Them from Doing So: Inappropriate Governance, Performance, and Adaptation in a Deregulated Industry." *Administrative Science Quarterly* 48 (2003): 433–65.

Office of the Federal Register. "Weekly Compilation of Presidential Documents." Washington, DC: National Archives and Records Service, General Services Administration, 1980.

Osnowitz, D. *Freelancing Expertise: Contract Professionals in the New Economy*. Ithaca: Cornell University Press, 2010.

Ouellet, Lawrence J. *Pedal to the Metal*. Philadelphia: Temple University Press, 1994.

Overdrive Staff. "Another Way to Buy." *Overdrive*, December 12, 2008a), http://www.overdriveonline.com/another-way-to-buy/ (accessed November 20, 2015).

———. "Inside Track." *Overdrive*, December 12, 2008b, http://www.overdriveonline.com/inside-track/ (accessed March 27, 2015).

Owner Operator Independent Drivers Association. *2007 Independent Driver Survey*. Grain Valley, MO: OOIDA, 2007.

Park, J. "Times They Are A-Changin': Can Owner-Operators Keep Pace?" *Heavy Duty Trucking*, February 10, 2010, http://digital.ipcprintservices.com/display_article.php?id=317776 (accessed March 27, 2015).

Partners in Business. "The Legal Status of Owner-Operators." Partners in Business Webinar Series, *Overdrive Online*, 2009b, www.overdriveonline.com/pib, accessed July 8, 2010.

———. "Partners in Business," *Overdrive Online*, 2010, http://www.overdriveonline.com/pib (accessed July 8, 2010).

———. *2009 Partners in Business: A Business Manual for Owner-Operators*. Tuscaloosa, AL: Randall-Reilly, 2009a.

Peoples, J., and M. Peteraf. "The Effects of Regulatory Reform on Company Drivers and Owner Operators in the For-Hire and Private Sectors." *Transportation Journal* 38, no. 3 (1999): 5–17.

Peoples, James. "Industry Performance Following Reformation of Economic and Social Regulation in the Trucking Industry." In *Trucking in the Age of Information,* edited by Dale Belman and Chelsea White III, 128–46. Burlington, VT: Ashgate, 2005.

Perry, Charles. *Deregulation and the Decline of the Unionized Trucking Industry.* Philadelphia: University of Pennsylvania Press, 1986.

Prottas, D. J., and C. A. Thompson. "Stress, Satisfaction, and the Work-Family Interface: A Comparison of Self-Employed Business Owners, Independents, and Organizational Employees." *Journal of Occupational Health Psychology* 11 (2006): 366–78.

Randall-Reilly. Media Kit. Tuscaloosa, AL: Randall-Reilly, 2010, http://www .randallreilly.com/markets/trucking/ (accessed March 27, 2015).

Recruiting Media. "Trucking's Top Rookie: Train. Retain. Gain," July 29, 2011, http://www.truckload.org/TCA/files/ccLibraryFiles/Filename/000000001191 /Trucking's%20Top%20Rookie%20White%20Paper.pdf (accessed November 20, 2015).

Rich, A. *Think Tanks, Public Policy and the Politics of Expertise.* Cambridge: Cambridge University Press, 2005.

Robertson, D. B. *Loss of Confidence: Politics and Policy in the 1970s.* University Park: Pennsylvania State University Press, 1998.

Robyn, Dorothy. *Braking the Special Interests: Trucking Deregulation and the Politics of Policy Reform.* Chicago: University of Chicago Press, 1987.

Roehl Transport. *Owner Operator Plan for Success.* Marshfield, WI: Roehl Transport, 2010.

Ross, Dave. "U.S. Trucking Overview and Outlook," January 27, 2012, http:// operationstimulus.org/documents/Acme%20Distribution%20Centers%20 Trucking%20Overview_1_27_12.pdf.

Russell, Thaddeus. *Out of the Jungle.* New York: Knopf, 2001.

Sage. *Free Truck Driver Training.* Sage Truck Driving School, http://www .sageschools.com/sage-employment.htm (accessed July 25, 2010).

SCDigest. "Carrier CEOs Says Driver Pay Must Rise to over 60,000," January 25, 2012, www.scdigest.com/ONTARGET/12–01–25–3.php (accessed October 2, 2013).

Seiber, Karl. "National Survey of Long-Haul Truck Driver Health and Injury." Federal Motor Carrier Safety Administration, Analysis, Research and Technology Forum. Transportation Research Board 93rd Annual Meeting, January 14, 2014.

Sloane, A. "Collective Bargaining in Trucking: Prelude to a National Conflict." *Industrial and Labor Relations Review* 19, no. 1 (1965), 21–40.

———*Hoffa.* Cambridge, MA: MIT Press, 1991.

Smith, Rebecca, David Bensman, and Paul Marvy. "The Big Rig: Poverty, Pollution, and the Misclassification of Truck Drivers at America's Ports, A

Survey and Research Report." Washington, DC: National Employment Law Project, December 8, 2010.

Smith, Robert Michael. *From Blackjacks to Briefcases: A History of Commercialized Strikebreaking and Unionbusting in the United States*. Athens: Ohio University Press, 2003.

Smith, V., and E. B. Neuwirth. *The Good Temp*. Ithaca: ILR Press, 2008.

Smith, Vicki. *Crossing the Great Divide: Worker Risk and Opportunity in the New Economy*. Ithaca: Cornell University Press, 2001.

Social Security Administration. "Wage Statistics for 2008," November 4, 2015, https://www.ssa.gov/cgi-bin/netcomp.cgi?year=2008]

Swain, D. H. *A Purpose Driven Career: Establishing a Career Path that Gives Drivers Something to Work For*. Worthington, OH: Trincon, 2007.

Transport Topics. "Top 100 For-Hire Carriers," http://www.ttnews.com/tt100 /TT100_web_FH09.pdf.

Truckinginfo.com. "Preparing for Change: Ray Kuntz, Chairman/CEO, Watkins and Shepard Trucking," May, 2009, http://www.truckinginfo.com/article /story/2009/05/preparing-for-change-ray-kuntz-chairmanceo-watkins-and-shepard-trucking.aspx (accessed November 20, 2015).

Truckload Carriers Association. *Dry Van Driver Survey Estimates $1.5 Billion Lost in Time Waiting*. Alexandria, VA: Truckload Carriers Association, 1999.

———. "The State of Independents: Recruiting and Retaining Owner Operators." Recruitment and Retention Conference, February 12, 2013.

Uchitelle, Louis. "Soaring Fuel Prices Take a Withering Toll on Truckers." *New York Times*, May 27, 2008, C1.

United States Department of Transportation. National Highway Traffic Safety Administration. "Traffic Safety Facts 2012 Data." Washington, DC: USDOT, 2014.

United States House of Representatives. "Hearing on the Effects of Misclassifying Workers as ICs." Washington, DC: House Committee on Ways and Means, 2007.

Upton, Rebecca L. "What Would Jesus Haul?: Home, Work, and the Politics of Masculinity among Christian Long-Haul Truck Drivers." In *Work and Family in the New Economy* (Research in the Sociology of Work, vol. 26), edited by Samantha K. Ammons and Erin L. Kelly, 101–26. Bingley, UK: Emerald Group.

Watson, Rip. "Fleet Bankruptcy Pace Slows." *Transport Topics*, April 27, 2009, http://www.ttnews.com/articles/printopt.aspx?storyid = 21783 (accessed June 8, 2015).

Williams, Christine L. *Gender Differences at Work: Women and Men in Nontraditional Occupations*. Berkeley: University of California Press, 1989.

————. *Still a Man's World: Men Who Do "Women's Work."* Berkeley: University of California Press. 1995.

Wright, Erik Olin. "Workers Power, Capitalist Interests and Class Compromise." *American Journal of Sociology* 105, no. 4 (2000): 1559–71.

Wyckoff, Daryl D. *Truck Drivers in America.* Lexington, MA: Lexington, 1979.

Zingales, Luigi. "Survival of the Fittest or the Fattest? Exit and Financing in the Trucking Industry." *Journal of Finance* 53, no. 3 (1998): 905–38.

Index

Page numbers in italics refer to illustrations and tables.

257